Author — Frances L. Knight

"This is more than a book on prayer it is a mini-course in Christianity."
—Leonard LeSourd
Past Publishing Editor/author

"We receive tens of thousands of manuscripts and only consider the top two percent, and yours is in an even higher percentage."
—Dr. Richard Tate
Tate Publishing & Enterprises

Virginia Greek, a devout 90 year old Bible teacher said, "What a blessing to read what the Holy Spirit gave to Frances! I feel it is Holy Ground and pray all will sense the Lord while reading it. I can't tell you how powerful it is… It is the book of the century… It should be in every hand in America."

"Frances wrote the most interesting and complete book on prayer that I have ever read anywhere, at anytime, by any author, even while working on my doctorate."
—Rev. Gene Horton Th. D.
Pastor/Author

CHRISTIANITY ALIVE!
with PRAYER POWER!

A Textbook for **LIFE**

CHRISTIANITY ALIVE!
with **PRAYER POWER!**

Frances L. Knight

Tate Publishing & *Enterprises*

Christianity Alive! with Prayer Power!
Copyright © 2010 by Frances L. Knight. All rights reserved.

No part of this publication may be reproduced, stored in a retrieval system or transmitted in any way by any means, electronic, mechanical, photocopy, recording or otherwise without the prior permission of the author except as provided by USA copyright law.

All scripture quotations, unless otherwise indicated, are taken from the *Holy Bible, New International Version*®. NIV®. Copyright © 1973, 1978, 1984 by International Bible Society. Used by permission of Zondervan. All rights reserved.

This book is designed to provide accurate and authoritative information with regard to the subject matter covered. This information is given with the understanding that neither the author nor Tate Publishing, LLC is engaged in rendering legal, professional advice. Since the details of your situation are fact dependent, you should additionally seek the services of a competent professional.

The opinions expressed by the author are not necessarily those of Tate Publishing, LLC.

Published by Tate Publishing & Enterprises, LLC
127 E. Trade Center Terrace | Mustang, Oklahoma 73064 USA
1.888.361.9473 | www.tatepublishing.com

Tate Publishing is committed to excellence in the publishing industry. The company reflects the philosophy established by the founders, based on Psalm 68:11,
"The Lord gave the word and great was the company of those who published it."

Book design copyright © 2010 by Tate Publishing, LLC. All rights reserved.
Cover design by Tate Publishing
Interior design by Nathan Harmony

Published in the United States of America

ISBN: 978-1-61739-769-1
1. Religion: Christian Education: General
2. Religion: Biblical Studies: Bible Study Guides
11.28.02

Dedication

I met Bob Knight during my first week at Baylor University, when I was seventeen. Through those years, the Baylor chimes echoed our love. Now, we have been married fifty-seven years.

I dedicate this book to my wonderful husband because he has continually supported and encouraged me through these forty years of studying, teaching, writing, and rewriting. He has had no personal motives other than for me to accomplish what I felt God was leading me to do in the writing of *Christianity Alive! with Prayer Power!*

Acknowledgments

I give my deepest appreciation to the Tate Publishing staff for their expertise in taking my manuscript and turning it into the book for which I had prayed.

I give a special acknowledgment to my personal friend and editor, Robin Holbert M.Ed., for her numerous hours during the early years of work on the manuscript.

I am grateful to my husband, Bob; our son, Gary, and daughter-in-law, Rita; our grandchildren, Savannah, Jonas and Natalie, Kendra, Christopher, and Sumer; and, our extended loving family; to Tina and JR Long, whom I love like family; to our pastor and his sweet wife, Bro. Gene and Phynetta Horton; to our Ladies Bible Study Class; and, to our special friends and church family for their continuing love and prayers.

Format

Christianity Alive! with Prayer Power!

Jesus said, "I am returning to my Father and your Father." John 20:17 (NIV)

"This, then, is how you should pray, Our Father..." Matthew 6:9–13 (NIV)

Establish a Relationship with God "Our Father!"	"Our Father
Learn more about Our Father	in heaven,
Revere Our Father's Almighty Name	hallowed be your name.
Desire Our Father's Universal Reign	your kingdom come.
God's Will: "Be Filled" with His Spirit Empowered *To Be* and *To Do*	your will be done, on earth as it is in heaven.
Ask Our Father "Thank You, Lord!"	Give us today our daily bread.
Repent to Our Father "I'm So Sorry, Lord!"	forgive us our debts,
Forgive Others "But, Lord...!"	as we also have forgiven our debtors.
Tempted, Tested and Triumphant	And lead us not into temptation,
Satan The Supreme Leader of Evil Defeated!	but deliver us from the evil one.
Victoriously Praise Our Eternal Father! "Lord! I see Your Glory!"	(For yours is the kingdom and the power and the glory forever.
"Amen" is not the End	Amen.)"

Table of Contents

Foreword 19

Preface 21

Introduction. 23

Prologue 25

I: Establish a Relationship with God as "Our Father". . .27

    Am I God's Child?. 31

    Islam/Israel/Christianity Origin 33

    Christianity has the Unique Plan:
    The Eternal Blood Covenant 35

    The Born Again Perspective. 50

II: Learn More about Our Father 59

    Know God the Key to Mountain Moving Faith 65

    See Our Father in Scripture. 67

    God Ministers in Three Persons:
    The Father, Son and Holy Spirit. 72

    God's Attributes. 74

God Created and Gave Man the Power to Rule . . 82

III: Revere Our Father's Almighty Name 87
Standing on Holy Ground 92
God's name: "I AM" 94
God Gave Jesus a Name Above All 95
Praise Emerges the Language of Victory! 99

IV: Desire Our Father's Universal Reign 107
Divine Travel Brochure to
Our Father's Glorious Kingdom 112
The Five Basic Phases in
The Kingdom of Heaven 115
    The First Phase: The Present Spiritual Kingdom . . . 116
    The Second Phase: Christians go to Heaven
    through Death and in the Rapture 123
    The Third Phase: Post Rapture Events 126
    The Fourth Phase: The Kingdom, and More 131
    The Fifth Phase: The Eternal Kingdom 134

V: God's Will: "Be Filled" with His Spirit
Empowered *To Be* and *To Do*! 137
The Body, Soul and Spirit of Man 143
The Father, Son and Holy Spirit
as They Relate to Man 144
Spirit Empowered "To Be" 145
How to "Be Filled" with God's Spirit 148
Steps that will lead us into the Spirit Filled Life 150
Evidence of the Spirit-filled Life 152

God Provides Spiritual Gifts with Special Abilities . 155
Spirit Empowered "To Do" 163
God Has Specific Assignments for Each Christian . 163
God Provides Sustaining Power. 170
When the Gifts Will Cease 171
"Thy Will be Done":
Baptism and the Lord's Supper Ordinances 172

VI: Ask Our Father—"Thank You, Lord!" 179

Twenty-Seven Basic Principles in Petitioning 183
Intercede for Others 218
Who Can Intercede 218
Interceding or Tattling and Accusing 220
The Intercessor Illustrated 221
The Intercessor Power Prayer. 222
The Power Prayer Foundational Principle
Pray in God's Will. 223
"Nevertheless, Not My Will But Yours" 224
How to Pray for the Terminally Ill 225
How to Pray for Those Who are Dying
with Classic Unsaved Symptoms 226
The Unpardonable Sin 227
A Tsunami Power Prayer for our Nation
May we pray together 229
Don't Forget to Say, "Thank You"
Does God See Us as One of the Nine?. 236

VII: Repent to Our Father—"I am So Sorry, Lord".....241
Five Steps from Sin to Answered Prayer 245
- Sin Recognized 246
- Sins Repented 251
- Forgiveness Received 254
- Obedience Reinstated..........................255
- Harmony Restored..............................255

Walking in His Footsteps 256

VIII: Forgive Others? "But, Lord!"..................259
- As We Also Have Forgiven Others? "But, Lord...". 264
- "Give and it shall be given unto you" Forgiveness 268
- The Stone Throwing Boomerang Principle 269
- Beware of the Root of Bitterness! 271
- We Must Also Forgive Ourselves.................. 274
- Forgiveness Heals 275
- Good News: Charges Have Been Dropped!...... 277

IX: Tempted, Tested, Triumphant 283
- We Live in a Mine Field of Temptation 287
- Good and Evil Often Look the Same 288
- Evil Lurks in the Paths of Temptation 289
  - Lust of the Flesh Physical......................291
  - Lust of the Eyes Material 292
  - Pride of Life—Spiritual 293
- Beware, Lest We Become the Stumbling Block!.. 300
- We Have Power to Escape 301
- God Will Help Us through Our Temptations 303

Steps to Power over Temptation 304
Temptations can be Terrifying 306

X: Satan the Supreme Leader of Evil—DEFEATED! 311

Exposing Our Enemy 316
    Satan's Reality 316
    Satan's Territory 317
    Satan's Power 321
    Satan's Rights. 321
    Satan's Strategy. 322
    Satan's Defeat and Destiny 330
Overcoming Our Enemy! 331
    Our Goal. 332
    Our Spiritual Position 332
    Our Authority in the Name of Jesus. 333
    Our Strength. 338
    Our Armor. 339
    Our Weapons. 340
    Victorious Overcomers 341
The Battleground for the Mind. 342
When Do We Battle Satan,
or Simply Trust Our Father? 342

XI: Victoriously Praise Our Eternal Father! 347

"Thy Eternal Kingdom, Power, and Glory" 352
    Glimpsing "Thy Eternal Kingdom!". 352
    Glimpsing "Thy Almighty Power!" 353
    Glimpsing "Thy Shekinah Glory!" 355

Forever 357
XII: "Amen" is not the End 361
    Our Concluding Prayer 366
    Author's Page for Readers 369
    Author's Statement of Faith 370
Image Gallery 371
Endnotes 381

Foreword

Rev. Gene Horton, Th.D.

I have been Frances Knight's pastor in the First Baptist Church in Rio Hondo, Texas for the past forty-one years. This is in regard to her life. First and most importantly, Frances is a committed born-again Christian. She believes the Bible to be the Word of God and lives a separated life that exemplifies her testimony. She is successful in all aspects of her life.

Frances is one of the most outstanding Christians I have ever known. She ministers to all people, regardless of race, creed or position in society. Many have come to Christ because of her love and compassion.

She is a gifted teacher and a true student of the Word, solid in doctrine. She has been a Ladies' Sunday school teacher in our church for forty-one years. And, for the past ten years, she has taught a widely attended Monday Morning Ladies Bible Study in our church.

Frances has written the most informative, interesting and complete book on the subject of prayer that I have ever read anywhere, at anytime, by any author, even while working on my doctorate. She has taught many seminars on prayer in denominational and non-denominational churches. And, she has taught prayer principles on television many times.

It is with pleasure that I am privileged to write the foreword in her book.

Preface

This book began on a day when great needs overwhelmed me. Not only did I have a desperate need for one of my sons, I also thought about the flow of prayer requests from heartbroken women in my classes: "Frances, please pray my son, who is on drugs... We have no food... My husband is addicted to pornography... We are facing bankruptcy... A young daddy asked, "Have you seen my wife and baby? They left two days ago..." As a church hospital layminister, I also thought of those who are suffering physically and families who are grieving.

While pondering these heart-rending needs, I thought of our loving Heavenly Father, with whom nothing is impossible, promising, "Ask and you will receive" (Jn. 16:24 NIV). I knew that only prayer could bridge the gulf between the abundant supply and the desperate needs.

On my knees at the foot of my bed, in tears I pleaded, "Father, I must learn to pray. I mean to pray with power to receive the big answers. How do I learn? Where do I go? What do I read?"

Then, these words clearly came into my spirit, "My child, I was asked that same question many years ago. Study the answer I gave to them then." I grabbed my Bible and quickly turned to the familiar passage where Jesus instructed his disciples, "This, then, is how you should pray: 'Our Father who art in heaven...'" (Matt.6:9 NIV). Jubilantly, I realized, "THIS IS THE FORMULA FOR POWER IN PRAYER!"

I intently studied every word and as the principles unfolded, for the next two years I taught a weekly, two-hour Ladies Bible Study class in church. When I filed away the "Amen" chapter, I looked at the scope of the files. Surprised, the same voice spoke again through my spirit, "Now, those are chapters for a book." The lesson plans became chapters.

At the first stage of my learning, I realized that "Our Father" was the most important factor in prayer. We could stop right there. I felt it imperative to know Him better. Since that life changing prayer when I asked God, "What do I read?" I have read the Bible through more than twenty times to learn more about him how he thinks, feels, what he promises, and how he responds to frail man's attitudes and actions.

As we continue to learn together, may Our Father draw us closer into that coveted realm of communion with him.

Introduction

This book is written in outline form that makes it easy to use as a text book for Sunday School Classes, Bible Study Classes, campus courses, sermons, and personal study.

At the end of each chapter, a Sample Prayer applies the principles in our prayer.

Then, A "Living Christianity Assignment" page suggests homework to apply the principles into daily living. The segments are: Bible Study, Prayer, and Works.

I pray that *Christianity Alive! with Prayer Power!* will inspire many people to go on a spiritually uplifting adventure through the Bible. I cannot imagine a more worthy goal than to learn more about God through his written word.

There are two books that I strongly recommend that will help the story to flow from Genesis through Revelation. The New "Panorama" Bible Study Course "The Plan of the Ages"[1] has eleven panels in picture form that make the sequence of events understandable. I made a fifteen-foot long wall chart for my classroom, using two of these books. I often refer to it to show where the lesson fits into the flow of the Bible. Several segments of the panels will be used as illustrations through this book.

The second book is *What the Bible is All About* by Dr. Henrietta Mears[2] (Foreword by Billy Graham) briefly explains each book in the Bible. I recommend reading her brief introduction, like

"Understanding Genesis." Then, read the book of Genesis. And, so on through the Bible.

For example: in her chapter "Understanding the Bible" she writes, "The Old Testament is an account of a nation [the Jewish nation]. The New Testament is an account of a Man [the Son of man]. The nation was founded and nurtured of God in order to bring the Man into the world" (Genesis 12:1–3). God Himself became a man so that we might know what to think of when we think of God (Jn. 1:14; 14:9). His appearance on the earth is the central event of all history. The Old Testament sets the stage for it. The New Testament describes it."

Christianity Alive! with Prayer Power! weaves it all together through The Lord's Prayer to explain every primary facet of Christianity and show how it works resulting in Power in Prayer as a way of life.

Prologue

IT'S ALL ABOUT LOVE: "GOD IS LOVE"

The Corridors of the Lord's Model Prayer Lead to Every Principle of Christianity. Each Step Leads to a Vibrant Life Close to God

Galatians 5:22 (NIV)

Basis for Prayer

He that cometh to God must believe that he is, and that he is a rewarder of them that diligently seek him.

Romans 8:15 (NIV)

I:
Establish a Relationship with God as "Our Father"

"Our Father"

> God sent the Spirit of his Son into our hearts, the Spirit who calls out, "Abba [Daddy] Father."
>
> Galatians 5:6 (NIV)

I:
Establish a Relationship with God as "Our Father"

"Our Father"

- Am I God's Child?
- How do I get into God's Family?
- Islam/Israel/Christianity Origin
- Christianity has The Unique Plan: The Blood Covenant
- The Born Again Perspective
- Sample Prayer: Establish a Relationship with "Our Father"
- Living Christianity Assignment

I:
Establish a Relationship with God as "Our Father"

"Our Father"

There can be no other question more important than "What is my relationship with God?" The answer can only be one of two choices: I am God's child, or I am not God's child. It is imperative for each of us individually to respond because how we live and where we will spend eternity depends on the answer. Beyond salvation, power in prayer begins and ends with the quality of our individual relationships with Our Father. It is so simple, yet so profound.

Am I God's Child?

Many people believe that we are all God's children because we are all his creation. This is a reassuring thought, but it is not true. To analyze our relationship with God we might ask ourselves more questions: Do I have a vague concept of God and mere respect for a Divine Creator? Am I relying upon good works, or trusting in a good philosophy for salvation? Do I only know *about* God, or do I know Him personally? What is my true perception of God?

In Pursuit of God, A. W. Tozer discusses common perceptions:

> It was Canon Holmes, of India, who...called attention to the inferential character of the average man's faith in God...God is an inference, not a reality. He is a deduction from evidence...He remains personally unknown to the individual. "He must be...therefore we believe He is."
>
> Others do not go even so far as this; they know of Him only by hearsay...and have put belief in Him into the back of their minds along with the various odds and ends that make up their total creed. To many others God is but an ideal, another name for goodness, or beauty, or truth; or He is law, or life...[3] Millions...go through life trying to love an ideal and be loyal to a mere principle.[4]

I read in the Valley Morning Star that a Harris Poll on American belief revealed that "Among Christians, ninety-nine percent believe in God."[5] Evidently, those who were in the remaining one percent who did not believe in God thought of themselves as being Christians, without understanding what they are supposed to believe to actually be one.

Misconceptions prevail for various reasons. For one, it is natural for people to see themselves as being good, which meets their personal criteria of Christianity. Then, there are those who base their faith on church membership. If we were to ask a man on the street if he were a Christian, he might say, "Yes, I'm a Baptist." He may proudly announce, "My family has been Catholic for years." This could be like saying, "I'm a Democrat or Republican." It is easy to adopt a religion without being born into God's family.

Some individuals have a second-hand religion and declare, "My dad was a preacher," or "My wife is a good Christian." Furthermore, they may even say, "I am a pastor, a deacon, or Bible teacher." With every good intention, involvement in church programs can be similar to activity in civic clubs; they both have official positions, committees and projects.

Since it is easy to deceive ourselves into believing we are what we would like to be, other people may have a clearer view of our lives than we do. I sat at a long banquet table near a Jewish friend who had lived in the small town for years and knew *his neighbors*. I overheard him thoughtfully analyzing those at the table who considered themselves to be Christians. Based on his concepts of Christianity, he concluded, "She is a Christian...he isn't...he is...she may be...."

Along with self-deception, I have also heard testimonies from people who said that they knew a lot about God and thought they were Christians, before they actually knew Him as a personal savior. A woman in my Bible Study Class said, "I thought I had it all down. Yet, I didn't know what I was believing. Now, I know." Our relationship with God must be on a personal level.

People all over the world know a lot about a distinguished person, like the president of a nation. But, only his children can pick up the phone and say, "Hello, Dad." Bible scholars, too, must be in God's family before they can address God with the personal endearment, "Abba, Father" (Rom. 8:15 NIV).

On a massive scale, multitudes of people miss the mark because of religious teachings that make no provision for salvation from their sin.

This includes Christian churches who preach spiritual principles—without ever explaining how to have eternal salvation. We can sing and praise among the best, but we can't face a totally righteous God, in eternity, when our lives have been blighted with sin. Evangelism means we spread the good news about salvation through Jesus' atoning blood.

Islam/Israel/Christianity Origin

Compare the two largest religions in the world Christianity and Islam. Abraham is the father of both religions. He had two sons: Ishmael was the first son, born to Hagar who was Sarah's handmaid; Islam claims their rights as descendants from the *first son*. Abraham's wife, Sarah, gave birth to Isaac; Judaism claims their rights because Issac was born from the *marriage.*

Christianity evolved from Judaism because they [gentiles] accepted the Jewish prophesied Messiah Jesus, heir to the Throne of King David: God promised King David, "Your house and your kingdom shall endure before Me forever; your throne shall be established forever." (2 Sam. 7:16 NASB). Centuries later, "God sent the angel Gabriel...to a virgin...give him the name Jesus. He will be great and will be called the Son of the Most High. The Lord God will give him the throne of his father David (Lu. 1:26–32 NIV).

"If you are Christ's, then you are Abraham's seed, and heirs according to the promise" (Gal. 3:26–29 NKJV).

In "According to Islam & Christianity Compare Basic teachings and Beliefs," Rev. Bruce Green, who has been a bridge-builder since 1983 between Muslims and evangelical churches, explains:

- CHRISTIANITY BELIEVES: Salvation is by God's grace, not by an individual's good works. Salvation must be received by faith. People must believe in their hearts that Jesus paid for their sins and physically arose again which is the assurance of forgiveness and resurrection of the body. This is God's loving plan to forgive sinful people.[6]
- ISLAM BELIEVES: Humans are basically good, but fallible and need guidance. The balance between good and bad deeds determines eternal destiny in paradise or hell. Allah's mercy may tip the balances to heaven, as his will is supreme.[7]

Both religions recognize sin as a problem that needs a solution. The Bible confirms: "*All* have sinned and fall short of the glory of God" (Rom. 3:23 NIV). Even one sin contaminates the soul. The penalty and solution: "The wages of sin is death, but the gift of God is eternal life in Christ Jesus our Lord" (Rom. 6:23 NIV). Justice *must* prevail unless redemption intervenes.

As Light cannot cohabit with Darkness, ultimately pure Righteousness cannot cohabit with Unrighteousness. God loves all people but the things they do break harmony.

Christianity has the Unique Plan: The Eternal Blood Covenant

The word *Covenant* means: The most solemn, binding agreement that could be made between two parties, tribes or nations. A *Blood Covenant is* the strongest bond possible.[8]

Since value equals price, defiance of God is the greatest sin and must require the highest price–sinless blood. Justice [eternal separation from God] *must prevail* when no shed blood has intervened to provide mercy. God designed a plan for redemption by giving *an extension of himself* to come to earth in human form [Jesus]: "For God so loved the world that he gave his only begotten Son, that whosoever believeth in him should not perish, but have everlasting life" (Jn. 3:16 KJV).

Blood is the heart beat of the Bible. "For the life of the flesh is in the blood: and I have given it to you upon the altar to make atonement for *your* souls: for it is the blood that maketh atonement for the soul" (Lev. 17:11 KJV). God's wonderful plan of salvation is the scarlet thread that weaves its way through the Bible from Genesis to Calvary.

Follow the Scarlet Thread:

(see page 371 for a larger image)

The Plan began in the beautiful Garden of Eden with Adam and Eve. I believe they were originally clothed in the glory of God. But they sinned by heeding Satan, the serpent, instead of obeying God. Their "Robes of Righteousness" disappeared and they were humanly naked.

An animal had to shed its blood so skin could clothe them. Consequently, they were cast out of the Garden of Eden *before they could eat of the Tree of Life* and live in this sinful nature forever separated from God.

The Scarlet thread [blood line of redemption] started right after the first sin with The Promise: "I will put enmity between you [Satan] and the woman, and between your offspring and *hers* [Jesus]; *he will crush your head* [destroy your control over mankind by paying for their sins with his blood] and you will strike his heel [give him a very hard time]" (Gen. 3:15 NIV).

I: Establish a Relationship with God as "Our Father"

(See page 372 for a larger image)

Exiled out into the world, Adam and Eve were prolific because "God blessed them and said..." Be fruitful and increase in number; fill the earth..." (Gen 1:28 NIV). The propensity to sin became out of control. When two of their sons were older, Cain, slew his brother Abel. The world became increasingly wicked. Generations later, God gave up on any repentance. He told Noah to build a huge boat; the cataclysmic flood is coming... It reduced the world population to eight: Noah, his wife, their three sons and their wives.

They left the ark and instead of dispersing and populating, as God instructed, their descendents grouped and built the Tower of Babel their own *humanistic* tower of worship. God divided their languages. Then, they regrouped and dispersed. Morally speaking, they were self-centered, self-willed and self-motivated. They needed a new nature.

God decided to start his own nation of people whom he could love and bless; and, wanted to receive their love in return. He chose Abraham from Ur of Chaldea from the world's wicked culture. He gave Abraham a heartrending test for two reasons: First, it tested his loyalty for the big assignment of being the father of His Chosen People. Second, it gave a symbolic picture of mankind's ultimate redemption that would happen about two thousand years later at Calvary on the same Mt. Moriah.

The test happened this way: God told Abraham to sacrifice his son, Isaac, for sins. His heart was broken. Yet, as he raised the knife, God provided a substitute lamb. Abraham passed the test of obedience. He also illustrated the process of redemption.

Abraham's son, Isaac, had a son named Jacob. Jacob had twelve sons. God changed Jacob's name to Israel and his sons became the Twelve Tribes of Israel. Henceforth, God's Chosen People would be called Israelites.

There was a severe famine and the Israelite family of seventy went into Egypt for grain. Jacob's son, Joseph, was already there, and had become second only to Pharaoh. During the next four hundred years they became a huge population. A new king arose who feared their number and put them under ruthless bondage (Exod. 1:1–14). They cried out to God, and he called Moses to deliver them from Egypt. [Read Genesis 37 through Exodus 14] God sent plagues upon the Egyptians to force the evil Pharaoh to let the Israelites go.

The Scarlet Thread continues: The night before their exodus, God instigated the first Passover Supper. "The Lord said to Moses, 'Tell the whole community of Israel...

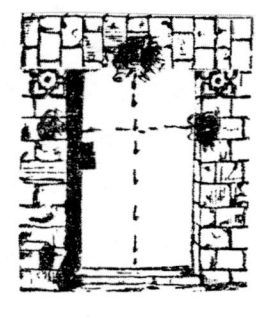

The animals you choose must be year-old males *without defect*...Take care of them until the fourteenth day of the month, when all the people of the community of Israel must slaughter them at twilight.

Then they are to take some of the blood and put it on the sides and tops of the doorframes of the houses where they eat the lambs.... On that same night I will pass through Egypt and strike down every firstborn both men and animals and I will bring judgment on all the [false] gods of Egypt [all sin]. I am the LORD.

The blood will be a sign for you on the houses where you are; and when I see the blood, I will *"pass over"* you. No destructive plague will touch you when I strike Egypt. This is a day you are to commemorate; for the generations to come you shall celebrate it [The Passover] as a festival to the LORD a lasting ordinance.

Exodus 12:5–14 (NIV)

The exodus of the Israelites brought them to the Red Sea with Pharaoh's chariots in pursuit. Moses had a serious prayer meeting with God. In essence God replied, "Moses, why are you calling to me, raise *your* staff and part the waters." They walked through on dry ground.

After a long trek, they settled in around Mt. Sinai. Slaves for four hundred years now had to be organized into a nation. On Mt. Sinai, God gave Moses the Ten Commandments—basic laws of right and wrong. The Israelites agreed, but broke all Ten before Moses came back down the mountain. God knew that the self-willed nature of mankind did not have the inner desire to live up to the standards of righteousness. The divine laws were like New Year's Resolutions which were doomed to fail. They needed a new nature.

The Brazen Altar at the Tabernacle

God also gave detailed instructions for worship when he designed The Tabernacle.

It was a large rectangular tent surrounded by an enclosure. The Brazen Altar for animal sacrifice was at the *entrance of the courtyard* because blood would have to be sacrificed *to pay for sins* before they could worship a Holy God. Since the blood from animals was inadequate for complete atonement, no one but the priest could go behind the thick curtain into the Holy of Holies. There, he would sprinkle blood over the Ark that contained the Ten Commandments. This signified God's atoning mercy over The Perfect Law which was impossible for humans to keep.

This ceremony of worship in the Tabernacle was another symbolic picture of redemption. Innumerable herds of animals were sacrificed through the centuries, until The Perfect Passover Lamb died at Calvary.

> Therefore, when Christ came into the world, he said: "Sacrifice and offering you did not desire, but a body you prepared for me; with burnt offerings and sin offerings [of inadequate animals] you were not pleased."
>
> ...Then I said, "Here I am" [Jesus volunteered] "It is written about me in the scroll I have come to do your will, O God...He sets aside the first [The Old Covenant] to establish the second [The New Covenant]. And by that will, we have been made holy through the sacrifice of the body of Jesus Christ once for all."
>
> Heb. 10:5–10 NIV

The New Testament IS the New Covenant:

Jeremiah prophesied:

> "The time is coming," declares the Lord, "when I will make a new covenant with the house of Israel and with the house of Judah. It will not be like the covenant I made with their forefathers when I took them by the hand to lead them out of Egypt, because they broke my covenant, though I was a husband to them," declares the Lord.
>
> "This is the covenant I will make with the house of Israel after that time," declares the Lord. "I will put my law in their minds and write it on their hearts. I will be their God, and they will be my people. No longer will a man teach his

neighbor, or a man his brother, saying, 'Know the LORD,' because they will all know me, from the least of them to the greatest," declares the LORD.

"For I will forgive their wickedness and will remember their sins no more."

Jeremiah 31:31–34 (NIV)

Isaiah prophesied the one to come [the prophet, John] who would herald to the world "Jesus is the Messiah!"

Comfort ye, comfort ye my people, saith your God... *The voice of him* [John, the Baptizer] *that crieth in the wilderness, Prepare ye the way of the LORD, make straight in the desert a highway for our God....* And the glory of the LORD shall be revealed, and all flesh shall see it together: for the mouth of the LORD hath spoken it.

Isaiah 40:1, 3, 5 (NIV)

About seven hundred years later the New Testament opens:

The Miraculous birth of the Prophet John and Jesus

Look at the miraculous birth of John, and of Jesus. [Read full account in Luke 1 and 2]

John's birth

Zachariah belonged to the priestly division of Abijah. His wife Elizabeth was also a descendant of Aaron... she was barren; and they were elderly. An angel of the Lord said,

Your wife Elizabeth will bear you a son, and you are to give him the name John... for he will be great in the sight of the Lord... he will be filled with the Holy Spirit even from birth. Many of the people of Israel will he bring back to the Lord their God. And he will go on before the Lord [Jesus], in the spirit and power of Elijah, to turn the hearts of the fathers to their children and the disobedient to the wisdom of the righteous to make ready a people prepared for the Lord.

Luke 1: 5–17 (NIV)

In those days John the Baptist came, preaching in the Desert of Judea and saying, "Repent, for the kingdom of heaven is near." This is he who was spoken of through the prophet Isaiah: "A voice of one calling in the desert, 'Prepare the way for the Lord, make straight paths for him.'"

Matthew 3:1–3 (NIV)

John was preaching repentance to pave the way for Righteousness.

Jesus' birth

God sent the angel Gabriel to Nazareth to a virgin, named Mary. He announced,

> You have found favor with God. You will be with child and give birth to a son, and you are to give him the name Jesus. He will be great and will be called the Son of the Most High. The Lord God will give him the throne of his father David, and he will reign over the house of Jacob forever; his kingdom will never end.
>
> "How will this be," Mary asked the angel, "since I am a virgin?" The angel answered, "The Holy Spirit will come upon you, and the power of the Most High will overshadow you. So the holy one be to born will be called the Son of God.
>
> Even Elizabeth your relative is going to have a child in her old age, and she who was said to be barren is in her sixth month. For nothing is impossible with God."
>
> Gabriel said, "I am the Lord's servant," Mary answered. "May it be to me as you have said." Then the angel left her.
>
> Mary hurried to a town in the hill country of Judea to tell Elizabeth about her good news. When Elizabeth heard Mary's

I: Establish a Relationship with God as "Our Father"

> greeting, the baby [John] leaped in her womb, and Elizabeth was filled with the Holy Spirit. In a loud voice she prophesied: "Blessed are you among women and blessed is the child you will bear! But why am I so favored, that the mother of my Lord [Jesus] should come to me? As soon as the sound of your greeting reached my ears, the baby in my womb leaped for joy"
> Luke 1:30–44 (NIV)

Leaping is more than a baby's ordinary movements inside its mother. Clearly, God's Holy Spirit connected the two babies and their mothers with divine revelation.

It would be easy to presume the boys grew up together, but I do not believe that is likely because personal friendship might have slanted John's prophetic herald.

When we look at the sequence of events in their lives we learn that they were destined, but their lives were not intertwined. Mary stayed with Elizabeth until it was time for John to be born. By then, Mary was about three months pregnant and she returned to her home. Just before her baby was born, she and Joseph made the long required trip to their birthplace for taxation. Jesus was born in Bethlehem.

They fled to Egypt when an angel told Joseph to "take Mary and the baby and leave quickly." Herod was killing all baby boys under two in an attempt to destroy, the one whom he thought would be his potential rival to his throne. They stayed in Egypt until Herod died.

Then, they returned to Nazareth where Jesus was reared.

John's lifestyle was vastly different. Elizabeth and Zachariah probably died while John was young. At some point, he went into the wilderness. "John's clothes were made of camel's hair, and he had a leather belt around his waist. His food was locusts and wild honey" (Matt. 3:4–5 NIV). "He lived in the dsert until he appeared publicly to Israel" (Lu. 1:80 NIV).

Keeping these facts in mind, it is probable that John and Jesus never met face to face until now, thirty years later, when divine revelation again connected them.

John introduced Jesus to the world

> These things took place in Bethany beyond the Jordan, where John was baptizing. The next day he saw Jesus coming to him and said, *"Behold, the Lamb of God who takes away the sin of the world! This is He on behalf of whom I said, 'after me comes a Man who has a higher rank than I, for He [Divine Savior] existed [eternally] before me.'"*
>
> John 1:28–30 (NASB)

God introduced Jesus to the world

As soon as Jesus was baptized, he went up out of the water. At that moment heaven was opened, and he saw the Spirit of God descending like a dove and lighting on him. And a voice from heaven said, "This is my Son, whom I love; with him I am well pleased" (Matt.3:17 NIV).

Jesus' ministry began. First, as a human, he proved that he could resist Satan in the Wilderness of Temptation. He lived in harmony with God and taught his disciples how to continue in his ministry of truth, love and compassion. Then, he died for us.

The Scarlet Thread ends at Calvary

Jesus died at Calvary on the *altar of the cross* to redeem mankind. For him, there was no last minute substitute. The scene was so horrific that God in his purity could not look upon the total degradation when his beloved sinless Son *became sin*. He assumed the forsaken darkness of every sin for all times. God turned his back on sin and Jesus cried out, "My God, my God, why have you forsaken me?" (Matt.27:46 NIV). The sky turned dark.

No one *took* Jesus' life from him. The *God person* of Jesus could lay his life down and take it up again. The human person of Jesus had such great love for mankind that he physically endured the agony of the cross because *he was seeing the great joy beyond the cross:* He would live forever in Glory with everyone who accepted his redemption!

> Let us fix our eyes on Jesus, the author and perfecter of our faith, *who for the joy set before him endured the cross,* scorning its shame, and sat down at the right hand of the throne of God.
> Hebrews.12:2 NIV [Read chapters 10–12]

When Jesus cried out in a loud voice, "It is Finished!" the plan of salvation was complete; the Lamb of God had paid the price for all. At that moment God sent an earth quake. "The earth shook and the rocks split." *The heavy veil that separated man from God's Holiness in the Tabernacle [in Jerusalem] was ripped from top to bottom.* (Matt. 27:50–51 NIV) [Also, Jn.19: 30 KJV].

Hallelujah! Now, instead of going through a priest, or any other intercessor, redeemed man can go straight into the Heavenly Holy of Holies and pray, *"Our Father."*

Furthermore, since redemption was paid in full, all believers can now eat freely of the Eternal Tree of Life! "Blessed are those who wash their robes [in the blood of Jesus], that they may have the right to the Tree of Life and may go through the gates into the city...." And, live forever in Glory! (Rev. 22:12–14 NIV)

(see page 376 for a larger image)

I am proud to wear the Star of David on my gold cross. People who know that I am an avowed Christian ask, "Why do you wear the Star of David?" I reply, "It represents what I believe. The Star of David is the Old Testament with Jehovah, Abraham, Israel, and King David.... The Cross represents the New Testament, which is the fulfillment of the Old Testament. When the prophesied *Israelite* redeemer, Jesus ... born of a virgin...in Bethlehem...legal heir to the Eternal Throne of *King David*, died to pay for our sins then, *Jehovah* became *"Our Father."*

Also, we Christians believe that we were once gentiles who were adopted into Abraham's family because we had faith in Israel's Messiah Jesus. "For you are all sons of God through faith in Christ Jesus. For as many of you as were baptized into Christ, have put on Christ. There is neither Jew nor Greek, there is neither slave nor free, there is neither male nor female; for you are all one in Christ Jesus. Again, *if you are Christ's, then you are Abraham's seed, and heirs according to the promise"* (Gal.3:26–29 NKJV).

Not only are we heirs to all of the promises that God gave Abraham, another scripture confirms an even greater heritage: "You received the Spirit of sonship. And by him we cry, 'Abba, Father.' The Spirit himself testifies with our spirit that we are God's children. Now if we are his children, then we are heirs of God and co-heirs with Christ" (Rom. 8:15–17 NIV).

In summary for those who resided in the Old Testament.

> It was not with perishable things such as silver or gold that you were redeemed from the empty [unfulfilled] way of life handed down to you from *your* forefathers, but with the precious blood of Christ, a lamb without blemish or defect. He was chosen before the creation of the world, but was revealed in these last times for *your* sake.
>
> 1 Peter 1:18–20 (NIV)

A Promise and a Warning

When I said that I was proud to wear the Star of David on my gold cross, I am genuinely proud of my spiritual heritage. God has made a special promise for those who love Israel. And, a warning for those who are enemies:

> And I will bless those who bless you [who confer prosperity or happiness upon you] and curse him who curses or uses insolent language toward you; in you will all the families and kindred of the earth be blessed (Gen. 12:3 AB).

"All the families... of the earth will be blessed" means Abraham's descendent, Jesus, would become the Messiah to save all mankind.

Dr. John Hagee (Cornerstone Church in San Antonio, Texas) believes Genesis 12:3 is an eternal covenant. He said that when they started blessing Israel, God started blessing them. The Cornerstone Church sponsors "A Night to Honor Israel."

Dr. Hagee wrote about the 2010 Washington Summit (July 20–22): "From the moment we began the Daughter's for Zion prayer meeting we could sense the presence of God at the Fifth Annual Christians United for Israel Summit in Washington, D.C. like never before."

Dr. Hagee has been to Israel at least 20 times and has met with every Prime Minister since Menechim Begin. John Hagee Ministries has given more than $3.7 million to bring Soviet Jews from the former Soviet Union to Israel. He has also written many books dealing with Jewish issues as they pertain to prophecy fulfillment.

We Must Make a Decision

This completes our Biblical overview about sinful man and God's plan for his redemption. Now, we must make certain that it is applied individually to each life. This requires a decision.

To better understand how crucial it is to accept God's Plan, I will use a secular illustration: Think of a lottery beyond imagination... you have the ticket with the winning number yet, you decide not to cash it in. Your salvation was bought we are talking about Eternity in Glory with God forever! Sad, but true not everyone will accept him as Lord.

Are churches today lax in proclaiming this vital Gospel of Eternal Salvation?

I have heard people from mainstream denominational churches say, "I have been to church all of my life and never heard how to get to heaven. Though all Christian churches celebrate Jesus' birth, death and resurrection as important Biblical events, many pastors do not explain that each person must *believe and receive* Jesus Christ as their personal savior.

The trend is motivational and prosperity sermons with few negatives. At least one person likes it that way: "I have worked hard all week and when I come to church I don't want to hear about sin, hell and agonizing death on the cross." It is easy to get caught up in the enthusiasm of singing *about* Jesus without knowing him personally. Also, it is easy for a pastor to presume that every person who sits in a pew is a Christian.

Through the centuries, Christian churches have emerged with different focuses. According to Wikipedia: Catholic is the largest Christian faith, claiming over one billion members around the world. Jesus on the Cross symbolizes their faith. The second largest is Baptist. Primarily in the United States, The Southern Baptist Convention has grown to sixteen million; they evangelize by sending more than five thousand missionaries over the word to spread the Gospel of salvation in one hundred fifty three nations.

The largest Christian church in America is Lakewood Church in Houston. Wikipedia describes the church and its theology: "It is Non-Denominational Evangelical with an attendance of 43,500 per week. It believes that the entire Bible is inspired by God ... and holds in account the belief in the Trinity, as well as the recognition of the death of Christ on the cross and resurrection.

From the commands found in the Bible, the church practices the following:

Salvation: Each service offers an Altar Call at the end in order for people to Accept Christ as Lord and Savior.

> **Water Baptism:** The church believes this as a symbol of the cleansing power of the blood of Christ and a testimony to faith in the Lord Jesus Christ. Baptism is practiced every Saturday night in the church's Chapel.
> **Communion:** The church deems this as an act of remembering what the Lord Jesus did on the cross. It is offered once a month.
> **Growing Relationship with Jesus Christ: Lakewood** believes that every believer should be in a growing relationship with Jesus by obeying God's Word, yielding to the Holy Spirit and by being conformed to the image of Christ."

Always smiling, Joel Olsteen's praise services are dynamic. His focus in preaching is to inspire his vast audience to claim God's promises, have a positive attitude, and go away feeling encouraged about life. Bob and I have attended both, John Olsteen's huge church and Joel Olsteen's mega church several times. They were both impressive.

On one of the largest television ministries, Joyce Meyer, helps me daily to *see myself*. She has given me, and multitudes of other women, insight into how to change our attitudes for a better life. She is a very effective teacher of Christian principles. Salvation is within her messages. I have been blessed by some of the best.

Every sermon *should* be motivational and God wants us to excel and be prosperous. But, he first wants to bless us with a glorious redemption and a transformed life. Then, he wants us to depend on him so he can bless us daily with our needs. Though, our *needs* may not be all of our *wants;* he has not promised that everyday would be Christmas in July. He wants us to have the greatest blessing of all Him, as "Our loving Father" and our daily provider.

Back to the basics: "Strait is the gate, *and narrow is the way, which leadeth unto life, and few there be that find it*" (Matt. 7:14 KJV). If every ministry would add the next four sentences to each message, it would motivate multitudes right into God's Presence and vastly increase the population in The Eternal City.

- Believe that Jesus died to pay the price for *your* sins.
- Believe he was buried and raised from the dead
- Ask His Holy Spirit to come live in *your* heart.
- Declare, "Jesus Christ is my Lord, now and forever!"

"If you confess with *your* mouth ["Jesus is Lord"] and believe in *your* heart that God raised him from the dead, you will be saved" (Rom.10:9 NIV).

Without receiving this message, there is no CHRISTianity only a philosophy of good principles.

The Born Again Perspective

Jesus said, "You must be born again" (Jn. 3:7 NIV). This means the *old nature* that was cast out of the Garden of Eden becomes the *new nature* of truth, goodness and love.

We were born physically, now we must be reborn spiritually. We may wonder, as Nicodemus asked, "How can a man be born when he is old? Surely he cannot enter a second time into his mother's womb to be born! Jesus answered, "I tell you the truth, no one can enter the kingdom of God unless he is *born of water [flesh]* and the *Spirit [spirit]. Flesh gives birth to flesh*, but the *Spirit gives birth to spirit*" (Jn. 3:4–6 NIV). In the *flesh*, a baby is contained in a literal sac of water. During physical birth the water bag breaks as the baby emerges.

Some believe that *"no one can enter the kingdom of God unless he is born of water"* means you have to be baptized to go to heaven. Study the previous paragraph again. Clearly, you must first be born *physically* and then *spiritually*.

When we analyze the spiritual rebirth, we see that our spiritual nature will be transformed. Transformed from what? Since Adam and Eve chose to listen to Satan rather than God, their descendants have the Adam nature. That means we all were born self-centered and susceptible to Satan's wooing; sin comes naturally.

When I spoke at a seminar a woman said, "I thought people were basically good." I replied, "Let's study a child's nature. For example, put two toddlers in a playpen with one toy between them. Probably, both will grab the toy declaring, 'Mine!' Break a candy bar, and both will claim the larger piece."

Obedience and moral values are learned, not instinctive. Scripture tells us to "Train a child in the way he should go..." (Prov.22:6 NIV). Every toddler tests authority in pursuit of his own desires. We have all seen a tiny hand edge toward a forbidden item. Temper tantrums become his supreme effort to get his way. A wise parent will immediately *teach* the child to obey.

When I was a child, my dad saved old nickels in a jar in the closet. I figured he would never miss it if I took only one each day to school to buy candy. One day he looked at his jar. The spanking that ensued taught me "Thou shalt not steal!"

God's Commandments, like New Years' resolutions, are quickly broken when we depend on our natural nature and its lack of self-discipline. Since Eve, mankind has failed.

Since Jesus, mankind can succeed. When Jesus' Spirit lives in our hearts, our nature becomes more like His. Then, we obey His rules not because he commanded, but because *we want to.*

Jesus tells us how to recognize those who still have their original nature, and those who have experienced the new birth: "You will know them by their fruits" (Matt. 7:20 NIV). As a Christian matures, he/she produces "the fruit of the spirit" which is "love, joy, peace, patience, kindness, goodness, faithfulness, gentleness and self-control" (Gal 5:22, 23 NIV). He tends to be dependable and helpful to others. Those who disregard God, produce self-indulging works.

Let's reconsider this familiar analogy: If we see a fowl that waddles and quacks grouped with ducks, we presume, "That is a duck." If we see a person mingling with people who have no apparent interest in God and are boasting about selfish interests, we know he is waddling and quacking like his father, Adam. Paul the apostle lists the natural characteristics.

> The acts of the sinful nature are obvious: sexual immorality, impurity and debauchery; idolatry and witchcraft; hatred, [vindictive and revengeful], discord, jealousy, fits of rage, selfish ambition, dissensions, factions and envy; drunkenness, orgies, and the like. I warn you, as I did before, that those who live like this will not inherit the kingdom of God.
> Galatians 5:19–21 (NIV)

Jesus' walk and talk was different. His deeds and words conveyed kindness and compassion for others. He was like His Father. Jesus said, "The Son can do nothing by himself; he can do only what he sees his Father doing, because whatever the Father does the Son also does" (Jn. 5:19 NIV). Christians grow to be like Jesus Christ, their Lord.

My pastor is a good example of a born-again spirit. He said that he was not raised in a Christian home and knew little about God. In high school he ran with beer drinking friends who did what was more or less typical during that era. He was popular in school, yet he testified that his life was without meaning and he had no desire to live. When a friend told him, "Jesus loves you," he said that he had never heard that before. He drove down a country road where he prayed with all his heart, "Please help me, forgive me and save me. I am ready to turn my life over to you...." Later, he wrote, "Right then and there...life came to my soul and a 180 degree change...."[11]

Becoming a Christian does not necessarily mean God will call us to be a pastor, or send us to Africa to be a missionary, as some people fear. God needs Christian parents, doctors, lawyers, scientists, teachers, business leaders, politicians, and workers in every area of life who reflect His attributes and serve with wisdom.

The spiritual transformation of the old nature is like a beautiful butterfly emerging from a cocoon. *"If anyone is in Christ, he is a new creation; the old has gone, the new has come"* (2 Cor. 5:17 NIV)! He will never again want to crawl. It is the beginning of a wonderful eternal relationship. "You have been *born again*, not of perishable seed, but of imperishable, through the living and enduring word of God" (1 Pet. 1:23 NIV).

Billy Graham simplified "How to be Born Again"

> The Bible says that without faith it is impossible to please God. But what does it mean to believe? It means to 'commit' to Christ, to 'surrender' to him. Believing is your response to God's offer of mercy, love and forgiveness....
>
> Belief is not just a feeling; it is the assurance of salvation. You may look at yourself in the mirror and say, "But, I don't feel saved I don't feel forgiven.' But don't depend on feelings for your assurance. Christ has promised, and He cannot lie. Belief is a deliberate act of committing one's self to the person of Jesus Christ, It is not a 'hanging on' to some vague idea. It is an act of trust in the God-Man, Jesus Christ...."
>
> Faith is not anti-intellectual. Faith involves a very logical premise that is, trusting that God's superior ability is able to save us.[12]

How Jehovah's Witness May Know They Are Going to Heaven

I admire the Jehovah's Witnesses for their diligence in witnessing. How many in other faiths would be so willing to give of their time and effort to share with others what they believe? From my conversations with them, it seems they do not have assurance that they will have eternal life in heaven.

Recently, two ladies came to my front door. During our conversation, I asked a question that confirmed my thoughts. I asked, "How do you get to heaven?" Long pause.

Then one said, "You have to study and then do good things like knock on doors to bring encouraging words to others." Then she confessed, "I do not believe I am going to heaven, because there are *only a few who will get there* and *the* 144,000 *have already been chosen.*"

In Dr. Tim LaHaye's Prophecy Study Bible (pgs. 1504-1507), the 144,000 *will be* 12,000 from each of the twelve tribes of Israel who will be sealed to become evangelists *during the Tribulation period.* (Revelation 7:3-17, NKJV). "*After* these things I looked...a great multitude *which no one could number of all nations, tribes, peoples.*" An elder asked, 'Who are these...these came out of the great tribulation, and washed their robes...in the blood of the Lamb."

Jehovah's Witnesses need not wonder. Everyone/anyone can accept salvation—right now.

"So That You May Know"

> I write these things to you who believe in the name of the Son of God so *that you may know* that you have eternal life.
>
> 1 John 5:13 (NIV)

> And this is the testimony: God has given us eternal life, and this life is in his Son. He who has the Son has life; he who does not have the Son of God does not have life."
>
> 1 John 5:11–14 (NIV)

> For it is by grace you have been saved, through faith—and this not from yourselves [you *did* nothing but believe], it is the [free] gift of God.
>
> Ephesians 2:8 (NIV)

> For God so loved the world that he gave his one and only Son, that *whoever believes in him* [Jesus] shall not perish but have eternal life.
>
> John 3:16 (NIV)

> For *all have sinned* and fall short of the glory of God.
>
> Romans 3:23 (NIV)

I: Establish a Relationship with God as "Our Father"

The *wages of sin is death*, but the gift of God is eternal life in Christ Jesus our Lord.
Romans 6:23 (NIV)

That if you confess with your mouth, "Jesus is Lord," and believe in your heart that God raised him from the dead, you will be saved...for it is with your heart that you believe and are justified, and it is with your mouth that you confess and are saved.
Romans 10:9–10 (NIV)

Everyone who calls on the name of the Lord will be saved.
Romans 10:13 (NIV)

Not of works, lest any man should boast" [No one can brag, "I did this or that"–Jesus did it all].
Ephesians 2:8–9 (KJV)

Response to the statement that few will go to heaven:

Enter through the *narrow gate*. For wide is the gate and broad is the road that leads to destruction, and many enter through it. But small is the gate and narrow the road that leads to life and *only a few find it.*
Matthew 7:13–14 (NIV)

The narrow road means there is only "one way" to heaven; and, that is "faith in Jesus Christ for paying the price for your sins." Though he has paid the price for all, "*Few that find it* means *relative* few will accept Jesus Christ as their Lord; most people don't want *anyone* to be their Lord. "The *broad worldly ways are independent of God, without his righteous restrictions.* As a result, the lost sinner will face judgment and have to pay for his own sins—which will be eternal separation from our Holy God.

Jesus answered, "I am the way and the truth and the life. No one comes to the Father except through me [because Jesus alone paid for man's sins. Now *that* is love]. If you really knew me, you would know my Father as well. From now on, you do know him and have seen him" [they are identical] (Jn. 14:6–7 NIV).

These scriptures and many more, clearly state that it is ONLY by faith in Jesus that we can know we will have eternal life in Heaven. It is not by studying and learning more; you can have a Ph.D. in Theology and dedicate your life to doing good things and still not make it to Heaven. Billy Graham and Mother Theresa had knowledge and good works, *but only their faith in Jesus reserved Heaven for them.*

Just say, "Jesus Christ is my Lord! And mean it with all your heart

Ask his Holy Spirit to come live in your heart. Thank Him for dying on the cross in your place. Praise Him always!

Eternal Life is in Heaven with God

> How great is the love the Father has lavished on us that we should be called children of God.
>
> 1 John 3:1 (NKJV)

Sample Prayer
Establish a Relationship with "Our Father"

Dear God,

I am not satisfied with my life. I believe that Jesus Christ, *your* only Son, came to earth and was born as a human baby. He lived a perfect life and died on the cross as a Blood Covenant to pay for my sins. He was raised from the dead and is alive today.

I ask you to forgive me for my sins and save my soul. I want to live for you. Please, Holy Spirit, come live in my heart. I now proclaim: "Jesus Christ is my Lord!"

Thank you for my Blood Covenant Relationship with The Eternal King of Kings.

Joy fills my heart as I can now call you *"Father!"*

_____   _____
(signature)   (date)

Living Christianity Assignment

Bible Study—Read the book of John. It tells us about Jesus as God's Son and how we can have a personal relationship with Him.

> Faith comes from hearing the message, and the message is heard through the word of Christ.
> Romans 10:17 (NIV)

Prayer—Reading books about prayer only teaches *about* prayer. Let's learn to pray by having conversations with *Our Father*. Don't forget this divine appointment.

> Ask, and it will be given to you.
> Luke 11:9 (NIV)

Works—Practice more love in *your* home. Make each family member feel special. Do not try to change them—just you.

> Faith without deeds is dead.
> James 2:26 (NIV)

II:
Learn More about Our Father

"Our Father in heaven"

> Let him who boasts boast about this: that he understands and knows me, that I am the Lord, who exercises kindness, justice and righteousness on earth, for in these I delight,' declares the Lord.
>
> Jeremiah 9:24 (NIV)

II:
Learn More about Our Father

"Our Father in heaven"

- Know God the Key to "Mountain Moving Faith"
- See Our Father in Scripture
- God Ministers in Three Persons: The Father, Son and Holy Spirit
- God's Attributes
- God Created and Gave Man the Power to Rule
- Sample Prayer: Learn More about Our Father
- Living Christianity Assignment

II:
Learn More about Our Father

"Our Father in heaven"

Prayer is more than saying a speech to God or reeling out a Want List. For power in prayer, joy of companionship will likely precede all else. That joy can only come as we learn more about our Father and live in a close relationship with him through prayer.

The simplicity of such a relationship was demonstrated as an older couple, returning from a vacation, slipped into our service. When our pastor spoke to them from the pulpit, a little girl promptly started toward the back to find her grandparents. The grandmother rose quickly, and the child started running and the grandmother scooped her up into her arms. The pastor didn't need to say another word the audience saw a living sermon of love.

When we come to Our Father in prayer, do we run to Him and does He scoop us up in His arms? He wants us to so much that He gave His only Son, Jesus, to make that relationship possible. Such love! Jesus came freely and gave His life for everyone so that God's children might be in one spirit with The Father, The Son, and The Holy Spirit. We must try to comprehend the magnitude of this relationship in order to realize Our Father's love for us.

Listen in on Jesus' prayer to his Father about us before he ascended:

> My prayer is not for them alone [disciples and early believers]. I pray also for those [through the centuries], who will believe in me through their message that all of them may be one, Father, just as you are in me and I am in you. May they also be in us.
> ...I have given them the glory that you gave me [The Holy Spirit], that they may be one as we are one: I in them and you in me. May they be brought to complete unity to let the world know that you sent me and have loved them even as you have loved me.
> Father, I want those you have given me to be with me where I am, and to see my glory, the glory you have given me because you loved me before the creation of the world.
> Righteous Father, though the world does not know you, I know you, and they know that you have sent me. I have made you known to them, and will continue to make you known in order that the love you have for me may be in them and that I myself may be in them.
>
> John 17:20–26 (NIV)

An overjoyed woman, who was laughing and crying at the same time, called the television station after hearing me over the air say, "Talking to God is like talking to *your* best friend. He loves you just as you are, and you can tell Him anything." Through her tears, she said, "I've always wanted a best friend. I did not know that I could talk to God like that. Now, *God* is my best friend."

I overheard my grandchildren talking about me, and I was startled by the casualness of the statement, "She pals around with God." I thought about that. Then, I realized it was not irreverent. Rather, it was merely their view of Grama's simple relationship with God.

Let's stop now and consider, "How well do I *really* know *Our Father*? Life in our spiritual family must be more than life in many modern homes where family members live together for years without knowing each other. Often, an "eat and run, you go *your* way and I'll go mine" attitude prevails. *Knowing* a person means more than knowing his name, address, phone number, and birthday. It means we know how he feels inside; we care about what makes him laugh or cry.

Do we know *Our Father's* heart? Do we care about His feelings? A vague acquaintance with Him results in shallow prayers. In church we may sing with gusto, "Sweet Hour of Prayer, which calls me from a world of care..." At home, our scanty prayers may be, "Thank you for this food" and, "Now I lay me down to sleep."

How do our prayers mature from the child's bedtime prayer, to the awesome prayer of Moses, "Lord, show me *your* Glory!" You and I are somewhere between the child and the spiritual giant. We must grow to be like Moses and *"seek God's face."*

King David is another example. He was a "man after God's own heart." This is because David sought God's face and also repented when he sinned. We may assume that David's close relationship with God began when he was a shepherd boy. Through those early years, while he was sitting on hillsides and looking at the stars, he was communing with God. Later, David wrote, in one of his psalms of endearment to the Lord, "Look to the LORD and his strength; seek his face always" (Ps.105:4 NIV).

Each of us must ask ourselves, "Do I seek God's hand more frequently than I seek His face? Or, do I seek his heart? When I have been with Jesus, does my face reflect his glory?

Know God the Key to Mountain Moving Faith

Our faith can move mountains of adversities: Jesus said, "Have faith in God... I tell you the truth, if anyone says to this mountain, 'Go, throw *your*self into the sea,' and does not doubt in his heart but believes that what he says will happen, it will be done for him.

Therefore...whatever you ask for in prayer, believe that you have received it, and it will be *yours*" (Mk. 11:22–24).

Most of us, who have made a serious attempt to learn to pray, have studied this Scripture and tried hard not to doubt that whatever we ask we shall receive. We attached our faith on our ability to believe rather than on God's ability to respond. Consequently, our mountain remains. It is important to note the verse above, with so great a promise, begins with "Have faith in God." This is how we acquire the necessary faith to receive.

The principle in light of the Lord's Model Prayer begins, *"Our Father,* who art in heaven..."Thinking about *Our Father* puts us in the right perspective since we often enter prayer discouraged and troubled by adverse circumstances. As we look to Him and ponder His love and power, He becomes larger than our mountains. Then, when we submit our petitions, we have faith, not that the circumstance will change, but rather in God who can change the circumstance.

Therefore, faith is simply confidence in God. There is no shortcut; there is no speaking to the mountain or confessions of the mouth that will instill faith without knowing God personally.

Let's start with the fundamental characteristics of God's nature as A. W. Tozer writes in *Pursuit of God:*

> A loving Personality dominates the Bible, walking among the trees of the garden and breathing fragrance over every scene. Always a living Person is present, speaking, pleading, loving, working, and manifesting Himself whenever and wherever His people have the receptivity necessary to receive the manifestation.[13]

I heard that a little boy had this receptivity. After his mother admonished him by saying, "God is watching you." He replied, "Yes, I know. He loves me so much He can't keep His eyes off of me." We all know what it is like to adoringly watch someone whom we love.

What a contrast when we see how some people view God. Hannah W. Smith writes in *God of All Comfort:*

> Because we do not know Him, we ... get all sorts of wrong ideas about Him. We think He is an angry Judge who is on the watch for our slightest faults, or a harsh Taskmaster determined to exact from us the uttermost service, or a self-absorbed Deity demanding His full measure of honor and glory, or a far-off Sovereign concerned with His own affairs and indifferent to our welfare.[14]

Our view of God affects our prayers. We are not likely to pray at all if he is a vague deity, or if we do not believe that He loves us. Whereas, if we know His love is great and His power unlimited, we will likely pray with great faith. Let's build our faith with Scriptures that reveal God's nature, character, and power

See Our Father in Scripture

"No one has ever seen God" (Jn. 1:18 NIV), because "God is Spirit" (Jn. 4:24 NIV). Yet, He allows man to see evidence of His Presence through manifestations of His Spirit. Primarily, Scripture records these as fire and a cloud, an intensely brilliant light of glory, a dove, and in Jesus.

God Revealed His Spirit through fire, a cloud and his Glory

God spoke through a *burning bush* when He told Moses to rescue the Israelites from Egyptian bondage (Exod. 3:2 NIV). Later, as Moses led them out of Egypt, "the LORD went ahead of them in a pillar of cloud to guide them on their way and by night in a *pillar of fire* to give them light" (Exod. 13:21 NIV).

After they arrived at Mt. Sinai where God gave Moses the Ten Commandments, "the glory of the LORD looked like a *consuming fire* on top of the mountain" (Exod. 24:17 NIV).

He "lives in unapproachable light, whom no one has seen or can see" (1 Tim. 6:16 NIV). Our mortal bodies must become immortal in order to withstand the brilliance of his glory.

When Moses said, "Now show me your glory" the LORD said, "I will cause all my goodness to pass in front of you, and I will proclaim my name, the LORD, in your presence.... But," he said, "You cannot see my face, for no one may see me and live."

> Then the LORD said, "There is a place near me where you may stand on a rock. When my glory passes by, I will put you in a cleft in the rock and cover you with my hand until I have passed by. Then I will remove my hand and you will see my back; but my face must not be seen."
>
> Exodus 33:18–25 (NIV)

Even after God protected Moses by hiding him in the cleft of a rock and covering him with his hand, just the effect of being near God's Glory was so strong that Moses' face had to be covered when he went back down the mountain.

When Moses finished building the Holy Tabernacle of Worship, God sent His approval when "The glory of the LORD filled the tabernacle" (Exod. 40:34 NIV).

In the New Testament, God's Glory illuminated Jesus when He, Moses, and Elijah supernaturally appeared. "There he was transfigured before them. His face shone like the sun, and his clothes became as white as the light" (Matt. 17:2 NIV).

When God was ready for His Salvation Message to be spread over the world, His brilliant glory had a profound effect on Saul of Tarsus; he fell to the ground blinded, and arose transformed to become the first evangelist Paul the Apostle. He was empowered to blaze a path through spiritually uncharted pagan lands with the gospel of Christ. Satan and all his fury could not stop him. Jeers, deprivation, floggings, shipwreck, serpent bites, and stoning could not deter him. He charged on, until the Romans shackled him in the death-row dungeon.

When I was in Rome, I stood in that cold, damp, stone dungeon and felt austere isolation. I imagined Paul feeling moments of terror, knowing his beheading was imminent. Even so, the power of God's glory sustained Paul till the end when he wrote,

> The time has come for my departure. I have fought the good fight, I have finished the race, I have kept the faith. Now there is in store for me the crown of righteousness, which the Lord, the righteous Judge, will award...to all who have longed for his appearing.
> 2 Timothy 4:6–8 (NIV)

God Revealed His Spirit as a dove

God chose the gentle dove to convey his presence when he announced to the world that Jesus was his Son: "As soon as Jesus was baptized, he went up out of the water. At that moment heaven was opened, and he saw the Spirit of God descending like a dove and lighting on him. And a voice from heaven said, 'This is my Son, whom I love; with him I am well pleased'" (Matt. 3:16, 17 NIV).

God Revealed Jesus through the ancient prophets

Since the New Testament is the fulfillment of the Old Testament, we must listen to the ancient prophets. Jesus fulfilled over one hundred prophecies identifying the Messiah who would become the King of Kings sitting on the Eternal Throne of David.[15]

First, Jesus was a double heir to the throne. From the tribe of Judah, Jesus' legal father, Joseph, was a descendant of King David's Son, Solomon (Matt.1; Lu. 1:32; Acts 13:22, 23–39). His mother, Mary, was a descendant of King David's older son, Nathan.[16]

Micah prophesied, more than five hundred years before Jesus' birth. "But you, Bethlehem Ephrathah, *Though* you are little among the thousands of Judah, *Yet* out of you shall come forth to Me The

One to be Ruler in Israel, Whose goings forth *are* from of old, From everlasting" (Micah 2:5 NKJV). The birth occurred about one thousand years after David had been born in Bethlehem; Jesus, heir to his throne, was born in the same obscure village.

Now after Jesus was born in Bethlehem of Judea in the days of Herod the king, behold, wise men from the East came to Jerusalem, saying, *"Where is He who has been born King of the Jews? For we have seen His star in the East* and have come to worship Him."

When Herod the king heard *this,* he was troubled, and all Jerusalem with him. And when he had gathered all the chief priests and scribes of the people together, he inquired of them where the Christ was to be born.

So they said to him, "In Bethlehem of Judea, for thus it is written by the prophet:"

> But you, Bethlehem, in the land of Judah, Are not the least among the rulers of Judah For out of you shall come a Ruler Who will shepherd My people Israel
>
> Matthew 2:1–6 (NKJV)

The ancient prophecies go on and on: He was...born of a virgin... called out of Egypt...rejected...came riding on a donkey...the deaf will hear, the blind see...a light to the Gentiles...new everlasting covenant...prophet like Moses, speaking God's words...hated without a reason...Came to do the will of God...Anointed by God...a priest after the order of Melchizedek...a new priesthood established...Passover sacrifice with no bones broken...hung upon a tree as a curse...thirsty during execution...accused by false witnesses...struck on the head...hands and feet pierced...soldiers cast lots for his coat...given gall and vinegar...beaten and spat upon.... [17]

Many of the prophecies are in the Psalms. And, Isaiah 53 is the classic prophecy chapter for Jesus on the cross.

We see God's Spirit through Jesus' attitudes and actions

His life exemplified love, mercy, and compassion as He healed the sick, raised the dead, fed the hungry, delivered those who were bound from demonic powers, and spoke words of forgiveness, peace, and hope. He told the woman caught in adultery, "Then neither do I condemn you... Go now and leave your life of sin" (Jn. 8:11 NIV).

Jesus read in the Synagogue from Isaiah about Himself, "The Spirit of the Lord is on me, because he has anointed me to preach good news to the poor. He has sent me to proclaim freedom for the prisoners and recovery of sight for the blind, to release the oppressed, to proclaim the year of the Lord's favor" (Lu. 4:18, 19 NIV).

I complimented a prominent man, Frank Boggus on his life of benevolent acts. Since we knew each other only socially, He said, "You do not *know* me." For fifty years I had seen his life, therefore, I knew his heart. We know God's heart because we have seen Jesus' life. Jesus said, "If you really knew me, you would know my Father as well. From now on, you do know him and have seen him" (Jn. 14:7 NIV).

God Revealed His Spirit in Jesus. The Father and Son Are One

The name Jesus means God with us. "He is the image of the invisible God, the firstborn over all creation" (Col. 1:15 NIV). "For in Christ all the fullness of the Deity lives in bodily form" (Col. 2:9 NIV). Jesus is "the radiance of God's glory and the exact representation of his being, sustaining all things by his powerful word" (Heb. 1:3 NIV).

In the beginning God, His Spirit, His Word were all one. God equates His Word to Himself. His Word took on human form and became Jesus in the flesh.

> Since the beginning, the Word was with God, and the Word was God. He was with God in the beginning. Through him [His Word spoken] all things were made; without him" (His

Word) nothing was made that has been made. In him was life, and that life was the light of men...The Word became flesh [Jesus] and made his dwelling among us.

John 1:1–4, 14 (NIV)

Being human, yet spotlessly pure, Jesus was qualified to redeem fallen man.

An angel of the Lord appeared to [Joseph] in a dream and said, "Joseph son of David, do not be afraid to take Mary home as *your* wife, because what is conceived in her is from the Holy Spirit. She will give birth to a son, and you are to give him the name Jesus, because he will save his people from their sins."

Matthew 1:20–23 (NIV)

All this took place to fulfill what the Lord had said through the prophet [Isaiah], "The virgin will be with child and will give birth to a son, and they will call him Immanuel" which means, "God with us."

Isaiah 7:14 (NIV)

God Ministers in Three Persons: The Father, Son and Holy Spirit

The Holy Spirit *is* the spirit of the Father and *is* the spirit of the Son. The Trinity ministers as three persons. Never call the Holy Spirit "It." He is a divine Person in the Trinity.

St. Patrick of Ireland used the Shamrock to illustrate the mystery of the Trinity. He asks, "Is this one leaf or three? If one leaf, why are there three lobes of equal size? If three leaves, why is there just one stem?" That made sense to me.

Similarly, this clover leaf grows in our yard. Surely, it was in the divine planning for the three leaves to be shaped as hearts, since God is Love.

The stem is the *spirit source* of three persons who are identical in nature and character. They function as three different persons in harmony with each other. The principle reminded me that Jesus said his spirit *is* our source. "*I am the vine; you are the branches.* If a man remains in me and I in him, he will bear much fruit; apart from me you can do nothing" (Jn. 15:5 NIV)

Another familiar example: Catherine Marshall in *Beyond Ourselves* writes that she heard a minister teach a simple lesson:

> "Children," he began, "When we speak of the Trinity, we mean the three Persons that go to make up God: God, the Father; Jesus Christ, the Son; and the Holy Spirit.
>
> Now look at these three jars. This one has water. This one has ice, and that one, steam. They all look different, don't they? Yet you know that ice is only frozen water. And, that when *your* mother boils water in a pan on the stove, steam rises from it. That means that water, ice, and steam are really the same...
>
> Now, the same thing is true of the Trinity... Jesus Christ, the water of Life, is different from the Father... The Holy Spirit, like the powerful steam that can drive an engine, is different from Christ and the Father, yet the same.[18] [They are identical in nature and character, but their ministries emphasize different characteristics]

Another simple illustration is in how one person functions in different ways: I am a wife, mother, grandmother, friend, Bible teacher, choir member and private corporation board member. The only person who knows me as a wife is my husband; he calls me, "Hon" [Honey]. To my grandchildren, I function as "Grama." Friends at church and at the office call me Fran or Frances. In all of the relationships, I am still Frances Knight.

God is My Father...Jesus is my Redeemer, Savior, my Rock and my Hightower, my Living Water and Bread of Life...The Holy Spirit is my Counselor and Comforter...I read in a Southern Baptist Sunday School lesson:

> *Our Father* is the Eternal Spirit. Jesus is God manifested as a human with a mission to redeem mankind. He returned to Heaven to be at The Father's right side. After Jesus ascended, The Holy Spirit came to earth to be the connector between God and man. He is the Spirit of God and The Spirit of Jesus and The Spirit who lives within the hearts of redeemed man. It is through Him our prayers flow to *Our Father* and he communicates with us, his children. He is the power of God and our source of spiritual strength.[19]

The Holy Spirit is also the common bond of love among all Christians. On television, I saw Glenn Beck's "Restoring Honor Rally" in Washington D.C. Kennedy Center. The huge auditorium was filled with like-minded people. The commentator said that he had been in many churches but had never felt anything like this. Trying to describe the feeling, he said, "It is like a family reunion." It *was* a family reunion; God's Holy Spirit bonded people who had never met.

One person said that it was so strange seeing a group of people huddled together in a hotel lobby praying. When they were finished, one said to another, "So glad to meet you, brother."

God's Attributes

God is Holy

Holiness is God's primary attribute, the moral essence of His Spirit: "Holy, holy, holy is the LORD Almighty; the whole earth is full of his glory" (Isa. 6:3 NIV). I believe glory is the radiating manifestation of the purity of God's holiness energized by the power of His love. God and His glory are inseparable; where He is, His glory shines.

God is the Only God

"This is what the LORD says Israel's King and Redeemer, the LORD Almighty: I am the first and I am the last; apart from me there is no God" (Isa. 44:6 NIV).

God Reveals His Basic Nature

God tells us the nature of His Spirit when His glory passed by Moses on Mt. Sinai, the Lord said He was "The LORD, the LORD, the compassionate and gracious God, slow to anger, abounding in love and faithfulness, maintaining love to thousands, and forgiving wickedness, rebellion and sin" (Exod. 34:6, 7 NIV).

God Never Changes

God is eternally the same: "I the LORD do not change" (Mal. 3:6 NIV). Worldly people change their moral values and try to establish what is right by popular acceptance of their evolving standards. Nevertheless, disregarding God's laws of righteousness is only to their destruction because the axis of life remains on God. Who he is eternally remains the same. "Jesus Christ *is* the same yesterday, today, and forever" (Heb. 13:8 NIV).

God is Self-Existent

God is Life: "As the Father has life in himself, so he has granted the Son to have life in himself" (Jn. 5:26 NIV).

God has All Knowledge

God knows all: "Known unto God are all his works from the beginning of the world" (Acts 15:18 KJV).

An amazing thing happened. God's spirit may speak through the lips of other Christians. Bob had prostate cancer. Before we left for M.

D. Anderson, our church prayed and friends came to our home and prayed. After we arrived in Houston, we searched for a post office to mail a letter. Finally, we found one some distance from the Medical Center. We waited in line...and then, we were called to a counter with a postal attendant who was a black woman. Bob expressed his approval of a small picture of Jesus on her cubicle wall, while I was thinking that black people have special faith in God born through their history of stress. Bob handed her the nondescript envelope. She looked straight into his face and said, "You are here for treatment at M.D. Anderson. Pack up your bags and go home, you are healed."

Bob and I were stunned. We just stared at each other trying to absorb the improbability of the circumstances and magnitude of the message. We drove in silence. Later, he said that he didn't have faith enough to cancel his radiation treatments. After six weeks, we packed up and went home. Now, after we have thought about the message many times, we are convinced that God healed him with the "Amen." That is the only explanation for the woman having knowledge that only God knew. His Holy Spirit speaks through his children.

Another illustration about how God's Holy Spirit gives information: I received a special letter from Sylvia Riddle who heard me speak at Calvary Baptist and Baptist Temple in McAllen, Texas *about fifteen years ago*. She wrote,

> On Monday, in a devotional I read in Jer. 6:16 (NLT) 'Stop at the crossroad and look around ask for the godly way and walk in it.' Yesterday, while still seeking and praying...; I picked up *another* devotional and there was that same scripture: 'Stop at the crossroad and look around ask for the godly way and walk in it.' Then, He reminded me of you!
>
> Yesterday I said to the Lord, 'I don't know if you still hand out double portions of anointing like Elijah-Elisha. But if you do, I would like Frances Knight's anointing to study, teach and live out your Word. The Lord's Prayer will be my prayer 'til he takes me (to Heaven) or, comes for me.'

My name was not important—God was reminding her of *"what I had said."* I had spoken truth about "the godly way to walk"; I had taught on "The Lord's Prayer."

God is Permanent Truth

What God has said is eternal true: "Heaven and earth will pass away, but my words will never pass away" (Matt. 24:35 NIV).

God is Love

God's love is the most powerful force in the world. Everything He does is ultimately from this viewpoint. "This is how God showed his love among us: He sent his one and only Son into the world that we might live through him. This is love: not that we loved God, but that he loved us and sent his Son as an atoning sacrifice for our sins" (1 Jn. 4:8–10 NIV). We must absorb the fact that God loves us.

God is Trustworthy

God is honest; he cannot lie. Believe his promises. What God has said is eternally true: "Heaven and earth will pass away, but my words will never pass away" (Matt. 24:35 NIV). "A man's word is his bond" is almost an archaic concept, according to liberal modern standards. It is not so with God because, "Not one word has failed of all the good promises he gave through his servant Moses" (1 Kings 8:56 NIV). We must also "Know therefore that the LORD *your* God is God; he is the faithful God, keeping his covenant of love to a thousand generations of those who love him and keep his commands" (Deut. 7:9 NIV).

God Gives

Notice the word *every*: "Every good and perfect gift is from above, coming down from the Father of the heavenly lights..." (Jas.1:17 NIV). God does not limit His giving: "For the LORD God is a sun and shield; the LORD bestows favor and honor; no good thing does he withhold from those whose walk is blameless" (Ps. 84:11 NIV). "My God shall supply all *your* need according to His riches in glory by Christ Jesus" (Phil. 4:19 NIV).

God Cares

Our Father doesn't want us to worry: "Cast all *your* anxiety on him because he cares for you" (1 Pet. 5:7 NIV). "Do not be anxious about anything, but in everything, by prayer and petition, with thanksgiving, present *your* requests to God. And the peace of God, which transcends all understanding, will guard *your* hearts and *your* minds in Christ Jesus" (Phil. 4:6, 7 NIV).

God Sends Angels

For it is written: "He will command his angels concerning you to guard you carefully" (Luke 4:10 NIV). "Are not all angels ministering spirits sent to serve those who will inherit salvation?" (Heb.1:14 NIV).

After our powerful session of prayer in out Ladies Bible Study Class, Carolyn Thompson, mayor of Elkton, Tennessee said, "…I had a vision; I got this mental image of an angelic force (I cannot say exactly how many but several) hovering over our 'little tabernacle.' I had a feeling of protection. I remember thinking, 'What are they going to do?' I got a clear impression that God is doing, and is about to do a great and mighty work here in this church.

> If you make the Most High your dwelling—even the LORD, who is my refuge. Then no harm will befall you, no disaster will come near your tent. For he will command his angels concerning you to guard you in all your ways;
>
> Psalm 91:9–11 (NIV)

I was driving across a railroad track. I glanced to the right and all I could see in the passenger window was the nose of a train. A flash thought: "He's got me! If I accelerate, it may hit the back door, spin the van, and I might live through it." Getting across the track was not even an option. I gunned it!

Trembling, I parked, put my face in my arms over the wheel and sobbed. The train slowed; the engineer looked out the window to see if I was alright. He had not blown his horn. There is no doubt in my mind that God had a mighty angel ready to shove me across the tracks.

Billy Graham wrote in his book, "Angels: God's Secret Agents":

> The great majority of Christians can recall some incident in which their lives, in times of critical danger, have been miraculously preserved an almost plane crash, a near car wreck, a fierce temptation. Though they may have seen no angels, their presence could explain why tragedy was averted. We should always be grateful for the goodness of God, who uses these wonderful friends called angels to protect us... [20] Scriptures are full of dramatic evidences of the protective care of angels in their earthly service to the people of God.[21]

God is Always Present

God reminds us of His presence throughout Scripture: "Am I only a God nearby... and not a God far away? Can anyone hide in secret places so that I cannot see him?" declares the LORD. "Do not I fill heaven and earth?" (Jer. 23:23, 24 NIV).

A golden chain connects our hearts so mine won't slip away.

When Bob and I faced grief, God's abiding presence sustained us during the months preceding our son's death. He comforted Ric too. Since doubts and fears frequently dominate a terminal patient's thoughts, Dr. Penny Jaffe asked, "Ric, there is something different about you, what is it?" He told her about being a Christian. Shortly before he died, he said, "Mother, God has never left me." Knowing that God also revealed his presence to Ric and provided him with supernatural assurance greatly comforted us during those days. It continues to provide solace.

Dr. Oscar Thompson professor of evangelism at Southwestern Baptist Theological Seminary conveyed God's abiding presence, comfort and sustaining power more profoundly when he told his class shortly before he died of cancer, "Friends, I've been all the way to the bottom and it is solid rock!" [22]

Our Father Has Tender Emotions

In Scripture, we see not only God's nature, character, and creation but also, His emotions. The Bible records every situation common to man, and also God's feelings about them. Yes, His judgment has fallen at times throughout man's history—but, not without warnings, pleadings, and grief on God's part.

We see evidence of God's sorrow when He said about His chosen people, the Israelites, "How I have been grieved by their adulterous hearts, which have turned away from me, and by their eyes, which have lusted after their idol" (Ezek. 6:9 NIV). When righteous judgment fell against Moab and Kirheres for their wicked ways, God mourned through the weeping prophet, Jeremiah, "Therefore I wail over Moab, for all Moab I cry out, I moan for the men of Kir Hareseth" (Jer. 48:31 NIV).

We see Jesus' love and feel the grief of His rejection as he laments over the wayward Israelites, "O Jerusalem, Jerusalem, you who kill the prophets and stone those sent to you, how often I have longed to gather *your* children together, as a hen gathers her chicks under her wings, *but you were not willing*" (Matt. 23:37 NIV).

God's love always reaches out to His children. Even while the Israelites were in foreign captivity because of their wickedness, God faithfully promised: "I myself will search for my sheep and look after them. I will search for the lost and bring back the strays. I will bind up the injured and strengthen the weak…" (Ezek. 34:11–16 NIV). Then, without any merit on the Israelites' part, God promised them a thousand year Utopia on this earth, and Paradise forevermore if they would only love and follow Him.

Jesus wept when Lazarus died (Jn. 11:35 NIV). This was more than wiping away a few tears. Lazarus, Martha and Mary were like family members. When Herod beheaded His beloved disciple, John, Jesus went off to be alone in His grief (Matt. 14:13 NIV). He loves us with the same intensity.

The closer we draw to Him, the clearer we will see Him. The effects of seeing Jesus sustained Stephen," (one of the seven deacons in the first Jerusalem church), before he was stoned to death. His spirit rose beyond the horrific circumstance when a heavenly scene captivated his attention. Stephen's face looked like an angels' as he "looked up to heaven and saw the glory of God, and Jesus standing at the right hand of God. 'Look,' he said, 'I see heaven open and the Son of Man standing at the right hand of God'" (Acts 7:55, 56 NIV).

Like Moses and Stephen, when you and I turn our eyes above the realities of this world, to truly seek the face of God, there will be a quiet glow of serenity in our countenance. The closer we draw to him, the more we will long to see him more clearly. In nothing but Christ! David Wilkerson writes:

> Ever since the Cross, all spiritual giants have had one thing in common… they became lost in the glorious vastness of Christ; and they died lamenting they still knew so little of Christ, yet wanted so much more knowledge of Him.
>
> So it was with all the disciples… with early church fathers; [Polycarp and Ignatius to Augustine, Francis of Assisi… and later] with Luther, Zwingli, and the Puritans; with the pious English preachers over the past two hundred years… Wesley, Fletcher, Whitefield, Mueller… And so it was and is with the pious Americans Tozer, Ravenhill, and many others.[5]

Though we cannot know God as well as we want to, we experience His involvement in every area of our lives. He empowers us to love Him, and our fellow man. He gives inexpressible joy and peace, even in the midst of our trials. He blesses, protects, and relieves our pains more times and in more ways than we will know.

A sweet Christian friend, whose son had just committed suicide, told me, with moist eyes and a serene smile, "Jesus has not left me for one moment. He has given me strength and comfort through these past few days that I never dreamed possible."

A loving family member wrote familiar words about God's unceasing love, "The Lord has blessed us. When we fall down, He picks us up. When we doubt He gives us faith. And, when we cry, He wipes our tears. When we falter He gives us courage. And, most of all, when we fail Him, He forgives us always. I now know why we love Him more than anyone else. He is *Our Father*, our best friend and counselor who is within reach at all times. It amazes me how long it takes for some of us to reach out for Him when His arms are open at all times. But, once we grab hold, we never want to let go."

God Created and Gave Man the Power to Rule

In the beginning God created the heavens and the earth.
Genesis 1:1 (NIV)

For in Him all things were created, both in the heavens and on earth, visible and invisible, whether thrones or dominions or rulers or authorities; all things have been created through Him and for Him. He is before all things, and in him all things hold together.
Colossians 1:16, 17 (NIV)

Then God said, "Let us make man *in our image*, in our likeness, *and let them rule*…So God created man in his own image, in the image of God he created him; male and female he created them."
Genesis 1:26, 27 (NIV)

There is no plausible conflict between creation and science. God created and scientists are trying to figure out how it was done. The universe is like a colossal puzzle and they find one small piece at a time. The reason some highly intelligent scientists cannot understand that there *has* to be a Divine Designer is because "He [Satan] has blinded their eyes and deadened their hearts, so they can neither see with their eyes, nor understand with their hearts..." (Jn.12:40 NIV).

God created us in His image, and gave us power to be. He created the incredible world and gave us eyes to see. It is all so amazing. For example:

When the Light of the World reflects upon the Living Water, droplets sparkle like a ballet of diamonds. At sunrise, gentle ripples twinkle across a lake. Grass on an ordinary lawn...leaves and flowers...glisten as in a fantasy. At sunset, we feel peace. How often does this marvelous production go unnoticed?

Visualize the vast oceans, the majestic mountains, and the dense forests. Hear the trumpeting elephant, the bleating sheep and purring kitten. See the hummingbird suspended in air. Touch the velvety rose and smell the fragrance. Watch the fluttering butterfly, see the flurry of snowflakes, and hold the newborn baby.

Look through the microscope and see cells multiplying and atoms dividing. Look through the telescope and scan the heavens. Eons of light years behind the farthest star, is much more. The galaxies are as the sands of the seashore synchronized to revolve in a twinkling heavenly ballet. The power of God's Word spoke it into place.

We have all seen God's awesome power as lighting lashed across the sky in a terrifying storm with its loud clashing thunder. In the midst of it all we have felt God's reassuring presence reminding us, "Do not be afraid, for I have created all things, I sustain all things, and I have promised, "I will never leave you..." (Heb.13:5 NIV).

When we think of his sustaining and perpetuating power, consider: Every seed knows exactly what to do.

As we daily contemplate the beauty and power of God's creation, our faith increases. We also fill our minds with treasured memories which may later sustain us during the bleak times of life when we must dwell upon what is good to find peace for our souls.

Now that we know more about Our Father in Heaven, and have reviewed the wonders of His creation, we feel like joining the vast choir of Christians throughout the centuries and jubilantly sing, "Oh Lord our God, How great thou are!"

How Great Thou Are
by Carl Boberg

Lord my God! When I in awesome wonder–
Consider all the worlds Thy hands have made,
I see the stars, I hear the rolling thunder,
Thy pow'r throughout the universe displayed,
Then sings my soul, my Savior God to Thee;
How great Thou art, how great Thou art![23]

Sample Prayer

Learn More about "Our Father"

Father, we come to you through the name of our Lord Jesus Christ. You are wonderful in every way. You *are* love! In your love, you are tenderhearted toward all your children. We thank you for your kindness and compassion; you never give us what we really deserve.

You give us mercy, even in our failings, because you understand how we have become who we are. You are guiding us toward a better life.

You are our Bread of Life and our Living Water. You are our Hightower to whom we can run when we have troubles. You are our Redeemer, our Shepherd and our Rock of stability.

We know that you want to hear and answer our prayers in greater measure than we ever thought possible. Help us not to wring our hands in doubt but have the assuring Mountain Moving Faith as we simply trust in you.

Thank you for hearing our prayer. We love you, Lord. Amen.

Living Christianity Assignment

Bible Study—Read Psalm 91 and Psalm 103. Try to memorize them.

> I will say of the Lord, "He is my refuge and my fortress, my God, in whom I trust."
>
> Psalm 91:2

Prayer—Go to your *Hightower* to be alone with your Father, and just talk.

> Praise the Lord, O my soul.
>
> Psalm 103:22 (NIV)

Works—Think of the way Jesus treated people: Be kind and courteous, patient and understanding, in your home to the young and the old... and to the sacker in the supermarket.

> He does not treat us as our sins deserve or repay us according to our iniquities. For as high as the heavens are above the earth, so great is his love.
>
> Psalm 103:10–11 (NIV)

III: Revere Our Father's Almighty Name

"Hallowed be your name"

> He will be called Wonderful Counselor, Mighty God, Everlasting Father, Prince of Peace.
>
> Isaiah 9:6 (NIV)

III: Revere Our Father's Almighty Name

"Hallowed be your name"

- Standing on Holy Ground
- God's Name: "I AM"
- God Gave Jesus a Name Above All

  - Our Salvation Is in His Name
  - Jesus Is Present in His Name
  - We Pray in Jesus' Name

- Praise Emerges—the Language of Victory
- Sample Prayer: Revere *Our Father's* Almighty Name"
- Living Christianity Assignment

III:
Revere Our Father's Almighty Name

"Hallowed be your name"

I sat at a small conference table with a visitor who, for years, had notoriously profaned God's name. After several expletives, I could not remain socially silent. So, I politely asked, "Larry, why do you profane God's name?" He looked surprised, blushed, and stammered defensively, "I don't do that."

He apparently had used God's name as a sentence filler and an emotional explanation point for so long, he didn't consider its significance: Hallowed *means* we regard God's name as being sacred and holy. Jesus taught us to pray, *"Hallowed be your name"* because God takes the reverence of His name seriously. One of the Ten Commandments is:

> Do not profane my holy name. I must be acknowledged as holy...
>
> Leviticus 22:32 (NIV)

> You shall not misuse the name of the LORD *your* God, for the LORD will not hold anyone guiltless who misuses his name.
>
> Exodus 20:7 (NIV)

> This is what the Sovereign LORD says: It is not for *your* sake, O house of Israel, that I am going to do these things, but *for the sake of my holy name*, which you have profaned among the nations where you have gone.
>
> Ezekiel 36:22 (NIV)

Standing on Holy Ground

While worshiping in a Messianic Jewish Synagogue in Houston, I noticed blank spaces for words in their writings. A member explained that many Jews still hold to the ancient tradition of not writing or speaking the most sacred word for God. Instead, they substitute the word "Lord" [Adonai].

When Moses was in God's presence at the *burning bush*, God said, "Do not come any closer...Take off *your* sandals, for the place where you are standing is holy ground" (Exod. 3:5 NIV). When we come into God's presence, we too, must remove our sandals; we must remove our sins and anything else that is between us and holy ground. "Just as he who called you is holy, so be holy in all you do; for it is written: Be holy, because I am holy'" (1 Pet. 1:15, 16 NIV).

Now that is a lofty goal. We all know that if we did everything perfectly and repented of all our sins, we still could never, in ourselves, be holy. We can only come before God in Christ our Savior's holiness. "This is how God showed his love among us: He sent his one and only Son into the world that we might live through him" (1 Jn. 4:9 NIV). Jesus said, "I am the vine; you are the branches" (Jn. 15:5 NIV). "If the root is holy, so are the branches" (Rom. 11:16 NIV).

From another view regarding our coming into God's presence, you and I are sometimes guilty of rushing through our prayer without coming to the holy place where we meet God. First, we must clear away the fog of human emotions involved in earthly circumstances. This is done by meditating about God's love, with a pure heart. Our Father wants to meet us in this holy place where there is power in prayer.

III: Revere Our Father's Almighty Name

During a special hospital visit, I felt I was standing on holy ground. Our eldest deacon, Mr. Huie, was very near death. I walked into his dark room. As I held his hand and talked about God's love, God's Presence was so strong that I thought, "This ground is holy." In awe, I sensed I should leave him alone with God. I briefly prayed, "Father, in Jesus' name, please heal Mr. Huie." Then, I quietly slipped away.

Within the week, he left the hospital and soon returned to church. Since he is a quiet person, he surprised everyone as he walked to the pulpit to speak. He said, "God raised me. Frances walked into my room during my darkest hour. As she held my hand and prayed, something happened. I felt God's great love and peace. It was the turning point in my recovery." God responded to our expressions of adoration.

Before I give further examples of healings through prayer let me say that I am not what some may call a "faith healer." I can do nothing, but pray. Only God has the power to heal. Though it is true I have seen amazing prayer answers, I have also prayed when seemingly nothing happened. God is lovingly in control; we seek Him.

Similar to Mr. Huie's recovery: I walked into the Critical Care Unit of the hospital to the bedside of a dying cancer patient. The family had gathered. I held his hand and said, "Charles, how are you doing?" He groggily replied, "I am dead."

I said, "No, Charles, you are not dead."

Confused, he said, "I'm not dead?"

"No, you are alive." He pondered the marvelous revelation and smiled like a child before Christmas as he repeated the message, "I'm not dead."

Once he felt secure in that truth, I changed the subject to God's love for him, and told him that God's Spirit was right here with him. After a short conversation about God's love, I explained how to have eternal life. He asked Jesus to come into his heart. That afternoon, Charles left the intensive care unit. In a few days he went home and returned to his job.

By bringing an awareness of God's presence into the room, God's power rescued Charles from the clutches of imminent death, gave him a chance to accept eternal life, and significantly added to his time on earth. What a difference a reverent recognition of God's presence made!

God's name: "I AM"

God's all-inclusive name is "I AM." When God told Moses to go to Egypt and bring the Israelites out of bondage, Moses said they would want to know the name of the God who sent him. God said to Moses,

> I Am Who I Am. This is what you are to say to the Israelites: I Am has sent me to you... This is my name forever...
> Exodus 3:14, 15 9 (NIV)

Concerning the name *"I AM,"* Dr. Pentecost, a well-known professor at the Dallas Theological Seminary wrote,

> It contains each tense of the verb 'to be' and might be translated, I was, I am, and I shall always continue to be. The 'I AM' of the burning bush now stands fully declared in the blessed Person of our Savior who said, *'I Am* the bread of life,' *'I Am* the good shepherd'... *'I Am* the light of the world,' *'I Am* the way, the truth and the life,' *'I Am* the resurrection and the life,' *'I Am* the true vine.' He is the eternal *'I AM'* 'the same, yesterday, today, and forever'... There is a depth here which no finite mind can fathom. *'I AM that I AM'* (Exod. 3:14 NIV) announced that the great God is self-existent, beside whom *there is no other* (Isa. 45:5 NIV). Without beginning, without ending, 'from everlasting to everlasting' (Rev. 22:13 NIV), He is God.[24]

The sacred covenant name for Israel's God was Yahweh (Exod. 3:15 NIV). *"Yahweh"* was later transliterated into English letters as *"Jehovah."*[25] This name represents the sum total of all of God's redemptive ministries clarified with different names.

Dr. Doug Alexander wrote "PRAISE JEHOVAH" identifying the ministries of God through his names.

Praise Jehovah
Praise the *Name of Jesus*,
He's my *Rock*, He's my *Fortress*, He's my *Deliverer*
Praise *Jehovah-Jireh*, Praise Jehovah-Jireh,
He's my *Source*, He's my *Sufficiency*, He's my *Provider*
Praise *Jehovah-Rophe*, Praise Jehovah-Rophe,
He's my *Health*, He's my *Healing*, He's my *Physician*
Praise *Jehovah-Nissi*, Praise Jehovah-Nissi,
He's my *Flag*, He's my *Banner*, He's my *Victory*
Praise *Jehovah-M'kaddesh*, Praise Jehovah-M'kaddesh,
He's my *Light*, He's my *Holiness*, He's my *Sanctity*
Praise *Jehovah-Shalom*, Praise Jehovah-Shalom,
He's my *Peace*, He's My *Comfort*, He's My *Security*
Praise *Jehovah-Rohi*, Praise Jehovah-Rohi,
He's my *Guide*, He's my *Shepherd*, He's my *Protector*
Praise *Jehovah-Tsidkenu*, Praise Jehovah-Tsidkenu,
He's my *Life*, He's my *Redemption*, He's my *Righteousness*
Praise *Jehovah-Shammah*, Praise Jehovah-Shammah,
He's my *Friend*,
He's my *Faithfulness*,
He's *Omnipresent*.[26]

God Gave Jesus a Name Above All

Jesus humbled himself and became obedient to death even on the cross! Therefore, God exalted him to the highest place and gave him the name that is above every name, that at the name of Jesus every knee should bow, in heaven and on earth and under the earth, and every tongue confess that Jesus Christ is Lord, to the glory of God the Father.

Philippians 2:8–11 (NIV)

Our Salvation Is in His Name

In Jesus' name we have eternal life: "These are written that you may believe that Jesus is the Christ, the Son of God, and that by believing you may have life *in his name*" (Jn. 20:31 NIV).

> Everyone who calls on the *name of the Lord* will be saved.
> Romans 10:13 (NIV)

> To those who believed *in his name*, he gave the right to become children of God.
> John 1:12 (NIV)

> Repent and be baptized, every one of you, *in the name of Jesus Christ* for the forgiveness of *your* sins. And you will receive the gift of the Holy Spirit.
> Acts 2:38 (NIV)

Jesus Is Present in His Name

Jesus said, "The Counselor, the Holy Spirit, whom the Father will *send in my name, will teach you all things and will remind you of everything I have said to you*" (Jn. 14:26 NIV). And, "Where two or three come together *in my name*, there am I with them" [through the presence of His Holy Spirit] (Matt.18:20 NIV).

We Pray in Jesus' Name

Powerful promises for prayer answers are in Jesus' name:

> And I will do whatever you ask *in my name*, so that the Son may bring glory to the Father. You may ask me for anything *in my name*, and I will do it
> John 14:13, 14 (NIV)

> In that day you will no longer ask me anything. I tell you the truth, my Father will give you whatever you ask *in my name*. Until now you have not asked for anything *in my name*. Ask and you will receive and *your* joy will be complete... In that day you will ask *in my name*. I am not saying that I will ask the Father on *your* behalf. No, the Father himself loves you because you have loved me and have believed that I came from God
>
> John 16:23, 24, 26, 27 (NIV)

An example of healing through the name of Jesus happened in my Sunday school class. A young woman routinely sat as close to me as possible because of her unreliable hearing aid. When she was a child her dad boxed her ears regularly as one form of severe punishment. He burst both ear drums when she was four. As a young adult, only her right ear was strong enough for minimal help by an aid.

As I began teaching the lesson, the thought occurred to me, "God wants His sweet daughter to hear like the rest of us." I took about one step forward and put my hands over her ears as I thought of the Scripture, "And these signs will accompany those who believe: *In my name* they will... place their hands on sick people, and they will get well" (Mk. 16:17,18 NIV).

And then, I quoted a scripture: "When Peter and John saw the lame man at the gate Peter said, *'Silver or gold I do not have, but what I have I give you. In the name of Jesus Christ of Nazareth, walk.'"* Likewise, I say unto you, "In the name of Jesus Christ of Nazareth, Hear! So be it as is prayed!" I stepped back and resumed the lesson (Acts 3:6 NIV).

After the class, she said, "I could hardly contain my joy until the class was over. I wanted to shout, *'I can hear!'* Sound, as a spotlight beam, began penetrating my ears. At first, it was as a pinhole and then it grew until the room was filled with sounds. I could even hear Mike Sullivan teaching in the next room." I thought, "If she couldn't hear Mike's dynamic preaching through the thin wall, she *had* to be deaf." Later, when we were outside, she said that she could hear the wind rustling the leaves in the trees.

The next class session I wanted to be sure the class knew that the healing occurred through Jesus' name, so I read Peter's response to the Scribes and Pharisees who, after seeing the lame man walking and leaping asked, "By what power or what name did you do this?" Then Peter, filled with the Holy Spirit, said to them: "*It is by the name of Jesus Christ of Nazareth,* whom you crucified but whom God raised from the dead that this man stands before you healed" (Acts 4:7, 8, 10 NIV).

Later, she went to her doctor to share the good news. He examined her ears and said, "There is *no way* you are hearing *anything* out of those ears." She went into the hall and talked to him through the wall. He said, "I don't know how you are doing that, but you aren't hearing out of *those* ears."

Years later, I talked with her on the telephone to verify her continued healing. I asked, "Are you wearing a hearing aid?"

> She said, "Oh, no, I can hear just as well as you can."
> I asked, "Could you have talked on the phone before you were healed?"
> She said, "Oh, no. The words would have been muffled and not understandable."

All of this time, I had wondered how God rerouted her hearing. Recently, I got a clue when a hearing aid specialist said that some people's hearing could be helped because of the vibrations to the bone behind the ear. Also, she said, "There is a sensory in the brain that had something to do with hearing."

Clearly, God can work within biological, psychological, spiritual, and atmospheric laws in his universe that scientists have yet to discover. And, he will do just that to answer prayers that are according to his will.

Praise Emerges the Language of Victory!

Praise is an outward expression that emerges from a deep, profound reverence for God. His ears are attentive when we pray, worship and praise Him. "I desire therefore that the men" [Men and Women in the Church] pray everywhere, lifting up holy hands..." (1 Tim. 2:7–9 NKJV).

King David, who wrote the Psalms of Praise, inspires us to begin our worship with praise: "Enter his gates" [the gates of The Tabernacle] with thanksgiving and his courts with praise..." (Ps.100:4 NIV). "But thou art holy, O thou who inhabitest the praises of Israel" (Ps. 22:3 KJV). "Shout for joy to the Lord, all the earth. Worship the Lord with gladness; come before him with joyful songs" (Ps. 100:1, 2 NIV).

Those of us who have sung the church hymns for many years sometimes sing ritualistically without putting our whole heart into the message of commitment and praise. Conversely, imagine how it would be if all worshipers were to enter sanctuaries over the world joyfully and enthusiastically singing, "Oh for a thousand tongues to sing, Blessed be the name of the Lord! The glories of my God and King, Blessed be the name of the Lord!"[27]

We would be spiritually harmonizing with myriads of angels around God's throne who praise Him day and night. If this were to happen, Christendom would be energized with unprecedented spiritual power.

In the Messianic Jewish Synagogue in Houston, there was deep reverence as well as great joy in their worship services. Young ladies dressed in flowing dresses danced to Israeli music. Bob and I felt as though we were in Jerusalem on the day of Pentecost, when God's Holy Spirit first descended to fill the hearts of believers. Wearing tradition Jewish caps and prayer shawls, they were praying to "Y'Shua Hamushiach Adonai," Jesus Messiah God Lord.

After the Israelites walked through the Red Sea on dry land, they praised God! It is very easy to praise in the wake of victory and blessings. David Wilkerson wrote, "They praised on the wrong side of the sea. They should have praised when they were trapped between the sea and the Egyptian army in anticipation of God provisions."

It is easy to get caught up in the spirit of praise when those around us are worshiping. God wants us to praise Him in the midst of, and through, all things good and bad. God can change seemingly hopeless circumstances, as we praise.

Let's look at four phenomenal turn of events that God caused to happen when His children praised. In the midst of worship, and in the midst of adversity, they are as follows:

God's Glory Filled the Temple

All the Levites who were musicians ... stood on the east side of the altar, dressed in fine linen and playing cymbals, harps and lyres. They were accompanied by 120 priests sounding trumpets.

> The trumpeters and singers joined in unison, as with one voice, to give praise and thanks to the LORD. Accompanied by trumpets, cymbals and other instruments, they raised their voices in praise to the LORD and sang: "He is good; his love endures forever." *Then the temple of the LORD was filled with a cloud,* and the priests could not perform their service because of the cloud, for *the glory of the LORD filled the temple of God.*
>
> 2 Chronicles 5:12–14 (NIV)

God destroyed the enemy's army

Imagine the bewilderment of the vast armies of the Ammonites, Moabites, and Mount Seir when they saw the approaching Israelite army with a choir on their front lines singing and praising God.

> King Jehoshaphat appointed men to sing to the LORD ... to praise him for the splendor of his holiness as they went out at the head of the army, saying: "Give thanks to the LORD, for

his love endures forever." As they began to sing and praise, the LORD set ambushes... [the invaders] destroyed each other.

2 Chronicles 20:21, 22 (NIV)

Jail doors opened

Beaten and bleeding, thrown into a maximum security cell, chained with no human way of escape, Paul and Silas sang and praised God. The prisoners listened in amazement: "Suddenly there was such a violent earthquake that the foundations of the prison were shaken. At once all the prison doors flew open, and everybody's chains came loose" (Acts 16:26 NIV).

Jericho's walls tumbled

Formidable Jericho was the first city to be conquered when the Israelites entered the Promised Land. They knew nothing of battle since they had been slaves for four hundred years. However, their worship was organized, detailed, and ceremonial. The rams' horns they blew were designed for praise, not battle. Shouts of praise and victory rose from obedience and confidence in God! He told them what would happen if they obeyed Him and praised and it happened! The LORD said to Joshua,

> March around the city once with all the armed men. Do this for six days. Have *seven* priests carry trumpets of rams' horns [for praise] in front of the ark. On the *seventh* day, march around the city *seven* times [seven is the scriptural number of completion], with the priests blowing the trumpets... When you hear them sound a long blast... have all the people give a loud shout; then the *wall of the city will collapse* and the people will go up, every man straight in...
>
> *When the trumpets sounded, the people shouted,* and at the sound of the trumpet, when the people gave a loud shout,

the wall collapsed; so every man charged straight in, and they took the city.

Joshua 6:3–5, 20 (NIV)

The greatest man of worship and praise in Scripture, King David, wrote, "I will praise you as long as I live, and in *your* name I will lift up my hands" (Ps. 63:4 NIV). He made instruments of music, organized choirs, and even joyfully danced while praising God with deep adoration:

> Praise God in His sanctuary;
> Praise Him in His mighty expanse
> Praise Him for His mighty deeds;
> Praise Him according to His excellent greatness.
> Praise Him with trumpet sound;
> Praise Him with harp and lyre,
> Praise Him with timbrel and dancing;
> Praise Him with stringed instruments and pipe.
> Praise Him with loud cymbals;
> Praise Him with resounding cymbals.
> Let everything that has breath praise the LORD!
>
> Psalms 150:1–6 (NAS)

Unchallenged, the greatest church in praise and worship is Yoido Full Gospel Church in Seoul, South Korea. The largest Christian Church in the world has 750,000 members. Dr. Mary Relfe writes in Moments with His Majesty:

> As I was ushered into a Minister's Prayer Parlor... off in the distance I heard as it were the sounds of Niagara Falls... logic convinced me that the sounds were from a huge choir and orchestra rehearsing in some remote section of that immense building... When the door was opened into the sanctum, I discovered that "music" wasn't the choir and orchestra, tens of thousands of Koreans filling every inch of space [53,000 on the first floor and probably a half-million more on the

top thirteen stories, who were likely watching on giant screens]. They were praying as loudly as their voices could project... What sights, what sounds, what scenes so sacred I felt like heaven had come down and glory filled my soul... I watch, listen, feel and sense the grandeur of that symphony of supplication. I had grown up in the Church, but never had I experienced anything like this.

My spirit bore witness that these prayers *were rising before the Lord as incense and the lifting up of our hands as the evening sacrifice* (Ps. 141:2). I remembered an experience of, and felt a kinship with Daniel, who devoid of strength; his face on the ground, said: "A hand touched me... and [a voice] said, 'Stand upright, for unto thee am I now sent.'" (Dan. 10:10–11). He touched me! Yes, He touched me! Strength surged into my body. I was uplifted in the Spirit and anointed to speak. [28]

On a much grander scale: "I [John] hears as it were the voice of a great multitude, and as the voice of many waters, and as the voice of mighty thundering, saying, 'Alleluia, for the Lord God omnipotent reigneth'" (Rev. 19:6 NIV).

When we are praising and worshiping God, our hearts are the closest to His throne. *Our Father* cherishes every word. Let us praise *Our Father* and His Holy Name, with every fiber of our being like our fellow Christians in South Korea. *That* is when God will raise us up and our insurmountable walls will *come tumbling down*. Edward Perronet penned one of the greatest praise songs that has ever been written:

> All hail the pow'r of Jesus' name
> Let angels prostrate fall!
> Bring forth the royal diadem
> And crown Him Lord of all![29]

Sample Prayer

Revere Our Father's Almighty Name

Our Father,

    We come to you in the almighty name of my Lord Jesus Christ. Please, forgive us for the times we have insulted you by not reverencing your name as we should. It is hard for us to comprehend awesome, pure divine holiness.

    We want to shout from the highest mountain, "I LOVE YOU, LORD!" I feel pure joy as I think of you; I praise you with all my heart, mind, and soul—*"Hallowed be your name"!* Amen.

III: Revere Our Father's Almighty Name

Living Christianity Assignment

Bible Study—Read Psalms 145–150. Revere and praise Our Father's holy name.

> Praise the Lord, O my soul; all my inmost being, praise his holy name.
> Psalms 103:1 (NIV)

Prayer—Praise even when it is the least logical thing to do, like Paul and Silas in adversity.

> Let them praise the name of the Lord, for his name alone is exalted; his splendor is above the earth and the heavens.
> Psalms 148:13 (NIV)

Works—Let your life reflect the Joy of the Lord.

> I will extol the Lord at all times; his praise will always be on my lips.
> Psalms 34:1 (NIV)

IV:
Desire Our Father's Universal Reign

"Your kingdom come"

> Seek first his kingdom and his righteousness, and all these things will be given to you as well.
>
> Matthew 6:33 (NIV)

IV:
Desire Our Father's Universal Reign

"Your kingdom come"

- Divine Travel Brochure to *Our Father's* Glorious Kingdom
- The Five Basic Phases in The Kingdom of Heaven

  - First Phase: Present Spiritual Kingdom
  - Second Phase: Christians go to Heaven
  - Third Phase: Post Rapture Events
  - Fourth Phase: The Millennial Kingdom
  - Fifth Phase: The Eternal Kingdom

- Sample Prayer: Desire Our Father's Universal Reign
- Living Christianity Assignment

IV:
Desire Our Father's Universal Reign

"Your kingdom come"

Don Piper visited Heaven for an hour and a half after his cataclysmic well documented death. In his book, 90 *Minutes in Heaven*,[30] the Baptist preacher gives us a glimpse beyond the veil. He also describes a persistent, unrelenting, powerful prayer during those ninety minutes by another Baptist preacher that brought him back to life.

Now, with a hint of what lies ahead, let's go on an adventure through Scripture highlighting events that await us. We will try to envision each Kingdom phase, which will ultimately lead us to *Our Father's* unfathomable Eternal Kingdom. The wonder of it all will exceed our mortal comprehension because God's word tells us that,

> No eye has seen, no ear has heard, no mind has conceived what God has prepared for those who love him" but God has revealed it to us by his Spirit. The Spirit searches all things, even the deep things of God.
>
> 1 Corinthians 2:9 (NIV)

Not only will we spiritually experience pure love, perfect peace and ultimate joy, the celestial will surpass our understanding of space, time, and beauty.

Our eagerness to see what is beyond this world should far exceed the astronaut's enthusiasm. What they saw and felt was indescribable. Later, words were not adequate for them to accurately convey their experiences. This was so with the Apostle John on the Isle of Patmos when he had the glorious vision of the future events in the Book of Revelation. And, with others, like Don Piper, who went to heaven and returned. The inexpressible wonder of it all will remain confined in their hearts.

The Holy Spirit of Jesus, who lives within us, will illuminate our understanding and help us to envision what lies ahead because he wants us to see His marvelous glory: Jesus prayed, "Father, I want those you have given me to be with me where I am, and to see my glory, the glory you have given me" (Jn. 17:25 NIV).

That reminds me of parents at Christmas time who can hardly restrain themselves from giving clues to their eager child about what is inside that huge package with a big red bow.

So, with my basic understanding, limited vocabulary, God's Word and the help of Jesus' Holy Spirit, let's explore together. I believe that we will all come away with a more fervent desire to pray, "Lord, Thy Kingdom Come!"

Divine Travel Brochure to Our Father's Glorious Kingdom

Destination

"...*your Father* has been pleased to give you the kingdom" (Lu. 12:32 NIV).

Cost

Entrance is free, "For God so loved the world that *He gave* His only begotten Son that whosoever believeth in him should not perish but have everlasting life" (Jn. 3:16 KJV). "For it is by grace you have been saved, through faith and this not from *your*selves, it is the gift of God not of works, so that no one can boast" (Eph. 2:8–9 NIV).

Value of the Gift

The value is so great it must be our highest priority: "The kingdom of heaven is like a merchant looking for fine pearls. When he found one of great value, he went away and sold everything he had and bought it" (Matt. 13:44 NIV). This would mean all that the merchant had was less valuable than what he had found.

Itinerary

We enter The First Phase of the Kingdom while we are on earth when Christ comes to live in our hearts. Jesus said, "… the kingdom of God is within you" (Jn. 17:21 NIV).

Briefly, we will leave this realm when our physical bodies dies and our spirits are instantly with the Lord (2 Cor. 5:6 KJV). Or, we may leave when we ascend in The Rapture to meet Christ in mid-air (1Thess. 4:13–18 NIV).

Then, we will face the Judgment Seat of Christ for rewards and admonishments for how we lived our Christian lives on earth (1 Cor. 3:13–15 NIV). After that, we will participate in The Great Marriage Banquet as the radiant Bride of Christ (Rev.19:7–10 NIV).

We will Join Christ's Second Coming to Earth (Matt. 24; Rev. 19 NIV) and reign with Him in the Millennial Kingdom. Then, during the final phase, we will live in His Eternal Kingdom!

Transportation

Divine Propulsion

Accommodations

Mansions in Glory! Jesus announced, "In My Father's house are many mansions; if it were not so, I would have told you. I go to prepare a place for you. And if I go ... I will come again, and receive you unto myself, that where I am, there ye may be also" (Jn. 14:2, 3 KJV).

Launch Time

Suddenly, at any moment we could meet the Lord. If our spirits are not already with him through physical death, "The Lord himself will come down from heaven, with a loud command, with the voice of the archangel and with the trumpet call of God ... and we will be caught up ... to meet the Lord in the air" (1 Thess. 4:16, 17 NIV).

Passport

Jesus is our passport. He said, "I am the gate; *whoever* enters through me will be saved" (Jn. 10:9 NIV). "I am the way and the truth and the life. No one comes to the Father except through me" (Jn. 14:6 NIV). There will be no spiritual illegals, those who have rejected Jesus.

We cannot afford to miss this trip; the alternative is unthinkable. Right now, each of us must check our passport.

I know a man who does not have one because of lack of commitment. Several years ago he called asking me to help him find a job. I knew, because he was a destitute drug addict, that a job would only be a temporary band-aid on his problems. He needed a complete overhaul.

I asked him if he would commit his life to God for help. He said, "I'm a Christian." I knew that since his confession to Christianity he had spent more time in bars than in church. He quickly defended his position, "The Bible says, 'Everyone who calls on the name of the Lord will be saved'" (Rom. 10:13 NIV). I quoted Jesus, "Not everyone who says to me, Lord, Lord, will enter the kingdom of heaven, but only he who does the will of my Father who is in heaven" (Matt. 7:21 NIV).

I then asked him, "Are you ready to turn from *your* sins and commit *your* life to Jesus Christ, so He can help deliver you from drugs and guide *your* life?"

"No," he said firmly, "I want to live my own life."

To compare this young man's *words only* Christianity with real Christians who are ready to go, look at what commitment means in a relationship. Most young women admire an outstanding young man, some even date him. But, only the one who says, "I do," marries him. Furthermore, no one has to drag the radiant bride to the church.

Similarly, many people admire Jesus and believe He is God's Son. They even date Him on Sundays, yet have no marriage intentions. Most people will readily declare their faith for a free ticket to heaven, as long as it doesn't cost them their old attitudes and lifestyle.

Jesus' bride is the Church. These are those who have committed to Him, "from this day forward forever." With this earnest vow we have our passport; we enter the First Phase of *Our Father*'s Kingdom proclaiming, "Jesus Christ is my LORD!" (Rom. 10:9–10, 13 NIV).

The Five Basic Phases in The Kingdom of Heaven

This is not an end-times study. Future events are skimmed only to expand our vision so we will desire to pray more fervently, *"Lord, Thy Kingdom Come!"*

The following Panorama of the Bible Study Chart[31], illustrates four of the five phases in *Our Father*'s Kingdom.

Christianity Alive! with Prayer Power!

First Phase	Second Phase	Third Phase	Fourth Phase
Today	(mid air) Rapture	*Post Rapture Events	Jesus' 2nd Coming

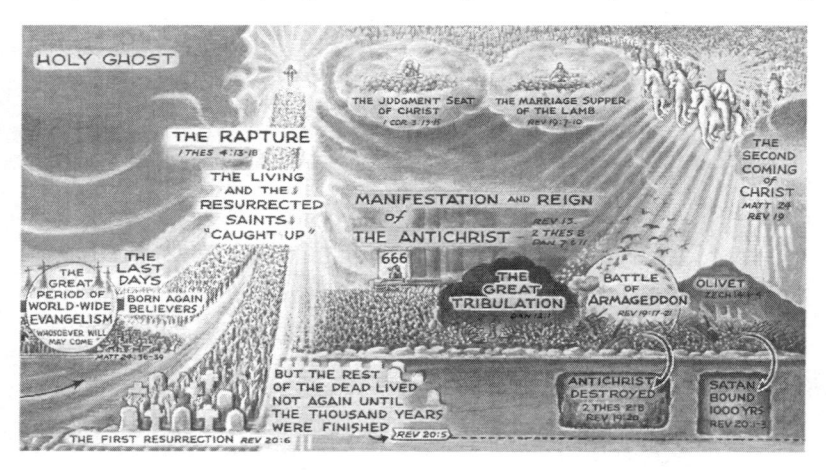

(see page 373 for a larger image)

There are theologians who believe the Rapture will occur before the Tribulation era. Others believe it will occur Mid-Tribulation or Post-Tribulation. Regardless, this text is only intended to show there are great events ahead for all believers. The most accepted Pre-Tribulation View is shown.

First Phase: The Present Spiritual Kingdom

We live simultaneously in two realms during the First Phases. Our feet walk on asphalt where we abide by rules of government and are confronted with daily challenges. While, our hearts reside in the spirit realm where God is *Our Father* and Jesus is our Lord. We get our instructions from above. The Holy Spirit guides us in God's way while we are on earth. And, he opens our eyes to see his creation.

This world is beautiful. Bob and I have peered from the tops of the Eiffel Tower and the Statue of Liberty and walked on the sands in Hawaii, Nassau, and the French Rivera. We have flown the skies, ridden a hydro jet boat across the Mediterranean and camels in Tangier, North Africa. We have seen tulip fields in Holland, and Disney World in Florida. We have skied in the Swiss Alps, and swam off Catalina Island. We have seen great treasures of the world in the Smithsonian in Washington, the Louvre in Paris... and, King Tut [Tutankhamen's] treasures. We were reverently awed in many great cathedrals, including The Sistine Chapel in Rome. And, we have seen the Dead Sea Scrolls.

We Simultaneously Live in Two Realms

The World		The Kingdom of Heaven
We reside physically, where		**Christ Reigns**
Satan is the god of this world		**Spiritually**
* Satan is "god" (small g)		* God is Father
(2 Cor. 4:4; 1 John 5:19)	"You must	* Jesus Christ is Lord
* *Self* rules	be born again."	* There are spiritual
* Three enemies are:	John 3:7 (NIV)	brothers and sisters
Satan, the flesh,		* Live by Laws of Love
And the world system		* Now, and forever
* It ends in Hell		* It ends in Heaven

Our Father's Kingdom on Earth Is Spiritual

Jesus said, "God is spirit, and his worshipers must worship in spirit and in truth" (Jn. 4:24 NIV), "My kingdom is not of this world" (Jn. 18:36 NIV), and "The kingdom of God is near...." (Mk. 1:15 NIV)! "I tell you the truth, some who are standing here will not taste death before they see the kingdom of God *come with power*" (Mk. 9:1 NIV).

As promised, on the day of Pentecost forty days after Jesus arose, His Holy Spirit *came in power* to set up His Kingdom in believer's hearts.

Since that time, Jesus' Holy Spirit has opened multitudes of believer's spiritual eyes to comprehend the realm of Our Father's Kingdom (Read Acts 2:1-47 NIV).

Jesus verified His follower's earthly residence and heavenly citizenship when He prayed to God, "My prayer is not that you take them out of the world but that you protect them from the evil one. They are not of the world, even as I am not of it" (Jn. 17:15, 16 NIV).

Joy overwhelmed my friend Robin Holbert when she read in Scripture, "Our citizenship is in heaven" (Phil. 3:20 NIV). She said, "I feel like my Mexican born friend after she left the United States of America Naturalization Ceremony at the Cameron County Courthouse and exclaimed, "I am an American citizen!" I can shout louder, "I AM A CITIZEN OF GOD'S KINGDOM!"

Jesus is Our King

Just before Jesus' crucifixion Pilate questioned Him: "You are a king, then!" "Jesus answered, 'You are right in saying I am a king. In fact, for this reason I was born, and for this I came into the world'" (Jn. 18:37 NIV). Centuries earlier, Isaiah had prophesied:

> For to us a child is born, to us a son is given, and the government will be on his shoulders and he will be called Wonderful Counselor, Mighty God, Everlasting Father, Prince of Peace.
>
> Of the increase of his government and peace there will be no end. He will reign on David's throne and over his kingdom, establishing and upholding it with justice and righteousness from that time on and forever. The zeal of the Lord Almighty will accomplish this.
>
> Isaiah 9:6, 7 (NIV)

The Kingdom Has Laws

The Old Testament Mosaic Laws burdened the Israelites with numerous do's and don'ts which were impossible to keep without divine empowerment. Jesus said,

> Do not think that I have come to abolish the Law or the Prophets; I have not come to abolish them but to fulfill them. I tell you the truth, until heaven and earth disappear, not the smallest letter, not the least stroke of a pen, will by any means disappear from the Law until everything is accomplished.
> Matthew 5:17, 18 (NIV)

Jesus simplified the Commandments and empowered the believer: "Until everything was accomplished," meant when the finished work of redemption for mankind was completed. It happened when Jesus announced on the cross, "It is finished" (Jn.30 NIV)! Love became the law.

The first Commandment, "You shall have no other gods before me" (Exod. 20:3 NIV) became "Love the Lord *your* God with all *your* heart and with all *your* soul and mind. This is the first and greatest commandment... the second is like it: Love *your* neighbor as *yourself*. All the Law and the Prophets hang on these two commandments" (Matt. 22:37-40 NIV). With this depth of love, multiple laws are not necessary because love does not kill, steal, cheat...

The Kingdom Has a Covenant

The Israelites disregarded The Covenant that God made with them. Therefore, God made an unbreakable New Covenant by sealing it with Jesus' blood and fulfilling it through the power of His Spirit: "This is the covenant I will make... declares the Lord. I will put my laws in their minds and write them on their hearts. I will be their God, and they will be my people" (Heb. 8:10 NIV).

Our Father's Children Have Different Characteristics

People of the world, focus on pleasure, prestige, and materialism. Without their realizing it, Satan himself is their default god. He has blinded their eyes to the truth with the dazzle of the world and the accessibility of sin.

> You followed the ways of this world and of the ruler of the kingdom of the air, the spirit who is now at work in those who are disobedient. All of us also lived among them at one time, gratifying the cravings of our sinful nature and following its desires and thoughts. Like the rest, we were by nature objects of wrath. But because of his great love for us, God who is rich in mercy, made us alive with Christ even when we were dead in transgressions... it is by grace you have been saved.
>
> Ephesians 2:2–5 (NIV)
> [Also read 2 Corinthians 4:4 and 1 Jn. 9]

An individual's philosophy of life is an identifying characteristic. I heard a valedictorian address that highlighted the world's humanistic philosophy as she expounded, "I am in control of my life and my destiny." Her closing summarized the principle, "The mind is everything!" Divine Rule was not in her philosophy.

Situation Ethics is the moral code of the world's people: "Do whatever seems right according to the situation." It is easy for a person to justify to himself in actions like deception, theft, adultery, and even murder because it seems right in his situation. The Apostle Paul writes, "Do you not know that the wicked" [the self-willed and unrepentant] will not inherit the kingdom of God?" (1Cor.6:9 NIV).

Since there are many people in the world who are considered to be good, distinguishing between the non-Christian and the Christian is not always easy. Scripture reminds us there are weeds among the wheat. They are so intermingled with the wheat that Jesus said,

IV: Desire Our Father's Universal Reign

> Let both grow together until the harvest. At that time I will tell the harvesters...collect the weeds and tie them in bundles to be burned; then gather the wheat and bring it into my barn.
> Matthew 13:30 (NIV)

The religious leaders in Jesus' era were considered to be the *most* holy. Yet, some were weeds. Jesus exposed them in one of his sermons: "I tell you that unless *your* righteousness surpasses that of the Pharisees and the teachers of the law, *you will certainly not enter the kingdom of heaven*" (Matt. 5:20 NIV).

Jesus describes the distinguishing traits of the Kingdom's citizens in the Sermon on the Mount, "...he began to teach them saying:

> Blessed are the poor in spirit [humble, non egotistical]...theirs is the kingdom of heaven.
> Blessed are those who mourn [tender hearted and compassionate], for they will be comforted.
> Blessed are the meek [power under control, teachable] for they will inherit the earth.
> Blessed are those who hunger and thirst for righteousness [Fervently desire more of God], for they will be filled.
> Blessed are the merciful [to others], for they will be shown mercy.
> Blessed are the pure in heart [righteous motives], for they will see God.
> Blessed are the peacemakers [settle controversies], for they will be called sons of God.
> Blessed are those who are persecuted [slandered, mistreated, homes burned, killed] because of righteousness, for theirs is the kingdom of heaven.
> Matthew 5:2–10 (NIV)

This means you and me. *Our Father's* children are supposed to have these characteristics right now. Surely, we will be humbled by this thought and inspired to pray, "Lord, let the true spirit of *Your* Kingdom fill my heart!"

Our spiritual attitudes influence how we react to circumstances. We cannot overlook the fact that while we are on the earth Christians and non-Christians alike have concerns with physical needs like food, shelter and clothing. At times, these needs are so overwhelming it is easy to lose our perspective.

Jesus promises help in our needs: "...so do not worry, saying, 'What shall we eat?' or 'What shall we drink?' or 'What shall we wear?'...*Your* heavenly Father knows that you need them. But seek first his kingdom and his righteousness, and [then] all these things will be given to you as well" (Matt. 6:31-33 NIV).

God who created the world and all therein will keep us; God who perpetuates the cycles of life promises to meet our needs! He will help one day at a time.

Christians have a Kingdom Commission on Earth

"Then Jesus came to them and said, 'All authority in heaven and on earth has been given to me. *Therefore go and make disciples* of all nations, baptizing them in the name of the Father and of the Son and of the Holy Spirit, and teaching them to obey everything I have commanded you. And surely I am with you always...'" (Matt. 28:18-20 NIV).

Christians Reign with Jesus from the Heavenly Perspective

Though our feet are on earth, "God raised us up with Christ and seated us with him in the heavenly realms in Christ Jesus...and has blessed us in the heavenly realms with every spiritual blessing in Christ" (Eph. 2:6; 1:3 NIV). Our hearts and minds will function more from the heavenly spiritual perspective.

IV: Desire Our Father's Universal Reign

Christians are Kingdom Ambassadors on Earth

We stand as official representatives of *Our Father*'s Kingdom as we live on earth helping others and gathering the lost into His realm. Having been reconciled, "We are therefore Christ's ambassadors, as though God were making his appeal through us" (2 Cor. 5:20 NIV).

Are Animals in Heaven?

This may seem inconsequential to many. "But, anyone whose beloved pet has ever passed away knows the pain of that loss and many of us have wondered: will we ever see our furred or feathered friends again? Drs. Jack and Rexella Van Impe have the answer, and it is a resounding yes! In their DVD "Animals in Heaven?," Dr. Van Impe, renown Bible scholar on prophecy, shows from the Bible and teachings of great theologians past and present, that:

> Heaven is a place that abounds with plant life and animal life! Every good thing on earth is but a shadow of its perfection in heaven so good pet friends will find their completion in heaven, too. And much more!" [32]

I don't think we need to split hairs over this one because if the joys of heaven are *beyond our imagination* (1 Cor. 2:9), this could not only include our family pets, but also an unimaginable variety of pets created just to surprise us. Love will abound!

The Second Phase: Christians go to Heaven through Death and in the Rapture

Through Physical Death

Many people sometimes, as Arthur Gordon wrote, "…think of death as a dark door when actually it is a rainbow bridge spanning the gulf between two worlds."[33] In fact, it will be Graduation Day on this side and Homecoming on the other. How can we be sad at this joyous occasion?

Yes, we will miss our loved ones, but only for a short time until our own Graduation Day. In Psalms we read, "Precious in the sight of the Lord is the death of his saints" (Ps. 116:15 NIV). They will go to sleep and awake in Glory! "Absent from the body, present with the Lord" (2 Cor. 5:6 KJV). Don Piper wrote,

> Simultaneous with my last recollection of seeing the bridge and the rain, a light enveloped me, with brilliance beyond earthly comprehension or description. Only that. In my next moment of awareness, I was standing in heaven... a large crowd in front of a brilliant, ornate gate... I stood speechless in the crowd of loved ones... The first person I recognized was... my grandfather. He looked exactly as I remembered him. "Donnie!" His eyes lit up... He embraced me, holding me tightly...
>
> ... they were more radiant and joyful than they'd ever been on earth. My great-grandmother, Hattie Mann... wasn't slumped over, She stood strong and upright and the wrinkles had been erased... As I stared at her beaming face, I sensed that age has no meaning in heaven.
>
> I had never felt such powerful embraces or feasted my eyes on such beauty. Heaven's light and texture defy earthly eyes or explanation. Warm, radiant light engulfed me. As I looked around, I could hardly grasp the vivid, dazzling colors. Every hue and tone surpassed anything I had ever seen...
>
> My most vivid memory... is what I heard... Praise was everywhere, and all of it was musical, yet comprised of melodies and tones I'd never experienced before... I felt so awestruck and caught up in the heavenly mood that I didn't look around. I was home; I was where I belonged. I wanted to be there more than I had ever wanted to be anywhere on earth... all worries... vanished... I felt perfect."[34]

Glory! This, testimony and scripture confirms that we shall know people in heaven. "Then we shall see [Jesus] face to face. Now I know in part; *then I shall know fully, even as I am fully known.* (1 Cor. 13:12 NIV)

In the Rapture When Jesus Returns

The greatest event for all Christians who are on earth at the moment our Lord Jesus returns—will be the Rapture. It could happen instantly. That means the *bodies* of Christians who have died will be the first to go up to be with Jesus. Even though their ashes may have been scattered over the ocean, their bodies will supernaturally reassemble and reunite them with their spirits, whom Jesus will have brought with Him.

One of the reasons we know that their spirits have been with Jesus since their physical death: Jesus told the thief hanging on the cross beside Him, "I tell you the truth, today you will be with me in paradise" (Luke 23:43 NIV). At the moment of death, the thief's spirit went to be with Jesus yet his body obviously went to the grave. During the Rapture, the thief's body and his spirit will be among those reunited.

Further confirming the immortality of the spirit, Jesus said, "Whoever lives and believes in me will never die" (Jn. 11:26 NIV). When it is time for us to leave our earthly bodies, our spirits will zip right on out and will instantly be with Christ: "Absent from the body...present with the Lord" (Cor. 5:6 KJV).

> Brothers, we do not want you to be ignorant about those who fall asleep [Christians who physically die], or to grieve like the rest of men, who have no hope. We believe that Jesus died and rose again and so we believe that God *will bring with Jesus* [the spirits of] *those who have fallen asleep in him.*
>
> According to the Lord's own word, we tell you that we who are still alive, who are left till the coming of the Lord, will certainly not precede those who have fallen asleep [died physically]. [They will leave their graves first to be with Jesus, then we will ascend.]
>
> 1 Thessalonians 4:13–15 (NIV)

The Second Part of the Rapture

After deceased Christian's bodies have vacated their graves, Christians who are alive on earth will ascend.

> We will not all sleep (physically die), but we will all be changed in a flash, in the twinkling of an eye, at the last trumpet. For the trumpet will sound, the dead will be raised imperishable, and we will be changed. For the perishable must clothe itself with the imperishable and the mortal with immortality…
> 1 Corinthians 15:52 (NIV)

Glory! All who are raptured will suddenly be like Him by the awesome power of His Presence. "… *we know that when he appears, we shall be like him, for we shall see him as he is*" (1 Jn. 3:2 NIV). At last, our transformed natures will have transfigured bodies.

The Third Phase: Post Rapture Events

The Judgment Seat of Christ

Another exciting event will be the rewards. "For we must all appear before the judgment seat of Christ, that each one may receive what is due him for the things done while in the body, whether good or bad" (2 Cor. 5:10 NIV). Jesus said, "Behold, I am coming soon! My reward is with me, and I will give to everyone according to what he has done" (Rev. 22:12 NIV).

This will be a time of mixed emotions rewards and accountability. Jesus will praise those for whom praise is due, and will admonish those who lived careless Christian lives on earth. For Billy Graham and Mother Teresa, who have toiled relentlessly and stayed faithful, I envision it will be like a Colossal Gloriously Divine Christmas.

This Judgment Seat has nothing to do with sin and eternal salvation. Only Christians will be there. This will be a private family affair between Jesus and the church who will soon become "The

Bride of The Lamb." After the judgment phase, there will probably be a lot of hugging and making up before the Marriage Banquet.

The Great Marriage Banquet

The Big Event will be The Great Marriage Banquet for Christ and His Bride! It will be splendor beyond imagination!

> Then I heard what sounded like a great multitude, like the roar of rushing waters and like loud peals of thunder, shouting: "Hallelujah! For our Lord God Almighty reigns. Let us rejoice and be glad and give him glory!
>
> For the wedding of the Lamb has come, and his bride has made herself ready. Fine linen, bright and clean, was given her to wear. [Fine linen stands for the righteous acts of the saints.] Then the angel said to me, 'Write: Blessed are those who are invited to the wedding supper of the Lamb!' And he added, 'These are the true words of God.'"
>
> Revelation 19:6-9 (NIV)

Try with me to envision the splendor of that feast. The best I can relate happened one evening when Bob and I drove into the small principality of Luxembourg. The city was lit like a fairyland. We wondered, "*What* is happening?" We learned the king's daughter would be married the next day. We stood wide eyed outside the palace watching dignitaries from all over the world arrive in spotless chauffeured limousines.

They wore the finest wedding garments: long-tailed tuxedos, elegant gowns and priceless jewels. We tried to imagine the grandeur inside the palace: glistening china and silver, sparkling crystal, breathtaking flower arrangements, an orchestra filling the hall with classical music, gourmet food by the world's best chefs, and waiters in long tailed tuxedos bustling around rechecking every detail

The Great Wedding Banquet for God's Son, the King of Kings and His Bride the Church will be of the highest realm in its splendor. I believe angels are joyously preparing the great feast right now. They are decorating the heavenly dining hall with celestial flowers. Eyes cannot see the full length of the table, which is set for millions.

The table settings are brilliant translucent pure gold dishes, knives, forks, spoons, and glistening crystal goblets. The delicate aroma of a vast array of heavenly manna is gently flowing through the gloriously magnificent hall. Angels in gleaming white gowns are eagerly rechecking every detail.

The vast Angelic Choir is rehearsing music divinely composed especially for the most glorious event in the Heavenly Realm—The Eternal Wedding!

A hush will settle over the royal assembly when the Bride of Christ, takes her place. Jesus will, "present her to himself as a radiant church, without stain or wrinkle or any other blemish, but holy and blameless" (Eph. 5:27 NIV). Our radiant bridal gowns of righteousness will be illuminated with God's glory, "Christ will shine on you" (Eph. 5:14 NIV). The bride's greatest joy will be when our *"eyes will see the king in his beauty"* (Isa. 33:17 NIV).

Joy Dawson wrote in *Intimate Friendship with God*, "We will see Him in all His majestic splendor, blazing glory, the fire of His purity, and the depth of His unfathomable love. Oh, the wonder of it all as we look into the eyes of Him who is infinite in wisdom and knowledge."[35] We will have no earthly desire to look back after attaining such glory.

Tribulation on Earth

While back on earth, for those who missed the Rapture, life will be the worst possible nightmare.

We may assume, after multiple millions of loved ones have vanished, there will first be profound grief for those who are left behind,

IV: Desire Our Father's Universal Reign

while they try to adjust to a very different way of life. Ironically, some godless churches will continue their services uninterrupted.

On the political scene, the Antichrist will rise in power. For the first three and one-half years, he will seem to have answers for the world's problems. And, with compelling charisma he will gain control of the world.

At the end of the first three and one-half years, he will diametrically change and will flaunt his hidden agenda: As Lucifer declared eons ago, "I will raise my throne above the stars of God; I will sit enthroned on the mount of assembly, on the utmost heights of the sacred mountain [Jerusalem]" (Isa. 14:13,14 NIV). The Antichrist will "set himself up in God's temple [on that sacred mountain], proclaiming himself to be God" (2 Thess. 2:4 NIV). Satan incarnates' reign of unprecedented terror will begin.

During this Tribulation period, cataclysmic things will happen: "giant hailstones will bombard the earth...a third of the sea will be turned to blood...water will be poisoned...locusts with the power of scorpions will sting until mankind cries for death. Even so, many will stubbornly refuse to repent" (Rev. 8:7; 9:21 NIV). Though the masses will still refuse righteousness, many will repent. Also, many will become martyrs for the Lord.

The Battle of Armageddon

Seven years ended, Satan will marshal his forces for the most dreaded battle of all times—The Battle of Armageddon!

Jesus! Conqueror of all evil, the King of Kings and Lord of Lords will descend to confront his challenger. The armies of heaven the Redeemed, who have left this earth, will be with him (Rev. 19:14–19 NIV).

> Immediately after the tribulation of those days THE SUN WILL BE DARKENED, AND THE MOON WILL NOT

> GIVE ITS LIGHT, AND THE STARS WILL FALL from the sky, and the powers of the heavens will be shaken.
>
> And then the sign of the Son of Man will appear in the sky, and then all the tribes of the earth will mourn, and they will see the SON OF MAN COMING ON THE CLOUDS OF THE SKY with power and great glory.
>
> And He will send forth His angels with A GREAT TRUMPET and THEY WILL GATHER TOGETHER His select from the four winds, from one end of the sky to the other.
>
> Matthew 24:29–31 (NAS)

John had this vision: "I saw heaven standing open and there before me was a white horse, whose rider is called Faithful and True. With justice he judges and makes war. His eyes are like blazing fire, and on his head are many crowns... and his name is the Word of God... The armies of heaven [the Redeemed] were following him, riding on white horses and dressed in fine linen, white and clean. Out of his mouth came a sharp sword... On his robe and on his thigh he has this name written: KING OF KINGS AND LORD OF LORDS" (Rev. 19:11-16 NIV).

Fierce battle will rage in the Valley of Armageddon (Rev. 19:17-21 NIV). The only weapon used by The Victor will be the sword that comes out of His mouth (Rev.19:21 NIV). That is the sword of the Spirit, which is the word of God (Eph. 6:17; Heb. 4:12 NIV).

I believe that this fatal proclamation by the King of Kings will again be: "It is Finished!" Jesus reminds Satan, with the same words He spoke on the cross, that He has already conquered evil by giving His life for the salvation of mankind. The moment of its total fulfillment was proceeding to its ultimate end.

The rest of them were killed with the *sword* [God's Word] that came out of the mouth of the rider on the horse (Rev. 19:21 NIV). I believe this will mirror the ambush God set to destroy the Ammonites,

Moabites, and Mount Seir when they attacked Judah (2 Chron. 20:22–24 NIV). In panic, Satan's troops will destroy each other.

Finally, an angel will bind Satan and throw him into the abyss and seal it for one thousand years (Rev. 20:1-3 NIV). Evil will cease.

To summarize, in Zion's Fire we read:

> Of all the real estate on planet Earth, why do the armies of the world converge on Israel for the battle of Armageddon? The biblical answer is clear. Jesus is the Son of David the Lion of the Tribe of Judah. He is the legitimate King of Israel, and His capital is Jerusalem. The Antichrist wants to capture Israel and, from God's holy city, rule the world. The Word of God is clear. He will not succeed. *Hallelujah!* [36]
>
> Israel will never be destroyed: "God has decreed that to destroy the nation of Israel you must first be able to destroy the sun, moon, and stars" (Jer. 31:35–36). As long as these heavenly bodies endure, so will Israel. An omnipotent, sovereign God has decreed it to be."[37]

The Fourth Phase: The Kingdom, and More
Jesus Returns to Earth and Reigns One Thousand Years

The long awaited Millennial Reign will begin. At that time, they will call Jerusalem "The Throne of the LORD..." (Jer. 3:17 NIV). With Jesus' descent, His feet will stand on the Mount of Olives. [This will be the same place from which He ascended after His resurrection.]

(see page 372 for a larger image)

His entrance into Jerusalem will be unlike the first when He rode a donkey with basically an entourage of women and children strewing palm branches. He will now enter the city with unprecedented pomp, majesty and glory. His entourage will be his called, chosen and faithful followers. (Rev. 17: 14 NIV).

As Jesus ascends King David's throne, "the twenty-four elders lie prostrate, worshiping and praising. The seventh angel sounded his trumpet, and there were loud voices in heaven: The kingdom of the world has become the kingdom of our Lord and of his Christ, and he will reign forever and ever" (Rev. 11:15 NIV). "Holy, holy, holy is the LORD Almighty; the whole earth is full of his glory" (Isa. 6:3 NIV)!

Earth's one thousand year utopia will begin (Rev. 19:11-13, 16 NIV). At last, King Jesus' righteous principles of truth, justice, mercy, love, and peace will prevail. And, God will pour His blessings upon the harsh desert land surrounding the holy city. It will become a lush fertile garden: "The desert shall bloom like a rose" (Isa. 35:1 KJV). "Instead of the thorn shall come up the fir tree, instead of the briar, shall come up a myrtle tree" (Isa. 55:13 KJV).

> The wolf also shall dwell with the lamb,
> The leopard shall lie down with the young goat,
> The calf and the young lion and the fatling together;
> And a little child shall lead them.
>
> Isaiah 11:6 (NKJV)

At the end of the millennial reign, Satan will be temporarily released. His spirit of evil will sweep the land and rally the largest army ever assembled for the Battle of Gog and Magog. Evil will confront righteousness for a final showdown!

The armies will surround Jerusalem. Then, faster than lighting, God will send fire from heaven and destroy them all! At last, Satan will be cast into hell and he will remain there forever (Rev. 20:7–10 NIV).

The Great White Throne

IV: Desire Our Father's Universal Reign

All *non-believers*, deceased and living, will go to the Judgment Seat of God which is The Great White Throne. Since their names will not be found among The Redeemed in the Book of Life, they will follow their default lord, Satan, to his eternal destiny.

The End of Planet Earth

The earth will be totally purged (perhaps with nuclear power), preceding the long awaited Eternal Kingdom.

> The heavens shall pass away with a great noise, and the elements shall melt with fervent heat, the earth also and the works that are therein shall be burned up. Nevertheless we, according to his promise, look for new heavens and a new earth, wherein dwelleth righteousness.
> 2 Peter 3:10, 13 (KJV)

The Fifth Phase: The Eternal Kingdom

Our final residence! The Glorious New Jerusalem where "the righteous will shine like the sun in the kingdom of their Father" (Matt. 13:43 NIV). John sees the city in his vision,

> Then I saw a new heaven and a new earth, for the first heaven and the first earth had passed away...I saw the Holy City, the new Jerusalem, coming down...from God, prepared as a bride...dressed for her husband. And I heard a loud voice from the throne saying, "Now the dwelling of God is with men, and he will live with them. They will be his people, and God himself will be with them and be their God."
> Revelation 21:1–3 (NIV)

Now that we have envisioned the glories of the future, we must come back to where we reside on earth. There is yet work to do. We must get busy telling others about Jesus and what awaits those who believe in Him. We must pray fervently for God's will to be done in the hearts of all mankind. And, that the fullness of His Kingdom will come soon. John Wesley wrote,

> Give me one hundred men who fear nothing but sin and desire nothing but God, and I care not a straw whether they be clergymen or laymen, such alone will shake the gates of hell and set up the kingdom of heaven on earth [Christ's glorious reign in the hearts of all people].[39]

In conclusion, when we persevere with the vision of Christ's Ultimate Reign in our minds, the fear of death will lose its grip and earth will lose its appeal. The thought of joining the King of Kings in the Millennial Reign, and living forever in the Heavenly New Jerusalem illuminated with God's glory, will inspire us to most fervently pray:

"Lord, May Your Kingdom Come!"

Sample Prayer

Desire Our Father's Universal Reign

Father, we thank you for making provisions for us to enter the Kingdom of Heaven when we accepted Jesus Christ as our Lord and his Holy Spirit came into our hearts.

Help us to know how to listen, understand and obey. Also, help us to serve humbly with your power and authority.

We cannot comprehend the full measure of rights, privileges and responsibilities that we have as representatives of the Kingdom of Heaven, while we are on earth. Thank you for giving us instructions, while our hands do the works that you want done.

IV: Desire Our Father's Universal Reign

We are eager for you to come get us in the Rapture. We are watching the eastern sky where you will suddenly appear with angels heralding your return. What a Glorious moment that will be when we are instantly caught up in the air to be with you always.

We dream of your Glorious Universal Reign. Thank you Lord, that it will be a reality.

We love you with all our hearts, minds and souls. Amen.

Living Christianity Assignment

Bible Study—Read Matthew and 2 Thessalonians and learn about the citizens of The Kingdom of Heaven.

> Blessed are the peacemakers, for they will be called sons of God.
>
> Matthew 5:9 (NIV)

Prayer—Meditate upon Our Father and His laws of love. Enjoy his presence.

> [Lord,] *Your* kingdom come, your will be done on earth as it is in heaven.
>
> Matthew 6:10 (NIV)

Works—Help and encourage others. Lift their spirits with a cheerful attitude. Tell others about the good news of Jesus Christ and His Kingdom.

> Let *your* light shine before men, that they may see *your* good deeds and praise *your Father* in heaven.
>
> Matthew 5:16 (NIV)

V:
God's Will:
"Be Filled" with His Spirit Empowered To Be and To Do!

"Your will be done on earth
as it is in heaven."

> [Ask] God to fill you with the knowledge of his will through all spiritual wisdom and understanding...that you may live a life worthy of the Lord and may please him in every way: bearing fruit in every good work, growing in the knowledge of God.
> Colossians 1:9, 10 (NIV)

V:
God's Will:
"Be Filled" with His Spirit Empowered To Be and To Do!

"Your will be done on earth as it is in heaven."

- "Be Filled" with His Spirit

    - The Body, Soul and Spirit of Man
    - The Father, Son and Holy Spirit as They Relate to Man

- Spirit Empowered "To Be"

    - How to Be Filled with God's Holy Spirit
    - Steps that will lead us into the Spirit Filled Life
    - Evidence of the Spirit Filled Life
    - God Provides Spiritual Gifts with Special Abilities

- Spirit Empowered "To Do"

    - God has Specific Assignments for Each Christian
    - God Provides Sustaining Power
    - When the Gifts Will Cease

- "Thy Will be Done": Baptism and The Lord's Supper Ordinances
- Sample Prayer: "Be Filled" with His Spirit Empowered *To Be* and To *Do*
- Living Christianity Assignment

V:
God's Will:
"Be Filled" with His Spirit
Empowered To Be and To Do!

"Your will be done on earth
as it is in heaven."

There are too many lifeless churches and powerless Christians. It is not supposed to be this way. God's Holy Spirit is an invisible Deity, a dynamic energizing force who transforms our nature and empowers us for service. In *Something More* Catherine Marshall likens the additional power in the Spirit-filled life to electricity vs. campfires and candles.[40] Peter was a flickering candle when he denied even knowing Jesus. Our churches and lives should be aflame in the light of God's glory. We should be more like Paul who blazed a path in uncharted lands. For us to have spiritual power, we must *be* filled with his Holy Spirit *to be* like Jesus and *to do* his will on earth. This is God's primary will.

> The people that do know their God shall *be* strong, and *do* exploits.
>
> Daniel 11:32b (KJV)

The mandate is clear: *"Be filled with the Spirit"* (Eph. 5:18 NIV). Jesus made it possible when He yielded and prayed, *"Your will be done"* in the Garden of Gethsemane, and submitted to an agonizing death for our salvation. Now, when we yield and pray, *"Your will be done,"* we enter into the victory of that salvation, which is God Himself in us and working through us. Paul wrote,

> I pray that out of his glorious riches he may strengthen you with power through his Spirit in your inner being, so that Christ may dwell in your hearts through faith. And I pray that you, being rooted and established in love, may have power, together with all the saints, to grasp how wide and long and high and deep is the love of Christ, and to know this love that surpasses knowledge that you may be filled to the measure of all the fullness of God. *Now to him who is able to do immeasurably more than all we ask or imagine, according to his power that is at work within us.*
>
> Ephesians 3:16–20 (NIV)

> [Ask] God to fill you *with the knowledge of his will* through all spiritual wisdom and understanding. And we pray this in order that you may live a life worthy of the Lord and may please him in every way: bearing fruit in every good work, growing in the knowledge of God, *being strengthened with all power according to his glorious might so that* you may have great endurance and patience, and joyfully giving thanks to the Father, who has qualified you to share in the inheritance of the saints in the kingdom of light.
>
> Colossians 1:9–12 (NIV)

We must be *filled with the Spirit* to have divine wisdom and insight into his spiritual world. Paul wrote,

> We speak of God's secret wisdom, a wisdom that has been hidden and *that God destined for our glory before time began.* None of the rulers of this age understood it, for if they had,

they would not have crucified the Lord of glory. However, as it is written:

"No eye has seen, no ear has heard, no mind has conceived what God has prepared for those who love him"

"but God has revealed it to us by his Spirit. The Spirit searches all things, even the deep things of God"

1 Corinthians 2:7–10 (NIV)

What does *empowered by God's Holy Spirit* mean? Let's clarify basic principles: 1. The Body, Soul and Spirit of Man; and 2. The Father, Son and Holy Spirit as They Relate to Man. Now, those principles are so profound we can only overview them.

The Body, Soul and Spirit of Man

Man is a spirit with a soul who lives in a body. Even a child can look into a casket and perceive the person who once lived inside, isn't there anymore. The soul and spirit are gone. Starting *before* our conception, God knew [in advance] who we would be before we were born (Jer. 1:5). For us, the beginning started when the sperm met the egg and sparked life. D.N.A mapped the individual.

Who would question that *Jesus* was alive at the moment of conception. (Read Luke 1:26–2:20 NIV.) He was not a disposable embryo; He was God's son sent from heaven on his way to Calvary.

It is easy for any medical student to identify the components of the body. The body is bone, muscles, organs, flesh and blood… Let's call the brain a command center with the ability to know, understand, evaluate and make decisions. It can calculate even to design the computer and the space ship that put a man on the moon. It sends messages to the senses to see, hear, taste, smell, and feel. It tells the feet when and how to run. When the command center is gone; the spirit and soul are gone.

Delving deeper, who can distinguish between the spirit and soul? We know that we were created in God's image (Gen. 1:27 NIV). "In knowledge, righteousness and holiness of truth"[41], with the capacity to love, feel, and care. I have heard it said that the soul is more the personality. Perhaps a eulogy explained it best: "He was all heart." Only God can accurately know the difference.

> For the word of God is living and active. Sharper than any double-edged sword, *it penetrates even to dividing soul and spirit*, joints and marrow; it judges the thoughts and attitudes of the heart.
>
> Hebrew 4:12 (NIV)

The Father, Son and Holy Spirit as They Relate to Man

The Father

The father is a spirit person without a body "God is spirit" (Jn. 4:24 NIV).

The Son, Jesus

"The Word" was first a spirit person without a body. "In the beginning was the Word [spirit], and the Word was with God, and the Word was God."…The Word *became flesh*…" Then, in a human body, he was called "Jesus" (Jn. 1:1, 14 NIV).

The Holy Spirit

The Holy Spirit is a spirit person without a body who lives in us and provides the guidance and power we need to walk as Jesus walked. When we think of the Holy Spirit as a person, it is easier to perceive when we use earlier Christian's terminology, "Holy Ghost." Meditate about that the Holy Ghost walking beside us, in us and through us. When we grasp the powerful concept *"in him,"* all things will be possible.

V: God's Will: "Be Filled" with His Spirit Empowered To Be and To Do!

Like Jesus, The Holy Spirit, has a mind of his own who is always working within the perimeters of God's will. He is the one who enables us *to be* more like Jesus and *to do* his work.

Spirit Empowered "To Be"

The availability of the spirit-filled life, promised in the Old Testament, is the fundamental principle of the New Testament Covenant that is sealed with Jesus' blood. Old Testament people lived under the Law, which, like new years' resolutions was easily broken.

God explains the promised indwelling Holy Spirit through the prophet Jeremiah: "I will put my law in their minds and write it on their hearts" (Heb. 8:10 NIV). Simplified, that means God's Spirit will change our nature so that our thoughts and desires will be more like his.

John promises the Holy Spirit through Jesus: Early in the New Testament God sent the last prophet, John, to introduce Jesus to the world as the promised Messiah. One day while baptizing, John said, "After me will come one more powerful than I … I baptize you with water, but he will *baptize you with the Holy Spirit*" (Mark 1:7, 8 NIV).

Near the end of Jesus' three year ministry, He told His disciples of His imminent death, with reassurance that His Holy Spirit would come back to guide them: "But I tell you the truth: It is for *your* good that I am going away. Unless I go away, the Counselor will not come to you; but if I go, I will send him to you" (Jn.7 NIV).

Christianity Alive! with Prayer Power!

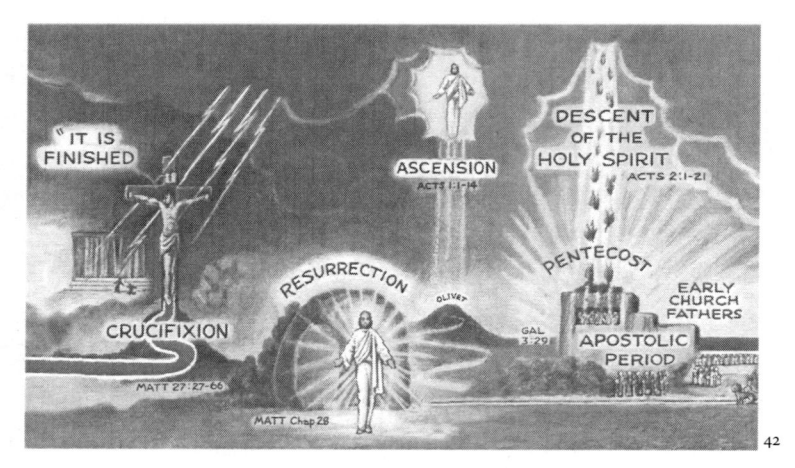

(see page 374 for a larger image)

Jesus gave further instructions: "I am going to send you what my Father has promised; but stay in the city until you have been clothed with power from on high" (Luke 24:49 NIV).

On the Day of Pentecost, the phenomenal event occurred. One hundred and twenty people, including Jesus' disciples, were obediently gathered in an upper room in Jerusalem when,

> Suddenly a sound like the blowing of a violent wind came from heaven and filled the whole house... They saw what seemed to be tongues of fire that separated and came to rest on each of them. All of them were filled with the Holy Spirit and began to speak in other tongues as the Spirit enabled them.
>
> Acts 2:1–4 NIV

When the citizens of Jerusalem and many devout Jews from other nations heard this violent wind they quickly assembled in the town square. The Spirit-filled men and women came forth boldly *proclaiming the mighty deeds of God* in the native languages of the foreign visitors. Everyone was amazed to hear these Galileans testifying in more than seventeen languages and dialects, such as Italian,

V: God's Will: "Be Filled" with His Spirit Empowered To Be and To Do!

Greek, Spanish, Hebrew, Arabic, Egyptian, Persian..."They ask one another, 'What does this mean'?" (Acts 2:5–12 NIV).

Skeptics mistook their exuberant joy for drunkenness. Peter explained the events according to the prophet Joel: "In the last days, God says, "I will pour out my Spirit on all people. *Your* sons and daughters will prophesy, *your* young men will see visions, *your* old men will dream dreams. Even on my servants...I will pour out my Spirit in those days, and they will prophesy" (Acts 2:17–18 NIV). (Also, read Joel 2:28–32)

On the mighty Day of Pentecost, Peter preached a dynamic sermon, in which he demonstrated the *spirit of prophecy which is the testimony of Jesus (Rev. 19:10)*.

> Men of Israel, listen to this: Jesus of Nazareth was a man accredited by God to you by miracles, wonders, and signs, which God did among you through him, as you yourselves know. This man was handed over to you by God's set purpose and foreknowledge; and you, with the help of wicked men, put him to death by nailing him to the cross. But God raised him from the dead, freeing him from the agony of death, because it was impossible for death to keep its hold on him.
>
> Brothers, I can tell you confidently that the patriarch David died and was buried and his tomb is here to this day. But he was a prophet and knew that God had promised him on oath that he would place one of his descendants on his throne. Seeing what was ahead, he spoke of the resurrection of the Christ, that he was not abandoned to the grave, nor did his body see decay. God has raised this Jesus to life, and we are all witnesses of the fact.
>
> Exalted to the right hand of God, he has received from the Father the promised Holy Spirit and has poured out what you now see and hear...Therefore let all Israel be assured of this: God has made this Jesus, whom you crucified, both Lord and Christ."

> When the people heard this, they were cut to the heart [deeply convicted] and said to Peter and the other apostles, "Brothers, what shall we do?" Peter replied, "Repent and be baptized, every one of you, in the name of Jesus Christ for the forgiveness of your sins. And you will receive the gift of the Holy Spirit. The promise is for you and your children and for all who are far off—for all whom the Lord our God will call."
>
> Acts 2:22–24, 29–38 (NIV)

Three thousand people were saved by faith in Jesus Christ that day. Everyone felt a sense of awe at the unusual things happening in their midst (Read Acts 2:14–43).

God's Holy Spirit dramatically changed lives. Earlier, Jesus' disciples had been spiritually weak. Peter, James and John could not stay awake with Jesus while he agonized in the Garden of Gethsemane. Thomas was a classic *doubter*. Peter even denied knowing Jesus *three times*. Now, they all preached with power, and had the courage to eventually die as martyrs.

On that mighty day of Pentecost the Christian Church era began. Since then, multitudes of Spirit-filled men and women have marched through the centuries empowered to be more like Jesus and to continue His work on earth.

To clarify the spirit-filled life we need to understand that it is not a one-time experience where we *arrive* at a high level of holiness. When sin slips in, power slips out. Rather, it is an empowered *lifestyle* of faithful love for God, and for humanity.

How to "Be Filled" with God's Spirit

We may ask, "What is the difference between being *born-again* into God's family" (Chapter 1) and being *baptized with His Holy Spirit?* Some people experience salvation and spiritual baptism at the same time, like it happened in my pastor's life. He immediately started proclaiming the glorious message of salvation to all who would listen.

V: God's Will: "Be Filled" with His Spirit Empowered To Be and To Do!

For me, it was different. My mother reared me, figuratively speaking, on the front row of a country Baptist church. I accepted Jesus as my Lord and Christian principles, along with walking and talking.

Yet, two experiences added high octane to my spiritual life.

When I was twelve, I was looking out of my bedroom window at the stars while thinking about God. *Then, suddenly, His Holy Spirit filled my room.* I felt *"God himself, is in my room!"* I was *consumed* in an aura of divine love, peace and joy. It was inexpressibly wonderful and I clung to the moment. I perceived that this would be a brief encounter so I sobbed as I pleaded with God, "Take me with you, I want to go to live with you forever, *Right Now!*" I could not possibly stay on this earth after I had been in His presence. Then, these words came gently and firmly through my spirit, "No, you cannot go now, I have work for you to do." His Spirit subsided.

With time, I drifted from that Glorious Mountaintop to the plains: "Satan knows that he doesn't have to drag Christians into deep sin to make them ineffective; sometimes he just needs to distract them so that they just stop growing and get involved in activities that have no real spiritual value. They become dormant in their walk with the Lord."[43]

My teenage years evolved around school and church. Later, as an officer's wife in the Air Force in Germany, I explored a more social world. Our non-inspiring chapel services were *generic ritual*. Conversely, in the Officer's Club we had friends and some required functions.

After two years, we were home in Harlingen, Texas. I was a typical mother involved in Cub Scouting, P.T.A., and Junior League. For seventeen years, I taught fashion design, sewing and tailoring to hundreds of students. Also, I taught a Sunday school class, though I knew that I didn't have the spiritual power that I should have had.

All of those activities were very important. But, God was not my *first* priority. I felt incomplete and I longed to be close to Him again.

In a sermon my pastor made a statement that recharged my life. He simply said, "Get *your* heart right with God." Instantly convicted, I prayed, "All right, Lord, my cigarettes too." Though this was socially popular in those days, I knew that it wasn't a good influence. With that simple prayer of repentance and turning my life totally over to God, I became vibrantly alive inside. It felt so good to finally be in tune with my Heavenly Father.

My life was set on a higher course. During the forty-plus years since then, my zeal as a Bible teacher and Christian writer has been undaunted. I have had an immensely satisfying lifestyle with my *Heavenly Father*, and with my fellowman.

> Total Commitment is the key
> to being filled with the Holy Spirit

Steps that will lead us into the Spirit Filled Life

You can hear about, read about and only know *about* the transformed and empowered life until you have experienced it. When you trust in Jesus with all *your* heart, mind, and soul, and turn to his lifestyle— you will *know*.

Desire

"Blessed are those who hunger and thirst for righteousness, for they will be filled" (Matt. 5:6 NIV). Jesus said in a loud voice, "If anyone is thirsty, let him come to me and drink. Whoever believes in me, as the Scripture has said, streams of living water will flow from within him ... By this he meant the Spirit, whom those who believed in him were later to receive" (Jn. 7:37–39 NIV).

Repent

Pray, "Search me, O God and know my heart; test me and know my anxious thoughts. See if there is any offensive way in me, and lead me in the way everlasting" (Ps. 139:23, 24 NIV). Meditate and let God reveal *your* sins. Put them out of *your* life and start doing what is right.

V: God's Will: "Be Filled" with His Spirit Empowered To Be and To Do!

When a friend repented, she broke her large collection of hard rock music records and returned a collection of stolen library books she had to her old high school, along with an apologetic letter. God is waiting for us to get serious. "If we confess our sins, he is faithful and just and will forgive us our sins and purify us from all unrighteousness" (1 Jn. 1:9 NIV).

Forgive

Determine to forgive. Write letters...make phone calls...arrange payments. Do not presume any matter is too old or trivial, and do not consider any offense too great to forgive. Though it may not be possible to restore relationships, forgiveness can heal lingering emotional injuries and establish a friendship on a new basis. "If you do not forgive men their sins, your Father will not forgive your sins" (Matt. 6:15 NIV). This is imperative! Though, it doesn't mean we should drag up a grudge that the other person doesn't even know about. That would be stirring up strife.

Apologize

To forgive [they are guilty] and to apologize [you are guilty] are not the same. "If you are offering *your* gift at the altar and there remember that *your* brother has *something against you*, leave *your* gift there in front of the altar. First go and be reconciled to *your* brother; then come and offer *your* gift" (Matt. 5:23, 24 NIV). I heard a preacher say, "I had rather apologize than agonize."

Invite

When the *closets of your life* are cleaned, ask God to "fill you with His Holy Spirit with the knowledge of his will through all spiritual wisdom and understanding...in order that you may live a life worthy of the Lord and may please him in every way: bearing fruit in every good work, growing in the knowledge of God" (Col. 1:9, 10 NIV).

Commit

Commit *your* life to God. In How to Obtain Fullness of Power, R. A. Torrey writes, "A surrendered will and life is the great key to receiving the Holy Spirit. Everything hinges on this. We may plead with God for the filling of the Holy Spirit, but unless we are yielded to Him to the very center of our being, nothing is likely to come of it."[44]

This reminds me of an experience with God's Holy Spirit that my granddaughter, Sumer, had when she was ten years old. She was on a pallet by my bed, and I was asleep. After a while, she started tugging on my arm excitedly, "Grama, wake up! God was right here in this room and he talked to me! We talked a whole fifteen minutes! I told Him, 'I give you my heart, not just a piece of my heart, but my *whole* heart.'" By this, I know that God has a special purpose for her life as she matures.

Believe

Believe that God wants you to have His Spirit indwelled. Do not rely on *your* feelings; trust His promises: "If you then, though you are evil, know how to give good gifts to *your* children, *how much more will your Father in heaven give the Holy Spirit* to those who ask him!" (Lu.11:13 NIV).

Praise

Praise God for hearing *your* prayer. Praise Him for who He is and for all He has done and is doing. By faith, Praise Him for filling *you* with His Holy Spirit.

Evidence of the Spirit-filled Life

There has been much discussion about *the evidence* of the Spirit-filled life. Many believe that a supernatural ability to speak in another language is the evidence. Even so, a righteous life must back up the claim.

V: God's Will: "Be Filled" with His Spirit Empowered To Be and To Do!

God made the primary proof clear: "This is how we know that he lives in us: We know it by the Spirit he gave us" (1 Jn. 3:24 NIV).

Also, "Whoever claims to live in him must walk as Jesus did" (1 Jn. 2:6 NIV). That obviously means our attitudes and actions are motivated from a heart that emulates Jesus.

I heard a minister say, "Transformed means to be changed from who we are to who he is. Renewing the mind means exchanging my thoughts and beliefs for God's thoughts and beliefs."

Another minister said, "You can tell where the Holy Spirit lives by the evidence in His *house*." Then he humorously compared the dorms on a college campus, "You can tell if girls live there by the tidy curtains ... and the sweet smell; if everything is basically in disarray, boys probably live there." Of course, girls *can* be messy and boys *can* be tidy. Regardless, if Jesus lives there, kind and gracious spiritual characteristics will prevail.

The fruit of the Spirit is love, joy, peace, patience, kindness, goodness, faithfulness, and gentleness, self-control (Gal. 5:22, 23 NIV).

Love will motivate *your* life: God's Spirit will help you to understand what it means to *"love God first"* and *"love your neighbor as yourself."*

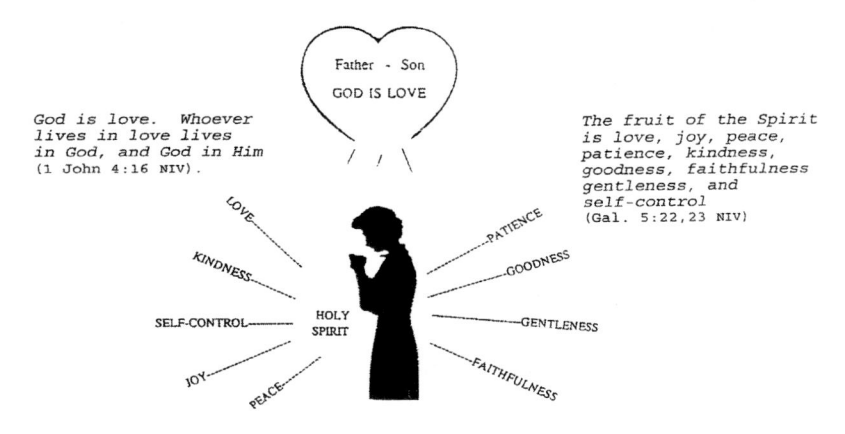

God is love. Whoever lives in love lives in God, and God in Him (1 John 4:16 NIV).

Father - Son
GOD IS LOVE

LOVE, KINDNESS, SELF-CONTROL, JOY, PEACE, PATIENCE, GOODNESS, GENTLENESS, FAITHFULNESS — HOLY SPIRIT

The fruit of the Spirit is love, joy, peace, patience, kindness, goodness, faithfulness gentleness, and self-control (Gal. 5:22,23 NIV)

You will radiate a Spirit of holiness: This means *purity* not *piety*. R. A. Torrey writes, "Holiness emphasizes the essential moral character of the Spirit. He is Holy in Himself. He imparts holiness to others."[45] *"Holy, holy, holy is the Lord Almighty"* (Isa. 6:3 NIV).

God abhors sin; you will too. This does not mean we are perfect, or that we will always make the right decisions, but we *will* feel uncomfortable when we sin. We will have an inner yearning to be right with God.

A woman asked my friend about her evidence:

"Are you filled with the Holy Spirit?"

She confidently replied, "Oh, yes!"

The inquirer asked, "What is *your* evidence?"

She answered, "I love my yardman!"

"That is *your* evidence?"

"Yes!" Gloria explained, "You see, a few weeks ago I looked out and saw him as a ragged, uneducated Mexican yardman. Today I see him as a loved child of God! Only God through His Holy Spirit within me could have wiped away the prejudices that had built up in me over a lifetime and left me with only love in my heart for that yardman!"

Others will sense Divine control of your life

Nebuchadnezzar said to Daniel, "I know that the spirit of the holy gods is in you" (Dan. 4:9 NIV). Similarly, on the Day of Pentecost the people, "recognized Peter and John as having been with Jesus" (Acts 4:13 NIV). They could see there was a divine presence in the way they looked and in what they were saying. With an aura of joy, they had command of divine truth.

Your priorities will change

Your life will be God-centered. Church, Bible study, and being with other Christians will become important. My pastor said that in his younger life he would drive by a church on Sunday and wonder why anyone would want to be there. Now, his place of choice is behind the pulpit.

You will desire to pray

As Jesus had the *spirit of sonship* with His Father (Gal. 4:6 NIV), so will you. Communion with *Our Father* will become a treasured privilege instead of a duty or responsibility. Besides specific prayer time, communication will simply flow back and forth.

You will pray in God's Will

The great Chinese Christian Watchman Nee writes, "Seldom are there those who pray aright. Many think of what they...wish to have, few pay attention to what God wants."[46] The Apostle Paul writes, "We have not received the spirit of the world but the Spirit who is from God, that we may *understand what God has freely given us*" (1 Cor. 2:12 NIV).

You will have special abilities

Your natural abilities will be amplified and God will give special abilities for a higher level of accomplishments. "Every good and *perfect gift* is from above, coming down from the Father of the heavenly lights..." (Jas.1:17 NIV).

God Provides Spiritual Gifts with Special Abilities

First, why there is little taught about *the power* in the gifts of the Spirit in our churches today? Many people believe that the Holy Spirit power was only for the apostles. It is probably because they have not seen such power in their churches.

A friend, who is graduating with a degree in theology, said that her denominational school's Harvard and Yale professors ignore Pentecostals and others who believe the gifts are relevant for today. Those intellectuals may accurately decipher Greek and Hebrew, but they may have missed the boat for spiritual power and don't know it. Worse yet, they are sidetracking their students.

Another friend said that she recently heard a pastor recite this common explanation to his congregation: "The gifts of the Spirit were no longer needed after the Bible was canonized."

It is true, Pentecostal power *has* waned through the centuries, but there is a reason why: sin, apathy, unbelief, lack of prayer, Bible study, and anointed spiritual leadership.

Historically, the time frame is about right when the gifts were deemed powerless. There was nothing wrong with the gifts; rather, the people. It was about 350 years after the apostolic era. In 373 AD, the historic Christian church agreed on the sixty-six books of the Bible. And, it was 382 AD, following the toleration of the faith by Emperor Constantine, that the Council of Rome decreed a seventy-three book Canon.

Since then in Christian history, the spiritual Dark Ages spanned centuries preceding 1000 AD and basically ended with the Reformation in the 1500's. During this time, only the papacy had Holy Scripture because each copy was inscribed by hand. They were not teaching Scripture because *they* were more concerned with power than prophecy. In 1455 the printing press made Holy Scripture available to the people.

Moving forward to 2011 AD, dusty Bibles are probably in most homes. It is easy to barricade ourselves within the doctrinal perimeters of our traditional beliefs. Consequently, there are congregations of ritualistic churchgoers who *"have a form of godliness but deny its power"* (2 Tim. 3:5 NIV).

Regardless of the historic reasoning that the gifts of the Spirit are not relevant for us today, it still does not correlate with what we read in God's word. What does *canonizing* [compiling] *the books of the Bible* have to do with the *Spiritual power of God's Holy Spirit* working in the lives of believers? They are not even the same subject.

In recent years, many churched and non-churched people sought a deeper relationship with our Lord. It became obvious when God responded with a new awaken in the 1900's and the supernatural gifts of the Spirit were evident.

Scampering for their Bibles and flipping pages to dormant principles reminiscent of the apostolic era, the book of Acts became their handbook. They could see themselves as the continuation of the book in the power of the Holy Spirit. Since Acts has only twenty eight chapters, some churches have called themselves "The Twenty-Ninth Chapter of Acts."

I became aware of the Charismatic movement in the early 1970's. I saw glimmers from other Christians and began to ask questions and search for answers. There was something different about them; *the joy of the Lord* seemed to be their common denominator.

Full Gospel Business Men's Fellowship International and Women's Aglow meetings flickered and flamed. In these meetings Protestants, Catholics and new converts seemed to be of one mind. Churches started (even in shopping centers), with non-traditional names like, "The Living Waters," "Spirit of Praise," "The Way of the Cross," and "Faith Pleases God." Some have become mega-churches with ministries that have siphoned members from traditional denominations.

God's Spirit has not lost His power. Nor has the New Covenant, sealed with Jesus' blood, been broken. Twenty-first century Christians need spiritual gifts now, just as in the apostolic era.

> When he ascended on high, he...gave gifts to men to prepare God's people for works of service, so that the body of Christ may be built up until we all reach unity in the faith and in the knowledge of the Son of God and become mature, attaining to the whole measure of the fullness of Christ.
> Ephesians 4:8, 12, 13 (NIV)

> God also testified to it by signs, wonders and various miracles and gifts of the Holy Spirit *distributed according to his will.*
> Hebrews 2:4 (NIV)

A common reason churches minimize Paul's message about the gifts in First Corinthians is because Corinth was a pagan culture and the new Christians were misusing some of the gifts. The church had the reputation for being confused. The same happens today from lack of understanding. A famous television minister said, "I have seen manifestations of the flesh and they call it the Holy Spirit."

From such incidents, many people have trepidation that God might give them something bizarre. Not so; God is a perfect *gentleman*. Everything he does is very good. We need to trust him to mold into us all that is necessary to be extraordinary in his kingdom's work.

As he did with the Corinthians, imagine Paul the Apostle behind the pulpit in our churches today saying, "I want to clarify the gifts and their use. Open your Bibles to First Corinthians the 12th chapter":

> Now about spiritual gifts, brothers, I do not want you to be ignorant…There are different kinds of gifts but the same Spirit. There are different kinds of service, but the same Lord. There are different kinds of working, but the Same God works all of them in all men.
>
> Now to each one the manifestation of the Spirit is given for the common good
>
> To one there is given through the Spirit the message of wisdom,
>
> to another the message of knowledge by means of the same Spirit,
>
> to another faith by the same Spirit,
>
> to another gifts of healing by that one Spirit,
>
> to another miraculous powers, to another prophecy,
>
> to another distinguishing between spirits,
>
> to another speaking in different kinds of tongues,
>
> and to still another the interpretation of tongues.
>
> All these are the work of one and the same Spirit, and *he gives them to each one, just as he determines.*
>
> 1 Corinthians 12:1, 8–11 (NIV)

V: God's Will: "Be Filled" with His Spirit Empowered To Be and To Do!

Then Paul compares the gifts and their use with the diverse functions of the body such as the eye, hand, and feet. We know that the eye sees for the whole body and the big toes keep the body in balance as we walk. Each part serves a different important purpose. He concludes,

> Now you are the body of Christ, and *each one of you is a part of it*. And in the church God has appointed first of all apostles, second prophets, third teachers, then workers of miracles, also those having gifts of healing, those able to help others, those with gifts of administration, and those speaking in different kinds of tongues
>
> 1 Corinthians 12:27, 28 (NIV)

Churches need the unique abilities of preachers, teachers, musicians, administrators, and translators. Add to this, the nursery workers who have been given extra love for babies, anointed secretaries, dedicated *Martha's* in the kitchen, fellowship organizers, and hard working custodians who have hearts to excel.

Our abilities must match our responsibilities. In *The Seasons of Life* Charles Swindoll presents a clever analogy of his frustration when he tried to emulate admired preachers' styles: "For over ten years in the ministry I, a rabbit, worked hard at swimming like a duck or flying like an eagle ... this rabbit quit the swim team and gave up flying lessons ... I learned it was okay to be me ... So relax ... cultivate *your* own capabilities."[47]

One day, while pondering the value of the spiritual gifts, I witnessed a prestigious marriage. Many sat in awe as the affluent groom committed his life and his possessions to his bride. This seemed like a fantasy in terms of wealth, power, and prestige. I thought of Christ as our heavenly bridegroom and His commitment to His church.

That night, I felt great love and joy being a part of Christ's spiritual bride (Eph. 1:22, 23; 5:25–27; Rev. 19:7 NIV). As I dreamed, words came to me, "All of my earthly possessions I give to you." When I awakened, I felt God's spirit had spoken to me in assurance of the heavenly riches that would eventually be ours as Christians.

The following night, the words persistently returned. "All of my earthly possessions I give to you." I tried to remove the word *earthly* so the message would correlate with my vision of heavenly streets of gold.

Thoughts persisted, "Now think. What were my earthly possessions?"

I replied, "I do not know of any." I thought about Jesus' life: "You did not have a 'place to lay your head'" (Matt.8:20 NIV). You provided money from a fish's mouth to pay taxes (Matt. 17:27 NIV). Also, they gambled away your robe at Calvary (Jn. 19:24 NIV).

Thoughts flowed. "The great riches I possessed on earth did not consist of things. This is what I give: I had a Spirit of sonship with My Father, and a spirit of love, joy, and peace. I was gentle, patient and understanding, with wisdom, knowledge, and discernment. I taught truth with simplicity, power, and authority. I proclaimed salvation to the lost with courage and boldness.

I cast out demons and healed the sick. I walked in confidence with God and man. As Peter and John said, "Rise and walk in the name of Jesus," you too have the power of my name. As the coin was in the fish's mouth, I have promised to meet your needs.

You have my continual abiding Presence. For I have vowed, "Never will I leave you; never will I forsake you" (Heb.13:5 NIV). All of my promises are yours. I love you, My Church, My Bride. My earthly possessions are yours.

I prayed, "Thank you, Lord. These treasures are my dream for they are far more beautiful than the glitter of flawless diamonds and the luster of pure gold. Beautiful jewels are the marvelous workmanship of your hands; whereas, your Spirit is the essence of you…"

The Gift of Love energizes the special abilities

Paul ended 1st Corinthians chapter 12 about spiritual gifts with, *"I show you a still more excellent way…"* Then, he sandwiched in the classic chapter on love before resuming his instruction about the gifts. Clearly, he was saying that Love is the motivation, the energizing power, the adhesive in the operation of the special spiritual abilities.

> If I speak in the tongues of men and of angels, but have not love, I am only a resounding gong or a clanging cymbal. Love is patient... kind. It does not envy... boast... is not proud... rude... self-seeking... easily angered, it keeps no record of wrongs. Love does not delight in evil but rejoices with the truth. It always protects... trusts... hopes... perseveres. Love never fails... And now these three remain: faith, hope, and love... the greatest... is love.
>
> 1 Corinthians 13 (NIV)

Jesus overflowed with energizing love. A woman who had been bleeding for years reached through the crowd just to touch His clothing, and she was healed instantly. "At once Jesus realized that power had gone out from him. He turned around in the crowd and asked, 'Who touched my clothes?'" (Mark 5:30 NIV).

God wants His children to be similar conductors, who allow his love to flow through them to others. Jesus said, "... these signs will accompany those who believe: In my name... they will place their hands on sick people, and they will get well" (Mark 16:18 NIV).

We have all felt the effects of love in a touch. A man's pat on the shoulder can give another man reassurance and comfort. A touch thrills a sweetheart and soothes a crying baby. Love in a touch is therapeutic. Tests have proven that new babies who are seldom touched are prone to wane, whereas those who are cuddled will, in normal circumstances, develop emotionally, mentally, and physically. When Christ's Spirit energizes the human touch, there will be a touch of the Divine. Miraculous things will happen.

A woman came to me thanking God for her healing that happened several years ago. I remembered seeing her limp to the altar when she asked our pastor to anoint her with oil, according to James 5:14. Due to a hip injury, she had been in severe pain for years. A small group gathered around touching her. I knelt and put my hand on her hip.

Tears welled when she said, "As everyone prayed, I felt surrounded by love. When someone touched my hip, warmth flowed through it, and my hip stopped hurting. At the end of the prayer I looked down to see who had touched me."

I replied, "I remember well. I did nothing but focus my attention on God and His Love in the name of Jesus Christ and asked Him to allow me to be a vessel through whom His love could flow."

As we realize the power of love more fully we understand why *our Father* tells us to "turn the other cheek" and "don't let the sun go down on our wrath." He does not want anger, bitterness, and resentment to interfere with our receptivity. Jesus' Spirit is still comforting and healing through His children with love.

In Chapter 14, Paul resumed his teaching on the gifts: "Follow the way of love and *eagerly desire spiritual gifts…*" Then, Paul highlights the most important gift: "… especially the gift of prophecy"… [Read 1st Corinthians chapters 12, 13 and 14]

Gifts can become a false doctrine when magnified beyond their purpose; some people place such emphasis on the more dramatic gifts that Jesus loses the limelight. We must keep our eyes on Him and simply use our individual divinely bestowed gifts as tools for worship and service.

You will have a servant nature

One of the most important signs of being filled with God's Holy Spirit is to have a servant nature: "By their fruit you will recognize them … every good tree bears good fruit" (Matt. 7:16 NIV). As Jesus felt compassion toward the sick, the lonely, the needy, and the lost, you too will desire to help them. "The Son of Man did not come to be served, but to serve" (Mark 10:45 NIV).

V: God's Will: "Be Filled" with His Spirit Empowered To Be and To Do!

Jesus exemplified the servant nature when he washed his disciple's feet. When I was a child, I enjoyed going to church with my Grandmother Taylor, who was a Primitive Baptist. I was intrigued with the *foot washing* ceremonies. She lived a life of love and service to her large family.

The power of God's Holy Spirit will work with you

One day I was wondering about the effective of my Christian life. That night I had a dream. *Symbolically,* when I touched people with my hand they were affected dramatically. It was like an electrical shock. I was curious about this so I gently touched several people to see what would happen.

Suddenly, something was thrown over me like an electric blanket with a short in it, and *I was jolted* with a stern admonition: "*Don't play with*" (manipulate) *my Holy Spirit!*" Clear instructions followed: "All you need to do is study my Word, commune with me, and follow me. Do this and no more. I will touch the lives of those around you *in my own way.*"

God's wise Holy Spirit works with us, through us, and around us when we obey His simple instructions. Furthermore, we need not see his results to know he is at work. Just obey him, trust him, and move forward.

Spirit Empowered "To Do"

It is not enough to simply *be* the kind of person God wants us to be. We must also *do* what God wants us to do.

God Has Assignments for Each Christian

God has specific assignments for each of his children. "*You did not choose me,* but I chose you and appointed you to go and bear fruit" (Jn. 15: 15 NIV). Early in this chapter, I gave my testimony about

God's Holy Spirit coming mightily into my room when I was young. Sensing the encounter would be brief, I pleaded with God to take me with him. His response was the calling upon my life: "No, you cannot go now, *I have work for you to do.*"

The rest of the verse, "… and bear fruit. I… appointed you to go and bear fruit that will last. Then the Father will give you whatever you ask in my name" (Jn. 15:15–16 NIV). That means *fruit* is more Christians. *Then*, he will provide, "whatever we ask in his name" to support our assigned ministry. (Many people claim the promise in the last part of the verse without reading the stipulation at the first.)

I believe that my assignment was to be a Ladies' Bible Teacher and a Christian Writer. *Fruit that will last* means dedicated women in the classes will teach others. It is true that through the years, women *have* become strong in prayer and many *have* gone forth in their own ministries. The number will increase exponentially as it will also include each person who is inspired to live *the message conveyed in scripture* throughout this book. Jesus has told each of us, "I have work for you to do: "Go into the world and spread the Gospel" (Matt. 28:19–20).

Like Jesus, we must, "be about Our Father's business." We do not have to be an evangelist or a theologian. Jesus sees our every effort to help others as a service unto him:

> I was hungry…you gave me something to eat, I was thirsty…you gave me something to drink, I was a stranger and you invited me in. I needed clothes…clothed me, I was sick and you looked after me, I was in prison…and you came to visit me… *whatever you did for one of the least of these brothers of mine, you did for me.*
>
> Matthew 25:35, 36, 40 (NIV)

Our Lord gives us inside information into *the family business.* He said, "I no longer call you servants, because a servant does not know his master's business… *everything* that I learned from my Father I have made known to you" (Jn. 15:15 NIV).

V: God's Will: "Be Filled" with His Spirit Empowered To Be and To Do!

A beautiful dream revealed to me the privilege of Christian service. In my dream, I prayed fervently about a desperate humanitarian need. A symbolic block of silver lay before me. I prayed that the silver would turn to gold. I looked down, and the Lord answered in an unexpected manner. My hands had turned to a beautiful, brilliant, pure, translucent gold! They were soft and gentle hands to help others and to communicate love in a touch. They were to be used in the kingdom's work, for God's glory.

Soon after the dream, I had an unusual opportunity to serve: I went to the hospital for a routine visits. Before leaving, I prayed, "Lord, is there anyone else you want me to visit?" Then, I remembered another member of our church. I thought her room number was 240A. As I approached the end of the hall, a desperate feeble cry came from an elderly woman's room, "Help me someone, Please!" I went to her bed. She grabbed my arm and began praising the Lord, "Oh thank you, thank you Lord! You sent someone to help me!" She was blind.

I quickly discovered a nurse had given her an enema and had not returned. I looked down the long empty hall. I buzzed the nurses' station to learn that her shift nurse had not come on duty. I could not leave her with such pleading. I saw some clean sheets and a gown stacked on a chair. Her nurse came in. Thinking I was her daughter, we worked together taking care of her needs.

Soon, we had her clean and peaceful in her dark world. She was still praising the Lord. I looked at my watch, prayed with her, and quickly left. I had no time to find the lady from our church. Curiously, I glanced back at the door. It *was* 240A. I felt awed when I realized God sends help to the cries of even His weakest children.

Though our everyday Christian services may not be this menial, love for our fellow man *will* supersede inconvenience in many ways. Then again, going far beyond what we call ordinary service, we all know that there are those who have special ministries such as: missionaries, medical doctors, and caregivers. Those who are more like

Mother Teresa, who spent her life in India caring for the hungry, destitute, diseased, and dying.

Jesus' ministry on earth lasted three years. That was only long enough to show His disciples what would have to be continued through the centuries. Just before Jesus ascended into heaven, He delegated to His followers the necessary authority, and commissioned them *to go*:

> *All authority in heaven and on earth has been given to me. Therefore go* and make disciples of all nations, baptizing them in the name of the Father and of the Son and of the Holy Spirit, and teaching them to obey everything I have commanded you.
> Matthew 28:18, 19 (NIV)

In Mark we read, "And these signs will accompany those who believe: In my name they will drive out demons [have authority over evil]; they will speak in new tongues [with new power]... they will place their hands on sick people, and they will get well" (Mk. 16:17–18 NIV).

> After the Lord Jesus had spoken to them, He was taken up into heaven and he sat at the right hand of God. Then the disciples went out and preached everywhere, *and the Lord worked with them*, [His Holy Spirit] *and confirmed his word by the signs that accompanied it."*
> Mark 16:19–20 (NIV).[48]

The power is in the last verse. Just as *"the Lord worked with them,"* through the power of His Holy Spirit and caused the healings and other supernatural occurrences to take place, *He also works with us and through us.* Jesus clarified the fact that *this includes us* in His prayer to *Our Father*:

V: God's Will: "Be Filled" with His Spirit Empowered To Be and To Do!

> As you sent me into the world, I have sent them into the world. My prayer is not for them alone. I pray also for *those who will believe in me through their message* [as the gospel is spread through the generations to us today], that all of them may be one, Father, just as you are in me and I am in you. May they [all Christians] also be in us so that the world may believe that you have sent me.
>
> John 17:18, 20, 21 (NIV)

Please reread that amazing verse. It is hard for us to comprehend the awesome fact that just as the Father, Son, and Holy Spirit are one, He wants our spirits to be in one with them: "Christ lives in me. The life I live in the body, I live by faith in the Son of God, who loved me and gave Himself for me" (Gal. 2:20 NIV). The truth of this verse is the power of the next verse:

> I tell you the truth, *anyone* who has faith in me will do what I have been doing. He will do even greater things than these, because I am going to the Father.
>
> John 14:12 (NIV)

First, let's clarify the word, *greater*. Since no one can improve on the quality of Jesus' works, greater would have to mean quantity. Jesus' perfect ministry went as far as he could walk, or ride a donkey, and he spoke to, even a crowd of five thousand (loaves and fishes)—without a microphone. Today, we have jumbo jets, the internet, and satellites that cover the world to help spread the gospel of salvation to many millions."

The Trinity Broadcasting Network (TBN) is the single largest TV network in the world. Since 1973, Paul Crouch and Jan Crouch have steadily expanded its outreach to spread the gospel of salvation throughout the world... According to their website: TBN is carried on over 275 television stations in the U.S. and on thousands of other cable television and satellite systems in over seventy-five countries, where their programming is translated into more than eleven languages.

Through TBN, Billy Graham's Crusades will continue going into the furthest reaches of the world. But now, they will go with a mega megaphone.

What are the works He wants us to continue? Jesus described His ministry when He stood in the Synagogue and read from the prophecy of Isaiah, concerning Himself: "The Spirit of the Lord is on me, because he has anointed me to preach good news to the poor. He has sent me to proclaim freedom for the prisoners and recovery of sight for the blind, to release the oppressed, to proclaim the year of the Lord's favor" (Luke 4:18, 19 NIV).

Since many people believe that the mighty Holy Spirit ministry was only for Jesus and His apostles, let's prove it applies to us today: Jesus trained other disciples. *First*, He called the Twelve together, and "gave them power and authority to drive out all demons and to cure diseases, and he sent them out to preach the kingdom of God and to heal the sick" (Luke 9:1, 2 NIV).

> After this the Lord appointed *seventy-two* others and sent them two by two ahead of him to every town and place where he was about to go...heal the sick who are there and tell them, "The kingdom of God is near you."
>
> John 10:1, 9 (NIV)

The seventy-two returned with joy and said, *"Lord, even the demons submit to us in your name."* Jesus replied, *"I saw Satan fall* like lightning from heaven" (God cast Lucifer from heaven and Jesus defeated him on earth; he no longer has any authority over you.) "I have given you authority to trample on snakes and scorpions (symbolic of Satan the serpent, all his evil spirits) and to overcome all the power of the enemy; nothing will harm you. However, do not rejoice that

V: God's Will: "Be Filled" with His Spirit Empowered To Be and To Do!

the spirits submit to you, but rejoice that *your* names are written in heaven" (Lu. 10:17–20 NIV).

Jesus got excited and "rejoiced greatly in the Holy Spirit" when He saw that his followers were learning to use the authority in His name over sickness and evil spirits while proclaiming the Kingdom of God.

> At that time Jesus, full of joy through the Holy Spirit, said, "I praise you, Father, Lord of heaven and earth, because you have hidden these things from the wise and learned, and revealed them to little children. Yes, Father, for this was *your* good pleasure."
>
> Luke 10:21 (NIV)

The colossal assignment to *go into the world* was not just for the apostles, the seventy-two, priest, preachers, and teachers. Jesus was commissioning *all* believers throughout the remaining history of mankind. It will require *every* Christian to witness for Christ where they are, and to reach out to others. And, he promised to work with us through the power of The Holy Spirit, just as he did for believers in that era: "And the Lord worked with them and confirmed his word by the signs that accompanied it" (Mk. 16:20 NIV).

Since then, the gospel branched out through the centuries. The Kingdom of God has been proclaimed from the Holy Land throughout Asia, the vast Roman Empire, and over the world— to us today. This obviously means that you and I must carry the torch for the ministry that Christ began.

The need is great. Jesus said, "Look on the fields; for they are white already to harvest" (Jn. 4:35 KJV).

"The harvest is plentiful, but the workers are few" (Lu. 10:2 NIV). I think of these Scriptures when I drive to church through a cotton farming area. When I see the huge white fields, I try to imagine how many individual cotton bolls are out there. The ones that are not brought in will be plowed under.

Clearly, that means numerous souls will be lost if they are not brought into His Kingdom. Since Jesus *has made us to be a kingdom and priests* to serve his God and Father, you and I have work to do. And, he did not unplug our *power* for service.

> ...and from Jesus Christ, who is the faithful witness, the firstborn from the dead, and the ruler of the kings of the earth. To him who loves us and has freed us from our sins by his blood, and *has made us to be a kingdom and priests* to serve his God and Father—to him be glory and power forever and ever! Amen.
>
> Revelation 1:5–6 (NIV)

> And he has committed to us [the redeemed] the message of reconciliation. *We are therefore Christ's ambassadors,* as though God were making his appeal through us.
>
> 2 Corinthians 5:19–21 (NIV)

God Provides Sustaining Power

For forty-three years my pastor, Rev. Gene Horton, has led the First Baptist Church in Rio Hondo, Texas. According to the Baptist General Convention of Texas statistician, that places him in the top *less than one percent* of all pastors, since the average pastoral tenure in *one church* is four and one half years.[49] I asked him, "To what do you attribute this longevity?"

He thoughtfully replied, "It *has* to be God's will: 1. God gave me the will to come. 2. He gave the congregation the will to want me to come. 3. He gave us the will to stay together."

The first two steps were probably true for the ninety-nine percent of the pastors who moved into their churches. Unless God specifically sends a pastor to another church, the third step is divine love that keeps the pastor and congregation together.

Bro. Gene has conducted numerous marriage ceremonies and family funerals. He prayed for us in our hospital beds and wept with

V: God's Will: "Be Filled" with His Spirit Empowered To Be and To Do!

us at the cemeteries. He said, "We have ridden the waves together." This shouldn't be extraordinary; it is the way church life should be. With God's sustaining power, we pray that our pastor will remain with us "Until death do us part."

When the Gifts Will Cease

As long as we need the gifts for service, we will have them. "God's gifts and his call are irrevocable" (Rom. 11:29 NIV). The next Scripture reveals when we will not need them.

> Where there are prophecies, they will cease; where there are tongues, they will be stilled...knowledge, it will pass...For we know in part and we prophesy in part, but *when perfection comes,* the imperfect disappears...Now we see but a poor reflection as in a mirror; *then we shall see face to face.*
> 1 Corinthians 13:8–10, 12 (NIV)

Jesus is the only perfect one. When he returns in the Rapture, perfection will have come. When we see Him *face to face* we will no longer need our unique gifts for earthly ministries, because we will have left this earth and will be with Him in the heavenly Realm.

When the Gifts will Cease[50]   **Jesus face to face**

(see page 375 for a larger image)

In conclusion, now that we have studied *our Father*'s primary will for our lives, we see that being filled with His Spirit is the only way we can be sensitive to his guidance in all areas of our lives, and be empowered to effectively carry on His work on earth.

In *Sit, Walk, Stand,* Watchman Nee writes our summary:

> God never asks us to do anything we can do ... Yet, by his grace we are living it and doing it. The life we live is the life of Christ lived in the power of God, and the work we do is the work of Christ carried on through us by his Spirit whom we obey.[52]

"Thy Will be Done": Baptism and the Lord's Supper Ordinances

There are two deeply spiritual ordinances that Jesus instructed believers to observe— Baptism and the Lord's Supper.

Baptism

Jesus' baptism was significant for five basic reasons:

1. John, the last of the Old Testament prophets, introduced Jesus to the world as the long awaited Messiah. These things took place in Bethany beyond the Jordan, where John was baptizing. The next day he saw Jesus coming to him and said, *"Behold, the Lamb of God* who takes away the sin of the world! This is He on behalf of whom I said, 'after me comes a Man who has a higher rank than I, for He existed before me'" (Jn.8–30 NASB).

2. Jesus symbolized his pending death, burial and resurrection by being *buried under the water and raised to life.*

3. God confirmed who Jesus was and announced his approval. As soon as Jesus was baptized, he went *up out of the water.* At that moment heaven was opened, and he saw the Spirit of God

V: God's Will: "Be Filled" with His Spirit Empowered To Be and To Do!

descending like a dove and lighting on him. And a voice from heaven said, "This is my Son, whom I love; with him I am well pleased" Matt.3:13–17 (NIV).

4. The ceremony initiated Jesus' ministry on earth.
5. He set an example for all believers to be baptized.

In baptism we are identifying with Jesus' death burial and resurrection by being lowered under the water and *raised to a new life in Christ*. It is an outward expression of what our heart believes.

It is the right thing to do. Jesus said to John before his baptism, "Let it be so now; it is proper for us to do this to fulfill all righteousness." Baptism is supposed to ceremonially initiate our earthly ministry, as it did for Jesus (Matt. 3:13–17 NIV).

Some congregations are taught that it is imperative to be baptized as a prerequisite to heaven. That was not true with the thief on the cross. The thief went straight to heaven, solely upon his faith in Jesus. "For God so loved the world that he gave his one and only Son, that *whoever believes in him* shall not perish but have eternal life" (Jn. 3:16 NIV). Jesus' blood secured our place in Heaven. Salvation happened in the heart through faith. Then, baptism symbolized it publically.

When emphasis is placed on baptism, it is easy to skip over the faith part, be baptized, and have a false sense of security.

As a matter of obedience, Jesus said, "Go … make disciples of all nations, *baptizing* them in the name of the Father and of the Son and of the Holy Spirit, *and teaching them to obey everything I have commanded you*. And surely I am with you always, to the very end of the age" (Matt. 28:19–20 NIV).

The early Christians obeyed: *"Those who accepted his message were baptized…"* (Acts 2:38–41 NIV). There were about three thousand converts after Peter's first sermon.

An Ethiopian eunuch, treasurer for Candace, queen of the Ethiopians, wanted to be baptized immediately after Philip explained to him salvation through Jesus Christ. "As they traveled along the road, they came to some water and the eunuch said, 'Look, here is water. Why shouldn't I be baptized?'... [They]... went down into the water and Philip baptized him" (Acts 8:36–38 NIV).

I was baptized when I was ten years old. I remember walking to the water with other converts and praying, "Lord, I don't understand all that baptism is supposed to mean, but I want it to mean all that it is supposed to." I felt that God and I had an agreement.

If anyone who has accepted Jesus Christ as Lord and has not been baptized, ministers will be glad to discuss their doctrine of faith. *Churches vary in their procedure.* The Baptist Church requires immersion for membership *as a testimony of what your heart already believes.*

The Lord's Supper

The second important ordinance is The Lord's Supper. It should be deeply meaningful; but, sometimes it is mere ritual. It depends on the each partaker's attitude. Their heart should be clean and deeply reverent.

Jesus and his disciples gathered to celebrate the ancient traditional Passover Meal: In the time of Moses, the night before the Israelites were to leave Egyptian bondage, God said to slay a lamb, put its blood over the doorpost of your homes and the death angel that will destroy the first born of every household will *Passover* you. (Read Exodus 12:5–14 (NIV)

During the Passover Meal, Jesus instigated the Lord's Supper as a New Covenant Memorial. He would soon *be* the ultimate Passover Lamb on the altar of the cross. Then, for all who have put the blood over the doorposts of their heart by faith in Jesus, will not die spiritually; the death angel will Passover and we will live forever.

> When the hour came, Jesus and his apostles reclined at the table. And he said to them, "I have eagerly desired to eat this Passover with you before I suffer. For I tell you, I will not eat it again until it finds fulfillment in the kingdom of God."

At this point, Jesus changed the ceremonial Passover Meal to become The Lord's Supper:

> After taking the cup, he gave thanks and said, "Take this and divide it among you. For I tell you I will not drink again of the fruit of the vine until the kingdom of God comes."
>
> And he took bread, gave thanks and broke it, and gave it to them, saying, "This is my body given for you; do this in remembrance of me."
>
> In the same way, after the supper he took the cup, saying, *"This cup is the new covenant in my blood,* which is poured out for you."
>
> Luke 22:7, 8, 14–20 (NIV)

> [Jesus said,] "This do, as often as you drink it, *in remembrance of Me"*
>
> 1 Corinthians 11:25 (NKJV)

The pure blood of the ultimate Passover Lamb sealed the *New Covenant of faith and love*, once and for all. (Read Hebrews 10:1–18)

Thy Will be Done "On earth as it is in heaven"

In closing, when we pray, *"Lord, Thy will be done"* we must include *"on earth as it is in heaven."* We ask the question, *how is it* in heaven that we want on earth? The answer is clear: God reigns supreme. Heaven is *filled* with God's Spirit of love, peace, and joy. His will is for it to the same for us on earth. For now, it is an earnest petition but in the Millennial Reign it will be fulfilled: Jesus will be the King of Kings and a "lion will lay down with a lamb."

Sample Prayer

"Be Filled" with His Spirit
Empowered To Be and To Do!

Our Father,

I commit my life to you and I ask you to fill me to overflowing with your Holy Spirit. Not for the sake of being holy, but for empowerment to be more like you and serve you with higher goals and greater accomplishments.

I want *your* Spirit to be so visible when others see me that they think of you.

Enlighten my mind to understand *your* Word. Open my ears to hear *your* voice and my eyes to see the world as you see it.

I want your love to flow through my life to bring comfort and healing to those who are discouraged or broken-hearted. And, I want my hands to help others and put into action that which my heart believes.

Help me to discern and grasp truth. *Your* will is my will, for I am *your*s. Amen.

V: God's Will: "Be Filled" with His Spirit Empowered To Be and To Do!

Living Christianity Assignment

Bible Study—Read Acts to see the power of the first church. Believers served as Jesus served with spiritual power. *Your* intellect must be impacted with the Word of God.

> In the last days, God says, I will pour out my Spirit on all people.
> Acts 2:17 (NIV)

Prayer—Ask God to fill you with His Holy Spirit so that you can serve more effectively in *your* ministry for Him.

> And you will receive the gift of the Holy Spirit. The promise is for you and *your* children and for all who are far off.
> Acts 2:38, 39 (NIV)

Works—Be more aware of people's emotional, spiritual, physical, and material needs. Find out what is important to them.

> Let us not love with words or tongue but with actions and in truth.
> 1 John 3:18 (NIV)

VI:
Ask Our Father
"Thank You, Lord!"

"Give us today our daily bread."

> Do not be anxious about anything, but in everything, by prayer and petition, with thanksgiving, present *your* requests to God.
>
> Philippians 4:6 (NIV)

VI:
Ask Our Father
"Thank You, Lord!"

"Give us today our daily bread."

- Twenty Seven Basic Principles in Petitioning
- Intercede for Others

  - Who Can Intercede
  - The Intercessor Illustrated
  - The Intercessory *Power Prayer!*

- The Power Prayer Fundamental Principle: Pray in God's Will
- "Never the Less, not My Will but *Yours*"
- How to Pray for the Terminally Ill
- How to Pray for Those Who are Dying with Classic Unsaved Symptoms
- The Unpardonable Sin
- Sample Prayer: Ask Our Father "Thank You, Lord!"
- Living Christianity Assignment

VI:
Ask Our Father
"Thank You, Lord!"

"Give us today our daily bread."

I remember a special time of asking and receiving when our first grandchild was small. Bob and I took Savannah to the toy store and intently watched her interests. We bought an adorable playhouse with a red roof and yellow shutters. She peeked out of the window, and said, "Grandpa, I need to kiss you."

This does not sound like deep theology, yet the simplicity of love in giving, and gratitude in receiving, is exactly what *Our Father* wants in response when He answers our prayers. "*Give us today our daily bread,*" can mean much more than the basic needs from Our Father's views: If you...though you are evil" (by basic nature), know how to give good gifts to your children, how much more will your Father in heaven give good gifts to those who ask him!" (Matt.7:11 NIV).

Twenty-Seven Basic Principles in Petitioning

Though *asking Our Father* for blessings is easy, there are principles that will strengthen our faith for larger prayer answers. In the following topics, we will see how to approach *Our Father*, make bold requests, and believe that we will receive.

Approach Our Father humbly

When Israel's King Solomon was young and faced the responsibility of governing a nation, he approached God humbly: *"But I am only a little child and do not know how to carry out my duties"* (1 Kings 3:7 NIV). We, too, must come to *our Father* with the same dependent relationship.

By contrast, I have heard some people pray arrogantly, *demanding* their *right*s as they *hold* God to His promises! If our children were to speak to us in such a manner, it is not likely they would receive a blessing.

We know that humility does not mean we are to think *less* of ourselves. Rather, we are to think *less* of *ourselves*. That is to say, we will spend more time thinking of other people's needs and less being preoccupied with our own.

An essential factor for humility is being honest about our sins. Daniel approached God with honesty when he received his great prayer answer, "While I was...praying, *confessing my sin, and the sin of my people Israel* and making my request to the LORD my God...Gabriel, the man I had seen in the earlier vision, came to me" (Dan. 9:20–21 NIV).

For a scene of humility, we might envision an old man in overalls sitting in a weathered rustic farm house at a table with his face bowed in his wrinkled hands. It is evident that he has seen many winters and has frequently sought God for his very existence through illnesses, storms, and famines. He has no false pride. Rather, he has serene confidence in his relationship with his Heavenly Father.

A Portrait of an Old Man
by - Ric Knight

The weathered old man was quite content,
Just rocking and thinking about the life he spent.
He smoked an old pipe in an old cedar chair,
The wind was blowing his white tattered hair.
His friends are few, his children are wed,
Not a soul to see that our old friend gets fed.
None will bother to take time to care,
None around for his secrets to share.
It bothers him not, that death lies in wait,
He's a happy old man, no grudges, no hate,
He says a soft prayer for his daily strife,
He manages to live, for God's in his life

God makes a great promise based on humility. It is not only for individuals but as God was deeply involved in the welfare of Israel throughout the Bible, he has made provisions for our nations today: "If my people, who are called by my name, will humble themselves and pray and seek my face and turn from their wicked ways, then will I hear from heaven and will forgive their sin and will heal their land" (2 Chron. 7:14 NIV). We all know that our nation desperately needs healing spiritually, morally and economically.

Take Time to Realize Our Father's Presence

Too often we rush through our prayers without experiencing God's nearness. Andrew Murray wrote, "We need time with God realize His presence... to consider and feel the needs we plead for; to take our place in Christ."[53]

Reading Scripture and thinking about God helps to kindle this awareness. Enjoy being with Him. In fact, *Abiding in Him* is a major principle for prayer answers. [7]"If you abide in Me, and My words abide in you, you will ask what you desire, and it shall be done for you" (Jn. 15:7 NKJV).

Have Proper Motives

Our Father expects us to have proper motives and be spiritually wise concerning things for which we ask. He is not an overindulgent Father who raises irresponsible children. He recognizes a demanding selfish attitude and forewarns, *"When you ask, you do not receive, because you ask with wrong motives, that you may spend what you get on your pleasures"* (Jas. 4:3 NIV).

For example, a "Name it and Claim it" principle emerged in some religious groups. They do such things as "lay hands on a Cadillac and declare, 'MINE,' in the name of Jesus!" We should ask, "Do I really need a Cadillac if so, why? Could it be ego?

This does not mean riches are bad. God gives, when he can trust us to use riches in a right way. Money is needed in every area of life. Certainly, Christian ministries must have funds. When we request riches, we need to analyze our reasons for asking because *"The LORD searches every heart and understands every motive behind the thoughts"* (1 Chron. 28:9 NIV).

Does he see a thirst to satisfy ego, pride, and power? Or does he smile when he sees a heart with a sincere desire to enrich lives and further his kingdom on earth? We may actually need a van more than a Cadillac.

Ask

The starting point for answered prayer is in the *asking*. "So I say to you: *Ask and* it will be given to you; seek and you will find; knock and the door will be opened to you" (Luke 11:0 NIV). Helen Steiner Rice wrote:

> ...If we send no ships out, no ships will come in,
> And unless there's a contest, nobody can win.
> For games can't be won unless they are played,
> And prayers can't be answered unless they are prayed...

Expect to Receive

Many times we plead to God for necessities when we should already be in the flow of blessings. The principles are engraved in stone. It could be that we do not have confidence in the principles and do not expect to receive. Study the Scriptures closely and inscribe them in our hearts.

> *Give, and it will be given to you.* A good measure, pressed down, shaken together and running over, will be poured into *your* lap. For with the measure you use, it will be measured to you.
>
> Luke 6:38 (NIV)

> Bring the whole tithe [ten percent, ref. Lev. 27:30–34] into the storehouse [church] that there may be food [to pay the bills] in my house. Test me in this, says the Lord Almighty, and see if I will not throw open the floodgates of heaven and pour out so much blessing that you will not have room enough for it. I will prevent pests from devouring *your* crops, and the vines in *your* fields will not cast their fruit, says the Lord Almighty. Then all the nations will call you blessed, for *your*s will be a delightful land, says the Lord Almighty.
>
> Malachi 3:10–12 (NIV)

Also, remember this: "Whoever sows sparingly will also reap sparingly, and whoever sows generously will also reap generously" (2 Cor. 9:6 NIV).

Is it possible that we need to get up off our knees and start sowing? The seed has to be put in the ground before it will reproduce and multiply. Then, we are getting our attention off ourselves and thinking of others. We all have *something* to give time, money, love, food.... It wasn't much, but I saw a man rummaging through a garbage can and bought him a hamburger. I can't get credit for the "widow's mite" but we know that Jesus was so pleased with her meager sharing that it is immortalized in God's word. He knows our ability to give and our willingness to share.

John R. Rice uses the analogy of "window shopping" when one prays *without expecting to receive.* After spending a morning with his wife downtown, He said, "I learned that a woman can shop half a day without... expecting to bring anything home!"[54]

Jesus promises "whatsoever we believe, we shall receive" which could also mean if we expect nothing; we receive nothing. Then, we think prayer doesn't work. I learned of this from Catherine Marshall's *Adventures in Prayer:*

> Sadly, sometimes we fail to catch God's vision for us because our capacity to dream has been atrophied by some condition which has given us a poverty complex. My first glimpse of this was in a former college friend... her widowed mother had taught her that those who hope for little or nothing will never suffer disappointment... this had been nothing less than excellent training in poverty expectation....[55]

This relates to an experience I had at the hospital while visiting a friend. After surgery, she was in great pain. Her pastor stood near her bed, and I asked him to pray for her. He started toward the door and said, "Let's come back when she is better." He obviously did not expect prayer to accomplish anything.

To me, that was precisely the time to pray. I had seen pain eased through prayer several times. For one, my aunt was in severe pain while awaiting surgery. I prayed, "Father, please ease her pain." She relaxed and slept.

Another example: Paula Cruz, a Christian nurse instructor, said that a patient with a possible cerebral hemorrhage was crying, "My

Head, My Head!" She held his head and prayed; God answered; the patient settles down and rested.

Medically speaking, there may be many opinions about *how* these things happened. Nevertheless, the only thing that is important in regard to prayer is, "We asked God, and we received answers." He works in his own ways.

Remember, it is Jesus' nature to want to bless and make whole. Thank him for wanting to do something wonderful in the person's life for which you are praying. We know that Jesus said, "I have come that they may have life, and have it to the full" (Jn. 10:10 NIV). Therefore, He wants us to trust Him, and expect to receive.

Gary Wilkerson wrote, "To expect little from God insults the King of vast resources, immense generosity, and unending compassion. Our churches need leader who expect."

Pray in the Spirit

Power prayers will *all* be prayed *in the spirit*. But, there are different ways we may express them:

- No words at all may come from meditative communication.
- We may express our prayers in our native language.
- Many people use a prayer language supernaturally endowed which is proclaimed to have special power.

The manner in which we express our prayers is not as important to *our Father* as the attitude of our hearts. He knows whether our requests are in harmony with His nature and character while seeking a purpose that is in line with His will.

To sum it all, Dr. Mary Relfe wrote: "Whatever dialect people speak, prayer is their native language; and is the only power on earth that commands the power of heaven."[56]

In *Pray in the Spirit*, Arthur Wallis writes, "The world has yet to see such a manifestation of the glory of God that can only come through a church...purified, praying in the power of the Holy Spirit."[57] If this were to happen we would see a mighty display of everything that extols God's power and His virtues.

Ask in Jesus' Name

We must remember that our right of access to God is through our Lord, Jesus Christ because he redeemed us from our sins. Amazingly, in his name, Our Father will give to us as he would to his son, Jesus. In this next verse Jesus told us *twice* to ask of the Father *in His name*. He assures us that we will receive, and it will be to our great joy.

> In that day [after I ascend and the Holy Spirit descends] you will no longer ask me [Jesus] anything. I tell you the truth, my Father will give you *whatever you ask in my name*. Until now you have not asked for *anything in my name*. Ask and you will receive, and *your* joy will be complete.
>
> John 16:23, 24 (NIV)

I always pray *in Jesus' name*. I remember a time when a member of our church was in the Critical Care Unit in the hospital with very serious heart problems. A member of my Sunday school class had worked in the unit for about twenty years and happened to be on duty that day. I went into the patient's cubicle and prayed.

When I left and was walking down the hall, the nurse came running after me, while tucking paper under her sweater. This was back in the days when the graphs of the patient's heart functions were printed on a strip of paper. With the excitement in her voice I could tell this was very important. "Don't tell anyone that you have seen this because I could lose my job."

Then she reeled out the paper "Look! This just doesn't happen the bottom part of her heart was dead and it started beating while you were praying." I could not read what she was showing me, but I do know that *the name of Jesus has God's power.*

Pray in Faith

Years ago, when I faced a personal heart-rending problem, a devout Christian said to me, "Keep your eyes on Jesus." I didn't fully understand what she meant. Now I know that we must hold on to our faith in Jesus' nature, character, and power. We are prone to lose our grip in view of adverse circumstances and discover we are sinking in the sea of human probability. We must hold to God's promises, against human logic and keep our eyes on Jesus and his promise: "Never will I leave you; never will I forsake you" (Heb.13:5 NIV).

In the days of Joshua, when the twelve spies returned from the giant-filled land of Canaan, ten fearfully and realistically reported, "We can't attack those people; they are stronger than we are" (Num. 13:31 NIV). Joshua and Caleb were faced with overwhelming evidence and a multitude of discouraging voices. Yet, "Caleb stilled the people before Moses and said, 'Let us go up at once, and possess it; for we are well able to overcome it'" (Num.13:30 KJV).

They quoted God's word declaring: "See, the LORD *your* God has given you the land. Go up and take possession of it *as the LORD, the God of your Fathers, told you.* Do not be afraid; do not be discouraged...The LORD *your* God which goeth before you, he shall fight for you, according to all that he did for you in Egypt before your eyes" (Deut. 1:21, 30 KJV).

We, too, are able to overcome figurative giants through faith in God's promises. One great reassuring promise is *"God is our refuge and strength, a very present help in trouble"* (Ps. 46:1 NKJV). These promises will conquer many of our fears.

A test for lack of faith: Are you *worrying* about the *giants in your land?* Are you wringing your hands; or, confidently trusting in God? The test is graded by the wringing of the hands.

Have Centurion Faith

Let's compare two kinds of faith: "Just say the word" and "If you had been here."

When Jesus entered Capernaum, a Centurion came to him. "Lord," he said, "My servant lies at home paralyzed and in terrible suffering" (Matt. 6:6 NIV).

Jesus said to him, "I will go and heal him."

The centurion replied, "Lord...just say the word, and my servant will be healed. For I myself am a man under authority, with soldiers under me. I tell this one, 'Go,' and he goes...'Do this,' and he does it" (Matt. 8:8 NIV).

When Jesus heard this, he was astonished and said to those following him, "I tell you the truth, I have not found anyone in Israel with such great faith" (Matt. 8:5–10 NIV). Then Jesus said to the centurion, "Go [home]! It will be done just as you believed it would. And his servant was healed" (Matt.8:13 NIV).

The Centurion was a pagan officer and militarily understood Jesus' power and authority better than Jesus' own people.

The Israelites had faith in a different way. Mary, Martha, and Lazarus were like Jesus' family. When Lazarus was critically ill, his sisters sent an urgent message to Jesus *to come* so that He could heal him.

Jesus lingered two more days then told his disciples, "Lazarus is dead, and for *your* sake I am glad *I was not there* so that you may believe. But let us go to him" (Jn. 11:14 NIV). Jesus knew that *if he had been there*, their faith would have compelled him to heal Lazarus. He had planned a greater miracle.

When Martha heard that Jesus was finally coming, she hurried out to meet him. She wept, "LORD, *if you had been here*, my brother would not have died" (Jn. 11:21 NIV). Even the devout Israelites who had gathered at their home said, "Could not he who opened the eyes of the blind man have kept this man from dying? [*if he had been here*]" (Jn.11:37 NIV).

After four days, Jesus prayed at Lazarus's tomb, "Father, I thank you that you have heard me. I knew that you always hear me, but I said this for the benefit of the people standing here, that they may believe that you sent me." When he had said this, Jesus called in a loud voice, "Lazarus, come out!" (Jn. 11:41–43 NIV). Lazarus came out.

To contrast the two types of faith: The Centurion said, "*Speak the word.*" The Israelites said, "*If you had been here.*" It is easy for me and you to believe that if Jesus *were here in the flesh*, there would indeed be miracles.

Do we trust Jesus to *speak the word* for healings in our homes, in distant cities and in other nations? May our faith be strengthened when we remember that He even raised Lazarus from the dead just to prove to His disciples that He is from God and *nothing* was impossible. After Lazarus died *Jesus was there.*

Jesus wants to *speak the word* through our lips empowered by the Holy Spirit who lives within.

Faith Sees the Answers

"Now faith is being sure of what we hope for and certain of what we do not see" (Heb. 11:1 NIV). Are we "stopped by the chains we have placed around our dreams?"[58]

Can we remove our paradigms and expand our vision into the realm of God's potential? For example, could we imagine a destitute drug addict with a clear mind and a holy glow, praising the Lord? I have seen redeemed lives and heard testimonies of it happening to many people.

One that stands out in my mind is a young *hippie* family in the sixties. They came to our church and walked center aisle right down to the front row. The daddy, mother and several children lived on the beach... long hair, beard, barefoot sandals, unshaven and unmarried. Also, the parents seemed a bit spaced out.

For several Sundays, they listened to the preaching. And then, the parents accepted Jesus as their Lord. Soon, they appeared in church, sober, clean shaven and cleaned up...with joy in their hearts...wanting to get married. Since then, they have been faithful in a missionary ministry.

Looking into the realm of God's potential, can we see the answers before we pray? In *Praying with Power for Others* Leonard LeSourd wrote:

> Visualize the person for whom you are praying as being in the presence of Jesus with His light shining around and through that person, penetrating every cell of that person's body... If emotions need healing, see them as becoming stable; if there are body ailments, see them as becoming whole...where Jesus is, there is Light.[59]

We must hold to our vision, day after day, in spite of the temptation to revert to the reality of the current circumstances. Continue believing that transformed lives are what God wants because he, "is patient...not wanting anyone to perish, but everyone to come to repentance." (2 Peter 3:9 NIV). God's power *will* be at work. Trust Him.

Be Specific

Jesus instructed us to pray, "Give us today our daily bread" (Matt. 6:11 NIV). *Today* specifies when the request is needed, *daily bread* states the need. "Bless the missionaries all over the world," can be a vague prayer requiring little faith.

Whereas, "Father, Rev. Johnson needs $5,150.45 by Thursday at 2:00 p.m." requires more faith. Jesus asked Bartimaeus to specify his need when He asked, "What do you want me to do for you?" The blind man said, *"Rabbi, I want to see"* (Mk.10:51 NIV).

Surprisingly, not all sick people want to get well. Jesus knew this when He asked a very sick man specifically, *"Do you want to get well?"*

(Jn.5:6 NIV). For some people, sickness provides attention, security, and relief from responsibilities.

For example, a preacher once asked a woman in a wheelchair, "May I pray for you?"

She quickly replied, "No, I have waited on my husband most of my life, and he is now waiting on me. I like it."

My younger son, Gary, was specific about a unique prayer request when he was a boy. He hated cats and this bothered him. He asked God to give him a love for cats. A few days later, he was amazed when he realized that tabby was his favorite pet. He said, "Mother, I will always have a cat." He continues to have a loving heart for all of God's creatures. And, he has a quiet confidence that God answers prayer. He said recently, "Mother, I have a special relationship with God." And, I know that is true.

Another illustration, this one with a *long list* of specifics, turned out to be a huge faith-builder for me. It is with mixed emotions that I write the following testimony, but I believe it will help many people who are going through deep water with a spouse, son, daughter, grandchild....

When Ric realized that his addiction was beyond his control, he and I were sitting in the car and he said, "Mother, I don't know what to do? In tears, we held hands and prayed, "Lord, we need a miracle..."

Later, in my private prayer I desperately pleaded, "Lord, we *must* have a miracle!" I thought, "Since we are starting below zero, I may as well go for the moon." I spelled out everything that it would take to get him back into the mainstream of life:

"Father, I am asking you to (1) deliver him from drugs (2) with his brilliant mind unharmed. (3) Give him a good job in a very large company (4) with secure benefits (5) where he can excel. Give him (6) a Christian wife, (7) a son, (8) a typical brick home (9) with two cars in the garage (10) and the appropriate mortgages. And, lead him to (11) a church (12) where he will be involved." To top it off, I added (13) a dog, (14) and a parakeet. That totals fourteen specifics.

Within two weeks, he was in a rehab center. God provided a counselor who was a Messianic Jew. They bonded. A huge unexpected blessing happened, he had an inside track in getting to know and spiritually help other young men. It could be that some of them would never have listened to an outsider. Later, he said, "Mother, I have seen young men come and go. I noticed that *only the ones who have Jesus* have the strength to make it through; the others go back into drugs, jail, or they die. Rehab became his mission field.

Near the end of his tenure, the specific prayer answers began to unfold: (1) He was totally freed from drugs (2) with his brilliant mind unharmed. (3) A lovely young lady came to the rehab center with a church group. Soon after he was dismissed, the wedding bells rang. My eyes welled with tears when I saw her beautiful wedding gown with its long train," (4) Fluor Daniel, a huge international company that builds refineries hired him as a computer programmer which required a brilliant mind. (5) Fluor had excellent employee benefits. (6) Ric loved his job and was respected for his ability.

(7) They bought a brick home, (8) and had two cars in the garage (9) with the appropriate mortgages. (10) They had the son of their dreams. Then, it was as though God wanted to show that he *delighted* in answering prayers. (11) The dog was not just a dog; it was a beautiful large white Great Pyrenees. (12) And, the *parakeet* was a delightful cockatiel whose favorite perch was on Ric's shoulder.

(13) God lead him to a good church. (14) He was a prayer partner with his pastor, was faithful and tithed his money. Later, the pastor spoke from his pulpit about the building of their second floor Sunday School classroom. In essence, "Ever big volunteer project generally starts with a large group that soon fizzles. On the night before Ric had to leave to go on a Fluor project, he worked all night alone. By morning, he had hung the last door."

During the time when God was answering my fourteen specifics, he was also working on an answer to a prayer that Ric had expressed in a poem:

> Help me live a Christian Life,
> Like Christians ought to do,
> Help me spread thy word oh God–
> So others might LIVE too.

I was praying for the mainstream in life and God overflowed its banks.

The sobering question is: "What if I hadn't prayed?" The Bible tells us that "You do not have, because you do not ask God" (Jas. 4:2 NIV). We need to stop for a minute and think: "How many *prayer answers* have I missed because I didn't pray?" Prayer can re-chart the course of many lives, even nations.

Ask for The Holy Spirit

"For everyone who asks receives; he who seeks finds; and to him who knocks, the door will be opened. Which of you fathers, if *your* son asks for a fish, will give him a snake instead? Or if he asks for an egg, will give him a scorpion? If you then, though you are evil [prone to sin by basic nature], know how to give good gifts to *your* children, *how much more will your Father in heaven give the Holy Spirit to those who ask him!*" (Lu. 11:10–13 NIV).

That means we are asking for the nature and character of Jesus in our lives with empowerment to live as he wants us to live. This will be a whole dimension above the ordinary.

Ask for Wisdom, Knowledge, and Discernment

A prayer with a sure answer is "If any of you lacks *wisdom,* he should ask God, who *gives generously* to all without finding fault, and *it will be given* to him" (Jas. 1:5 NIV). This prayer pleases God.

When young King Solomon of Israel started his reign, appearing in a dream God said, "Ask for whatever you want me to give you."

Solomon replied, "*Give me wisdom and knowledge, that I may lead this people…*" (2 Chron. 1:7, 10 NIV). God replied,

> Since this is *your* heart's desire and you have not asked for wealth, riches or honor, nor for the death of *your* enemies, and since you have not asked for a long life but for wisdom and knowledge… therefore wisdom and knowledge will be given you….
> (2 Chronicles 1:11, 12 NIV)

King Solomon also prayed, "Give *your* servant a discerning heart to govern *your* people and to distinguish between right and wrong" (1 Kings 3:9 NIV).

King Solomon revealed his divinely inspired wisdom, knowledge and discernment when two new mothers and one baby were brought before him. One infant had died during the night and the dead son's mother switched babies. They both claimed the living child. The king called for a sword and said that he would divide the baby so each mother could have half. Obviously, he did not plan to do that, but the real mother surfaced quickly "Don't kill him! Give him to her!" (1 Kings 3:22–27 NIV).

As it did for King Solomon, discernment helps us to see situations for what they are. It enables us to read other people's emotions. For example, exuberant happiness could be a cover up for a great disappointment. With discernment, we may also recognize a scheming attitude or know there is an ulterior motive, a hidden agenda.

God was so pleased with young Solomon's request that he threw in everything: "*I will also give you wealth, riches and honor, such as no king who was before you ever had and none after you will have*" (2 Chron. 1:12 NIV). When we ask for wisdom, knowledge and a discerning heart, God may add blessings for us too.

There is nothing wrong with esteem and prosperity, if they are used wisely. Unfortunately, the plush life and fame led to King Solomon's downfall. He had about nine hundred wives and concubines. Then, giving in to their coercions, he built temples for their pagan gods. With this evidence, we know that Solomon did not always use the wisdom God gave him.

A modern example: Since wisdom tells us how to use knowledge, it was sadly lacking in the management of the giant Enron, Inc. that caused its implosion. Brilliant men used their knowledge creating unprecedented schemes with no regard to the multitude of investors who suffered devastating losses. It is not hard to find other examples of highly educated people who lack wisdom and become unscrupulous in their dealings.

We parents would be impressed if *our* children were to ask us to give them "wisdom, knowledge, and a discerning heart" before they asked for a myriad of other things. We would, if we could, gladly pour it in. *Our Father* feels the same way about us.

God wants us to grow as Jesus grew, "in wisdom and stature, and in favor with God and men" (Luke 2:52 NIV).

Ask for Our Father's Opinion

Perhaps our greatest continual need is God's opinion before we make decisions. It pleases him when we seek his counsel. Throughout Scripture, God noted that various men either asked for, or did not ask for his advice. King David, a man after God's heart, frequently sought God before making decisions. God answered with directions for victory in his battles and his life.

When the Philistines were ready to attack the Israelites, "David inquired of the Lord, and he answered, 'Do not go straight up, but circle around behind them and attack them in front of the balsam trees. As soon as you hear the sound of marching in the tops of the balsam trees, move quickly because that will mean the Lord has gone out in front of you to strike the Philistine army" (2 Sam 5:23,24 NIV). They did and they won.

We know of the infamous time when David *did not want God's opinion* before committing adultery with Bathsheba. As a result, he suffered major consequences when one sin led to the next. He had a man killed, his baby died, and his family lived in turmoil thereafter. David already *knew* God's opinion.

We might ask, "Do I want to be like David when he *wanted* God's opinion, or when his lust dictated his decision? Either way, we too will live with the results.

There were other times when Israel did not ask God's opinion: "The shepherds [spiritual leaders] are senseless and *do not inquire of the Lord;* so they do not prosper and all their flock is scattered" (Jer. 10:21 NIV). "All their kings fall, and *none of them calls on me*" (Hos. 7:7 NIV). "They set up kings *without my consent*; they choose princes *without my approval*. With their silver and gold they make idols for themselves to their own destruction" (Hos. 8:4 NIV).

Hopefully, we will learn from the Israelite's mistakes. We can save ourselves a lot of heartbreak if we will include God's opinion in making all of our decisions. Then, unlike David in his time of temptation and the other Israelites in times of decision, we must have a strong resolve to ask for and abide by God's opinion.

Hear God's Voice

When we ask God for his opinion, we need to be prepared to hear his answer.

Though it may be rare, I have heard people say that God spoke to them through an audible voice. Then toning it down a bit, there are other times when a message may be so clear that it *seems* like an audible voice. We all know that a guilty conscience can shout!

Since God is a spirit, and the Holy Spirit resides in our spirit, we can pick up on messages from God through our mind, our conscience, our awareness, impressions, circumstances, and words from others.

Most importantly, as we read God's written word we comprehension. His voice could be a sense of knowing what to do. Sometimes we have a strong impression that helps us avoid disaster.

One morning during my meditation, I heard a sound like in a tiny wind tunnel coming from a window. I prayed, "Lord, are you speaking to me through the wind? The loving reply came immediately in my spirit. "Yes, I am speaking to you through the wind, through the moon, through the stars, and through the intricate details of the flowers, fruits and plants in which you marvel and for which you praise me. I speak to you anyway you will listen."

He may first have to get our attention. Most parents remember a time when we held our children's sweet faces, looked them straight in the eyes and said, "Now, listen to me!"

In whatever manner, we may be assured that *Our Father* is eager to speak to his children and to hear them speak. Similarly, one of my greatest joys is hearing the sound of my grown children and grandchildren's voices when they call.

"For the eyes of the LORD move to and fro throughout the earth that He may strongly support those whose heart is completely His" (2 Chron. 16:9 NAS).

Nothing is too Trivial

Some say, "Don't bother God with small things." In *Beyond Ourselves*, Catherine Marshall responds:

> By all means you should bother the Father with details. Jesus...was constantly 'bothering the Father' with the practicalities of life with people's health problems, with securing the money for Peter's temple tax, with supper for a crowd of hungry listeners, with the wine running out at a wedding reception.[60]

I love to ask God to help me find lost items. It is a delight because He knows where *everything* is. And, it is His nature to want to help his children. One time, I glanced at my hand and saw the center diamond on my wedding ring was missing. I frantically prayed, "Lord, you know where the diamond is, *PLEASE!* Help us find it!"

I remembered that I had been playing the piano with gusto, so I searched every crevice. Then, I searched the carpet around the piano...and throughout the house. Bob kept going back to the piano. With the flashlight, he started pushing down each key. On an obscure ledge, the diamond sparkled, "Here I am!" I believe it could have been lost forever if we had not asked God.

My purse was stolen in Washington D.C. when an extra million people were in town. A good man opened a dumpster and found a purse that didn't look like it should be thrown away. All the thief had taken was my money and cell phone. The man mailed the purse to me with my driver's license and credit cards, and would not accept a reward. No one can tell me that God didn't do that!

An amusing thing happened years ago when I asked God to help me find a report card that one of my young sons had delayed in giving to me. I prayed, "Father, where is the report card?" *Immediately* after my prayer, I walked through a tidy room and absent-mindedly picked up a pillow and fluffed it. Something was inside. I unzipped and found the card. After we discussed a certain grade, he asked me how I found it. I said, "I asked God." He shook his head and replied, "I should have known." I think God smiled while answering that little prayer.

Hindrances Can Be Subtle

Small hindrances often demolish our intercession. Gloria Leigh humorously wrote about her pesky obstacles in prayer:

> It seems like every time I resolve anew to be a mighty prayer warrior...Satan deploys a task force over to my house. They pull the alarm buzzer and all the little off-duty demons jump up, slide down the pole and suit out...The head honcho announces,

VI: Ask Our Father "Thank You, Lord!"

'All right you guys, get over to 34 Los Amigos she's decided again to start praying more!' So they jump in the van and roar over...

They start their demolition job, but as I head to my Prayer Station, I notice a picture hanging crookedly that I'm sure was straight a few minutes ago. While fixing it, I see smudgy finger prints on the wall...I get a sponge...while looking for Ajax, I spill rice in the pantry...the faucet drips...the phone rings...the clothes dryer rings. I cleaned up the rice while I prayed.

"Sorry, Father! There've been so many interruptions. What were we talking about? Oh, yes! Power! I want the power of the Early Church Christians." I can't believe there is so much rice in one box...[61]

Such hindrances relegate us to *praying on the run*. It is difficult to have an in-depth conversation with God while waiting for the traffic light to change. We make our speeches, and leave before God has a chance to speak.

Then again, let's look at *minute* prayers from another perspective. If we are accustomed to staving off hindrances and having uninterrupted, quality time with God we will be ready for instant prayers. I heard an African American preacher explain that *"praying always"* is like a bird sitting on a limb. He is not always flying, but he is ready to go. Sometimes "Help!" is a short urgent prayer that instantly communicates to *Our Father*.

Unfortunately, in this hurried world many people spend hours commuting. This can become a prayer closet, under the guise of dozing. Also, the laundry room and the bathroom can be Prayer Retreats.

Sometimes we are just *too* busy! I remember a time when I was kneeling at the prayer altar and heard giggles behind me; I was wearing two different shoes.

Reasons Prayers are not Answered

David Wilkerson gives six reasons our prayers can be aborted:

- When they are not according to God's will.
- When they are designed to fulfill an inner lust, dream, or illusion (Ps.66:18 NIV).
- When we show no diligence to assist God in the answer (2 Thess.3:10 NIV).
- When a secret grudge is lodged in the heart against another (1 Tim.2:8 NIV).
- When we do not expect much to come of them.
- When we ourselves attempt to prescribe how God should answer.[62]

Some prayer hindrances are not so subtle. We can sabotage our prayers by being disrespectful; in some homes it explodes into yelling, door slamming and tire screeching. The principle is clear: "Husbands...be considerate as you live with your wives, and treat them with respect...*so that nothing will hinder your prayers*" (1 Peter 3:6–8 NIV). An inspiring book to read is The "Marriage Maze"—Shining His Light on Your Journey, by Joyce Akin.

Respect also applies to wives for their husbands. In fact, we must "Show proper respect to everyone" (1 Pet. 2:17 NIV), regardless of age or gender. God expects us to be gracious; he wants us to have power in prayer.

Have an Earnest Desire

Hannah, the mother of the Prophet Samuel is an example of one who had an earnest desire. Before he was conceived, she went to the LORD's temple to pray for a child. "In bitterness of soul Hannah wept much and prayed to the LORD...Eli [the priest] observed her mouth...her lips were moving but her voice was not heard. Eli thought she was drunk" (1 Sam. 1:10, 13 NIV).

She answered Eli's inquiry, "I was pouring out my soul to the LORD." The priest was so impressed with her sincerity that he said, "Go in peace and may God grant you what you have asked" (1 Sam. 1:12–15 NIV). After her baby was born, she fulfilled her vow to God by giving Samuel to Eli to rear for service in the Temple.

The prophet, Jeremiah, had an earnest desire when he bewailed Jerusalem's destruction: "Streams of tears flow from my eyes because my people are destroyed. My eyes will flow unceasingly, without relief, until the LORD looks down from heaven and sees" (Lam. 3:48–50 NIV).

The most intense desire goes beyond human compassion into a realm motivated by God's Spirit: "The Spirit himself intercedes for us with groans that words cannot express" (Rom. 8:26 NIV). In this depth of grief, the feeling can be so strong it would seem *your* heart could break. The prayer arduously *labors through* until inner peace gives assurance the answer is received. Theologically, this is called "travailing in prayer."

I have learned that anytime your heart feels heavy and concerns seem to be coming from all directions, it is time to get alone with *Our Father* and just pour it all out. He will patiently and compassionately listen. Then, you will likely feel clean and at peace inside while he is working on the answers.

Pray in Agreement

Agreement is a powerful form of prayer. This means two or more people share an ardent desire. Jesus promises, "Again, I tell you that if two of you on earth agree about anything you ask for, it will be done for you by my Father in heaven. For where two or three come together in my name, [for my name] there am I with them" (Matt. 18:19, 20 NIV). When Jesus' spirit is with them, the prayer request will be in His will.

Agreement means more than nodding the head in affirmation. For example, at the prayer altar a broken hearted woman asked me to pray for her mangled son after he was in a car wreck. Since I had two sons, I felt her grief as though her son was mine, and we wept together as we prayed with one desire.

Sad to say, numerous churches have forgotten the power in *agreement prayer*, and have disbanded their prayer meetings. Nevertheless, "*two or three*" gathered in agreement can pray the meetings back in again. This is the power of the church.

Pray with Fasting

I cannot stress enough the importance of fasting for spiritual breakthroughs. Fasting lends power to prayer. Our receptivity is clearer because we are drawing closer to God. As a result, "Satan will flee" (Jas. 4:7). Arthur Wallis, in *God's Chosen Fast* writes,

> Fasting is designed to make prayer mount up as on eagles' wings...usher the supplicant into the audience chamber of the King...extend to him the golden scepter...drive back the oppressing powers of darkness and loosen their hold on the prayer objective. It is calculated to give an edge to a man's intercessions and power to his petitions.[63]
>
> Jesus fasted and set the example for us. He did not say, "*If* you fast" but "*When* you fast...*your Father*, who sees what is done in secret, will reward you."
>
> Matthew 6:16, 18 (NIV)

Dr. Mary Stewart Relfe, founder of the international ministry, The League of Prayer, wrote about her experiences with Dr. Yonggi Cho who started his 750,000 member church with only a few family members and friends. Through prayer and fasting it became the largest Christian church in the world

She said that all Christian churches in South Korea, large, small, rich, or poor have prayer meetings in their sanctuaries before the sun comes up, 365 days a year. She asked why the senior pastors generally lead these prayer meetings. The consistent response was, "That is where the power is." She wrote:

> I had the privilege of attending the world's largest, early-morning prayer meeting at the Myung-Sung Presbyterian Church, pastured by Kim Sam Hwan. The group I was with had to call ahead for reserved seats at the 6:00 a.m. meeting packed with 4,000 people. This however, was the third such service that morning; others were held at 4:00 a.m. and 5:00 a.m. The usual early-morning prayer meeting attendance…is 12,000.
>
> The largest Baptist, Methodist, Presbyterian, Holiness and Pentecostal churches in the world are all in South Korea. Many have asked church leaders, "How did this happen?" They received the same answer, "Prayer."
>
> More than 200 churches have purchased mountains on which they have built prayer retreat centers. Some are large, such as Pastor Cho's…where 3,000 people are always present and more than 10,000 on weekends…At one prayer mountain…I visited, the only food service was a medically designed diet for withdrawal from prolonged fasts. 21 day fasts are not uncommon. 40 day fasts are also seen at times. [64]

Dr. Cho said, "Churches in American have lots of programs, Churches in Korea have lot of prayer. Your churches build Family Life Centers. Korean churches build Prayer Mountains…"

A period of fasting preceded many great biblical events:

- Moses fasted and God gave the Ten Commandments
- Queen Esther and the captive Jewish nation fasted and God spared them from annihilation (Esther 4:16 NIV).

- When the wicked citizens of Nineveh repented and fasted, God spared their city (Jonah 3:7 NIV).
- Jesus began His ministry by fasting, and overcame Satan's temptations in the wilderness.
- His disciples fasted before choosing deacons.
- The church at Antioch fasted before sending Paul as the first missionary.

There are wrong and right ways to fast. Of course, we know the wrong way is to concentrate on the suffering aspect. Another is to consider fasting as *spiritual bribery* in an attempt to bargain with God. In the classic chapter on fasting, Isaiah 58, we read that God is not impressed unless our lifestyle is right. We must:

> Loose the chains of injustice...set the oppressed free...share *your* food with the hungry...provide the poor wanderer with shelter...when you see the naked, to clothe him, and not to turn away from *your* own flesh and blood... *Then*... the Lord will answer; you will cry for help, and He will say, "Here I am."
> Isaiah 58:6–9 (NIV)

In proper fasting, we rearrange our priorities. *Our reason for fasting must be more important than food. The true spirit of fasting is simply seeking God.* One morning, a radiant young woman greeted me before Sunday school and said, "I started reading my Bible and talking with the Lord early yesterday morning. I enjoyed it so much that I didn't do anything else. Last night, I realized I hadn't eaten all day."

I believe Jesus went into the wilderness *to be alone with His Father* and was so caught up in His presence that He fasted forty days. Our fasts *must be unto the Lord*.

The attitude of the heart is primary. There are no set rules. Let's look at three basic examples in Scripture:

- The Partial Fast: Daniel eliminated only certain foods, *"I ate no choice food; no meat or wine touched my lips"* (Dan. 10:3 NIV).
- The Normal Fast: In Jesus' fast, it is believed that he abstained from all food, but not from water because water is not mentioned: *"He ate nothing during those days"* (Lu. 4:2 NIV).
- The Total Fast: Queen Esther proclaimed an absolute fast: *"Do not eat or drink for three days, night or day"* (Esther 4:16 NIV).

An Essential Fast: We all should regulate whatever is a needlessly wasting our time. For example: television, mall browsing and games. Prioritize for Bible Study and prayer. What a huge difference it will make in *your* spiritual power.

Warning: Those who have health problems should use common sense in fasting liquids and some foods. It could be damaging for *anyone* to go totally without liquids for more than three days. Also, some medications must be taken with food. Diabetics could abstain from watching television, or something else they simply like to do.

Note: If you break your fast, just resume.

I remember an example of victory after a group had fasted. Every diabolical scheme imaginable had hindered our plans for witnessing at an outdoor gospel concert near a teen nightclub. At five o'clock p.m. the gospel band, Puppet Team, and staging vehicles arrived. They had just enough time before seven o'clock to set-up.

The sky turned dark and lightning flashed. I thought, "Oh No!" Rain started *pouring* down! I searched the sky for hope; there was none. Precious minutes ticked away. Stranded in my car, I dreaded looking at my watch... seven o'clock sharp! Defeated. I thought, "We'll just have to go home."

"No," I decided! So I braved the deluge and dashed for an empty building. I found the gospel team there praying. My faith grew when I saw the strength of their faith. I knew there was extra prayer power in agreement. I also remembered God had heard Elijah's prayer about rain (1 Kings 18:42–45 NIV), and I knew God loved us too. We pleaded, "Lord, this work is for *your* Kingdom, please stop the rain! Give us a starry night. And, I added, *"without even a mist."*

Within minutes the rain stopped. Someone shouted, "Look! A rainbow is beyond the teen center." By eight o'clock p.m. the band came alive praising God. Traffic circled and curious teens started gathering under a starry sky. I held out my hand, to verify this was from God, and did not feel *even a mist*.

Many people have unyielding problems. Perhaps it is critical illness … financial problems, need a job … conflict in relationships.…

Several years ago, I fasted for three days without food only water and tea. It was for a church friend who had chronic excruciating pain. Her doctor refused to do exploratory surgery because, with time, he was convinced it was a psychiatric problem. It looked like she was destined to suffering. God was the only answer. After my session of prayer and fasting, she went back to her doctor. He said, "Well, I will operate but I'm telling you now, I won't find anything." He operated and found the problem.

Recently, I fasted for four days and nights. I was troubled by the problems that an extended family member was having which could result in divorce. It almost seemed sinister. The Scripture came to my mind, "And [Jesus] said unto them, 'this kind can come forth by nothing, but by prayer and fasting' (Mark 9:29 KJV). I decided to go into battle, and set my goal for fasting: four days and nights with only water or tea.

At the end of the fast, I was amazed that I was not very hungry. I felt such peace that I remembered the Scripture where Jesus told his disciples, "I have food that you know nothing about" (Jn. 4:32 NIV). Drawing close to God was deeply satisfying.

There was instantly a major breakthrough in this special person's life. And, as an added bonus, I had been lagging in my work on a major seminar. Now, my inspiration and creativity went into high gear.

When God's children travail in prayer with fasting for a purpose that glorifies His name... and persevere through the powers of darkness, God will answer.

Use Authoritative Prayer

In The Prayer Ministry of the Church, the great Chinese preacher Watchman Nee states: "Authoritative prayer is that which occupies a most significant place in the Word."[65] He adds, "The principal work of over comers is to bring the authority of the heavenly throne down to earth."[66] J. A. McMillan writes,

> Authoritative intercessors are men and women whose eyes have been opened to the full knowledge of their place in Christ... The Word of God has become a battle chart on which is detailed the plan of campaign of the hosts of the Lord... Deeply conscious of their own personal unworthiness and insufficiency, they yet believe God's statement concerning their identification with Christ in His throne power... they realize that heavenly responsibility rests upon them for the carrying forward of the warfare with which they have been charged."[67]

Watchman Nee concludes, "This is not something that can be *worked up* at a time of crisis. It is a fruit of obedience to God and of a resulting spiritual position... It is something we must have already if it is to be available in a time of need."[68]

Frances J. Roberts gives a powerful summary:

> Presume not to labor to build with the right hand without holding the sword in the left (Neh. 4:18 NIV). It is vigilance COMBINED with prayer that spells victory. Devotion must be coupled with warfare to be fruitful. Holy ecstasy must be mixed with holy boldness, and love must be blended with courage. Only to pray is not enough. Prayer must rise from the battlefield of spiritual conquest.[69]

We will discuss authoritative prayer in more detail in the chapter, "Satan The Supreme Leader of Evil Defeated!"

Cry Out to the Lord

Our prayer enters a new dimension when the intense desires of our heart burst forth with deep emotion! Renowned men of God have written about Don Gothard's book, *The Power of Crying Out:*[70]

> Dr. Charles Stanley, Senior pastor of the mega church First Baptist, Atlanta Ga., wrote, "The principles found in The Power of Crying Out have made an indelible impact on my life. I have seen them work in the lives of others and would encourage everyone to learn these principles and practice them."
>
> Dr. Gary Smalley wrote, "Bill Gothard's book has reawakened in me a strong desire to cry out to my Lord with passion and expectancy."
>
> Dr. Adrian Rogers, three term president of the Southern Baptist Convention, the largest American Protestant denomination with sixteen million members, wrote, "[The]...teaching has been transformational in my life, giving me a foundational understanding of biblical truths, especially on authority."
>
> Byron Paulus, President of Life Action Ministries, wrote, "Until God's people cry out in desperation, there will be little hope for revival. The truth recaptured in this book could be used of God to recapture our nation."

Jesus was the ultimate in crying out to God. In the Garden of Gethsemane, in the midst of his desperate prayer, "An angel from heaven appeared to him and strengthened him. And being in anguish, he prayed more earnestly, and his sweat was like drops of blood falling to the ground" (Luke 22:43–44 NIV). The prayer gave him spiritual strength to fulfill his mission at the cross to redeem us all.

VI: Ask Our Father "Thank You, Lord!"

King David, a man after God's own heart, frequently raised his voice in prayer. There were times when his life was at stake. Throughout the psalms we read such Scriptures as:

> Evening and morning and at noon I will pray, and cry aloud, and He shall hear.
>
> Psalm 55:17 (KJV)

> In my distress I called upon the LORD, and cried out to my God; He heard my voice from His temple, and my cry came before Him, even to His ears.
>
> Psalm 18:6 (KJV)

I vividly remember a time when my friends, Pattie and Laurie, and I were floating on a raft in the surf off Padre Island. A large wave swamped us and we were caught in the undertow. I felt like I was in a washing machine. It was a viscous cycle. The washing machine kept churning. I didn't know which way was up; there was no way out. Seconds counted. Our husbands were fighting the surf to find us. God heard our terrified heart cries.

> The eyes of the LORD are on the righteous, and His ears are open to their cry... The righteous cry out, and the LORD hears, and delivers them out of all their troubles.
>
> Psalm 34:15, 17 (KJV)

> Hear my cry, O God; Attend to my prayer.
>
> Psalm 61:1 (KJV)

> I cried to the LORD with my voice, And He heard me from His holy hill. Selah.
>
> Psalm 3:4 (KJV)

> O LORD my God, I cried out to You, And You healed me.
>
> Psalm 30:2 (KJV)

> To You I will cry, O LORD my Rock: Do not be silent to me, Lest, if You are silent to me, I become like those who go down to the pit. Hear the voice of my supplications when I cry to you, when I lift up my hands toward your holy sanctuary.
> Psalm 28:1, 2 (KJV)

My daddy and mother cried out to the Lord. He was testing his new car and was driving at the maximum speed limit. In those days, the doors opened into the wind. I was three years old and leaned on the handle, and out I went. My face hit the highway and I rolled into the ditch. They thought my right eye was gone. Frantically, they raced to the hospital. Their prayers were answered when the doctor lifted the flesh covering my eye, and it was still there. I remember the lights in ER ... the pain, surgery, and fear. Clearly, God answered their prayer, saved my eye, and saved my life. Also, even with many stitches, I do not have disfiguring scars.

We all know that God is not deaf. Crying Aloud has power when it conveys the intense desires of the heart.

Persevere

Persevere means don't give up ... keep pressing on ... give every ounce of energy mentally and physically that it takes to reach your goal.

My grandson, Christopher, is an organized and goal oriented young man. He went to state twice with his cross-country track team in his Four-A high school. Competition was tough. I watched a practice run. Before he finished the course, I wanted him to quit because I was more concerned about his heart than a trophy. He persevered with all of his mental and physical strength.

In With Christ in the School of Prayer, Andrew Murray recognizes the casualness of many prayers: "How many prayers are wishes, sent up for a short time and then forgotten, or sent up year after year as a matter of duty, while we rest content with the prayer without the answer."[71]

We must not, as E. M. Bounds writes, merely have "a little talk with Jesus, as the tiny saintlets sing but must demand and hold with iron grasp the best hours of the day for God and prayer, or there will be no praying worth the name."[72] We must tenaciously pray until the answer is assured. Perseverance in prayer can literally snatch from the powers of darkness those held in bondage by sickness, disease, adversity, and hopelessness.

In *The Purpose in Prayer*, E. M. Bounds writes, "...pray till hell feels the ponderous stroke...pray till the iron gates of difficulty are opened, till the mountains of obstacles are removed, till the mists are exhaled and the clouds are lifted, and the sunshine of a cloudless day brightens."[73]

Jesus gave a parable that instructed His disciples to never give up:

> Suppose one of you has a friend, and he goes to him at midnight and says, 'Friend, lend me three loaves of bread...' Then the one inside answers, 'Don't bother me...' I tell you, though he will not get up and give him the bread because he is his friend, yet because of the man's boldness he will get up and give him as much as he needs.
>
> Luke 11:5–8 (NIV)

This does not mean we have to beg God. I believe he appreciates our sincerity by our determination.

True perseverance is not rambling with many words which Jesus declared as meaningless (Matt. 6:7 NIV). Rather, our faith must be unrelenting in our petition. We must *"be alert and always keep on praying for all the saints"* (Eph. 6:18 NIV).

Daniel held firm for twenty-one days, when a heavenly messenger came to him and said, "*Since the first day* that you set *your* mind to gain understanding and to humble *your*self before *your* God, *your* words were heard, and *I have come in response* to them. But the prince of the Persian kingdom [demonic] resisted me twenty-one days. Then Michael, one of the chief princes, came to help me..." (Dan.10:12,12 NIV).

It may be that God will dispense a mighty angel to intervene for us, while our answers are on the way. "Are not all angels ministering spirits sent to serve those who will inherit salvation?" (Heb.1:14 NIV).

Commit and Wait

Payday is not always at five thirty p.m. on Friday. After we commit our petition to *our Father*, we must patiently wait for the answer. This principle is simple yet difficult to do. Often we pray and then pick up our worries and continue hauling them around.

An excellent tract entitled, "Victorious Praying" gives the following illustration regarding "Prayer of Committal": "Suppose you take... [*your* watch] to the watchmaker and ask him if he can repair it. He... replies, 'Yes,' and you say, 'Thank you,' and then you–*leave with your watch...*" As a result, the watch does not get repaired.[74]

It is hard for us to give up control in some matters. To commit, we must relinquish the situation to God's ability, and His trustworthiness.

Like the watchmaker, God needs time to work. He may have to reckon with many circumstances and stubborn wills. Then again, God has His own timing in some matters. Abraham and Sarah prayed for a son when they were young; their hair turned white with age before Isaac was miraculously born.

While we wait for our prayer answers, we must not *worry about the watch*. Rather, we must *have confidence in the Watchmaker*. "They that wait upon the LORD shall renew their strength; they shall mount up with wings as eagles" (Isa. 40:31 KJV).

Be Patient There is a Process

Sometimes the answers are instant and sometimes they take time to go through a process of development. Things could get worse before they get better. When praying for a lost person, he/she could feel convicted and express major rebellion.

A few years ago I needed a new kitchen. So, I asked my husband for one. Believe me, it did not happen instantly. Things got a whole lot worse before hot biscuits came out of my new oven. My campfire was a single burner in the garage. Demolition was memorable. After the dust settled, rebuilding began tile, paint, cabinets, appliances, wallpaper... the clock on the wall.... Time was still ticking. Cabinets had to be filled.

In our prayers, what is going on in the background may not be visible; the processes may be tedious and long. Regardless, with confidence in Our Father's love, we need to start thanking him because we know the answers are on their way.

Sometimes God says, "No"

Like parents, sometimes *our Father* says, "No." There may be reasons that are beyond our understanding. When this happens, we must not think that God does not hear. Rather, we must believe He will utilize whatever circumstance we find ourselves in, for a greater purpose. Norman Vincent Peal wrote, "Ask for what you want, but be willing to take what God gives you. It may be better than what you asked for."[75]

In time, you may be very glad that he said, "No!" For example, you may have prayed fervently to marry tall and handsome and he did not turn out to be the man of your dreams. Later, you found your true love. Many people have prayed fervently while speeding to the airport. We have all heard stories about people missing their flight and their plane went down.

In essence, my plane went down. God did not answer my prayer in the way I prayed, my son died. I did not ask God, "Why?" Though I was grieved, I knew that he had a higher purpose for my life, and for Ric's testimony, that would comfort and encourage many people.

The reason I had that assurance was because the next verse was engraved in my heart: "*All things* [good and bad] *work together for good* to them that love God, to them who are the called according to his purpose (Rom. 8:28 KJV).

I realized Ric didn't die he just moved to Heaven. Each day is one day closer to the time when we will all attend *Our Father's* glorious family reunion.

In our prayers, we should trust God to give us what is best in his wise long range plan. We should trust his judgment and end our prayers, "Nevertheless, Thy will be done." Let God have the last word, and it may be "No," for now.

Intercede for Others

As we pray for ourselves, we must also pray for others: "*Our Father…give us.*" One of the highest ministries in the Kingdom's work on earth is intercession. Intercessors are essential because, for various reasons, many people do not pray.

The intercessor literally stands between God and man, *pleading the cause of man* and *bringing God's will to prevail on the earth*. Souls are saved, godly men are raised, bodies are healed, needs are met, and Satan's work is thwarted

Who Can Intercede

For power as an intercessor, God requires righteousness. He told Jeremiah to, "Go up and down the streets of Jerusalem, look around and consider, search through her squares. If you can find but one person who *deals honestly and seeks the truth*, I will forgive this city" (Jer. 5:1 NIV).

God spoke through Ezekiel, "I looked *for a man* among them who would build up the wall and stand before me in the gap on behalf of the land so I would not have to destroy it, but I found none" (Ezek. 22:30 NIV). God did not want to destroy the land, but it would be necessary because of the Israelite's sins. *If, however, He could find one man* who would confess their sins and ask for forgiveness, his merciful nature could prevail.

VI: Ask Our Father "Thank You, Lord!"

God grieved when He found none. God questioned Israel, "When I came, why was there no one? When I called, why was there no one to answer? Was my arm too short to ransom you? Do I lack the strength to rescue you?" (Isa.50:2 NIV). Without human free-will intervention, judgment against sin would be mandatory.

To find the ultimate free-will example, we go back centuries earlier when Moses staked his eternal life for the errant Israelites. He pleaded, "Forgive their sin but if not, then blot me out of the book you have written" (Exod. 32:32 NIV). Now *that* is intercession! God spared the whole Israelite nation.

God provided the ultimate *human* intercessor: "Christ Jesus, who died... was raised to life is at the right hand of God and is also *interceding for us*. (Rom.8:34 NIV). He interceded for us with his blood for our righteousness, and with his prayers for our blessings.

Important! Notice in Jesus' prayer for believers that he didn't mention sins or faults:

> My prayer is not for them alone [disciples and early believers]. *I pray also for those [through the centuries], who will believe in me* through their message that all of them may be one, Father, just as you are in me and I am in you. May they also be in us...
>
> I have given them the glory that you gave me [The Holy Spirit], that they may be one as we are one: *I in them and you in me*. May they be brought to complete unity to let the world know that *you sent me and have loved them even as you have loved me*.
>
> Father, I want those you have given me to be with me where I am, and to see my glory, the glory you have given me because you loved me before the creation of the world.
>
> Righteous Father, though the world does not know you, I know you, and they know that you have sent me. I have made you known to them, and will continue to make you known in order that the *love you have for me may be in them and that I myself may be in them*.
>
> John 17:20–26 (NIV)

Interceding or Tattling and Accusing

Do We Intercede With Jesus	or	**Do We Accuse With Satan?**

"Father, I know it is *your* will that none should perish.

I ask you to bless [name] _____.

Please forgive his sins and transform his life to become *your* adored child who honors you."

"Father, he drinks, and he runs around

He won't take care of his family, and his children need him.

He won't work and pay his bills"

Jesus The Intercessor

Christ Jesus ... *is at the right hand of God and is also interceding for us.*

Romans 8:34 (NIV)

Satan The Accuser

... the accuser of our brothers, our brothers, who accuses them before our God day and night.

Revelation 12:10 (NIV)

Unlike Jesus' prayer, other people's faults sometimes inspire our prayers. If we are not careful about our attitude toward the one for whom we are praying, we may be agreeing with Satan, the master accuser, who stands before God tattling night and day" (Rev. 12:10 NIV). Consequently, our one-sided gossip sessions will not likely result in blessings.

Rather, ask for God's greatest blessing: "May the power of your Holy Spirit overshadow and transform him/her into your image. Then, bless them in every area of their needs."

The Intercessor Illustrated

The chart below will help us to see our intercessory position between God and man. God sees intercessors who they are, and their deep concerns. Look at the top of the page on the right and see a list of biblical intercessors and God's response to them. Their prayers made a big difference in people's lives and circumstances. Those *who received the prayer answers* had no part in the faith required for the answers.

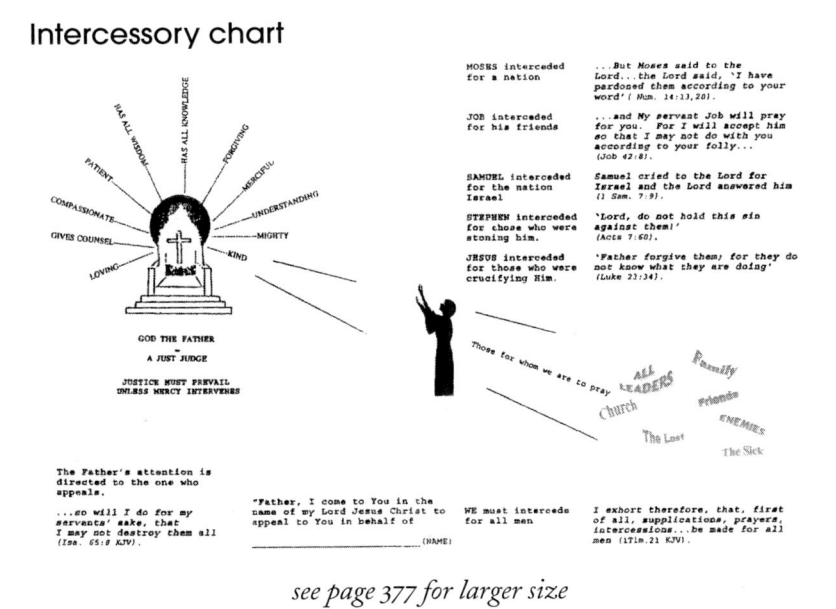

Intercessory chart

MOSES interceded for a nation
...But Moses said to the Lord...the Lord said, 'I have pardoned them according to your word' (Num. 14:13,20).

JOB interceded for his friends
...and My servant Job will pray for you. For I will accept him so that I may not do with you according to your folly... (Job 42:8).

SAMUEL interceded for the nation Israel
Samuel cried to the Lord for Israel and the Lord answered him (1 Sam. 7:9).

STEPHEN interceded for those who were stoning him.
'Lord, do not hold this sin against them!' (Acts 7:60).

JESUS interceded for those who were crucifying Him.
'Father forgive them; for they do not know what they are doing' (Luke 23:34).

GOD THE FATHER
A JUST JUDGE
JUSTICE MUST PREVAIL UNLESS MERCY INTERVENES

Those for whom we are to pray: ALL LEADERS, Family, Church, Friends, The Lost, ENEMIES, The Sick

The Father's attention is directed to the one who appeals.
...so will I do for my servants' sake, that I may not destroy them all (Isa. 65:8 KJV).

"Father, I come to You in the name of my Lord Jesus Christ to appeal to You in behalf of _____ (NAME)

WE must intercede for all men

I exhort therefore, that, first of all, supplications, prayers, intercessions...be made for all men (1Tim.2:1 KJV).

see page 377 for larger size

"Mercy Triumphs over Judgment" (Jas. 2:13).

As you and I stand in the center position between God and man we must first, be keenly aware of The One to whom we are pleading. *Know* Our Father's nature and character.

Then, we must see the ones for whom we are praying with understanding, compassion, and an earnest desire for God to intervene in their behalf. In essence, we are bringing the two together. It is *our* faith; that furnishes the *confidence in God* to which He will respond. In our confidence, we *know* that with him there is nothing impossible. And, we *know* that His love overflows with a desire to transform and bless.

As we study the chart, it is important for us to understand that justice must prevail, unless mercy intervenes. That means if there is no repentance, or righteous intercession then judgment will fall! Can we comprehend what that means?

(God) said to Moses, "I will have mercy on whom I have mercy, and I will have compassion on whom I have compassion" (Rom. 9:15 niv). Jesus' merciful and compassionate blood intervened over the impossible demands of The Law (Old Testament).

The Intercessor Power Prayer

"Lord, May your Holy Spirit come and work mightily, according to your transforming power, in the life of _____" (name).

This prayer has merit because we do not ask the unregenerate or wayward person to do anything. Rather, we go straight to God, who is totally dependable. And, we ask Him to do with unreserved power that which is the mission of The Holy Spirit: To Transform Lives.

When His Holy Spirit comes, He will do basically three things: He "will convict the world of guilt in regard to sin and righteousness and judgment" (Jn. 16:8 niv). This means

- He will cause a person to be miserable about his/her sins.
- He will reveal Jesus Christ as Righteousness.
- He will give an awesome sense of impending judgment against unrighteousness.

The Power Prayer Foundational Principle: Pray in God's Will

The key to answered prayer is in asking for something that God wants to do anyway. We see God's will through his nature and character. We read about his will in Scripture. An important guide would be to ask the question that young people are taught, "What would Jesus do?" Then pray accordingly.

> This is the confidence we have in approaching God: that if we ask anything according to his will, he hears us. And if we know that he hears us ... whatever we ask ... we know that we have what we asked of him.
>
> 1 John 5:14–15 (NIV)

When God's spirit inspires us to pray, it will be for a purpose that is in His will. "In the same way, the Spirit helps us in our weakness: We do not know what we ought to pray for, but the Spirit himself intercedes for us..." (Rom.8:26 NIV).

Scriptures that Confirm God's Will

When we write our "Will," we are documenting that which we want to legally happen. God wrote his Will: "[He] ... wants all men to be saved and to come to knowledge of the truth" (1 Tim. 2:4 NIV). "The Lord is ... not wanting anyone to perish, but everyone to come to repentance" (2 Pet. 3:9 NIV).

God wants no one to go to hell. It was not designed for people: Everlasting fire was "prepared for the devil and his angels" (Matt.

25:41 NIV). In fact, God has done everything possible to keep people from going there except transgress a person's free-will.

He loved the sinful people of the world so much that, "He gave his only begotten son that whosoever believeth in him should not perish but have everlasting life" (Jn. 3:16 KJV). In Jesus' mind, it was well worth the temporary unfathomable agony, the lashings, the crown of thorns, the nails, and the spear to pay for mankind's sins. His great love kept him nailed to the cross. Greater than his pain, was his desire for us to have a glorious life with him forever.

God's will is to give the Holy Spirit. "If you then, though you are evil [prone to sin in basic nature] know how to give good gifts to your children, [by contrast] how much more will your [Divine] Father in heaven give the Holy Spirit to those who ask him" (Luke 11:13 NIV)!

The Holy Spirit is eager to fulfill his mission. "When he, the Spirit of truth, comes, he will guide you into all truth...He will bring glory to me by taking from what is mine and making it known to you" (Jn. 16:13, 14 NIV). And, not only will he enlighten and transform, he will continue his work by teaching, inspiring, and guiding: It is "God who works in you to will and to act according to his good purpose" (Phil. 2:13 NIV).

Surely, as we pray in God's will with the transforming power of The Holy Spirit, we shall see transformed lives.

"Nevertheless, Not My Will But Yours"

Many people will not pray "nevertheless, not my will but *yours*" because they believe it would be *doubting* and would negate their request. They are probably clinging to this scripture: "I tell you the truth, if anyone says to this mountain, 'Go, throw *your*self into the sea,' *and does not doubt in his heart* but believes that what he says will happen, it will be done for him" (Mark 11:22–24 NIV).

We hear Jesus' desperate plea to his Father that ended, "Nevertheless, not my will, but *yours*." He was agonizing in the

Garden of Gethsemane over the excruciating spiritual and physical pain that awaited him: *"Abba,* Father," he cried out, "everything is possible for you. Please take this cup of suffering away from me. *Yet* [nevertheless] I want *your* will to be done, not mine" (Mark 14:36 NLT). He trusted God's higher plan.

How to Pray for the Terminally Ill

When we are praying for someone who is terminally ill, we should first ask God's Holy Spirit to help us to pray. God may give us great faith to believe for a miracle; or it may be, he has a higher plan. We should not hesitate to relinquish to *our Father* the final decision. Remember, dying is not the worst thing that can happen. Sometimes, *not* dying can be the worst. Above this, God's broader vision knows the effects on other people lives that this *life or death* would cause.

For example: With a mother's death, family members could be deeply touched during the funeral sermon and turned to Jesus for eternal salvation. Whereas, at no other time would their hearts be so softened. If, only by her death, even one family member would have eternal life, a greater divine purpose has been accomplished.

Three years ago, Ruth had stage four cancer, and the doctor said that she had only a few more days to live. Our Bible Study Class and many others prayed for her. Now, she is radiantly alive.

Recently, Margie came to our Ladies Bible Study Class with a terminal diagnosis. Mega doses of chemotherapy had virtually destroyed her kidneys putting her precariously close to stage four renal failure with rapidly dropping values on her kidney evaluations. The prognosis: "Nothing can be done. You will get progressively worse requiring dialysis and kidney transplants with over eighty thousand people on the waiting list ahead of you, or you will go into acute renal failure and die.

Another devout Christians had prayed for Margie before she came to our Ladies' Bible Study. In class, about eighty women were praying when we felt the presence of God's Holy Spirit in a profound way. Several women seated at the table with Margie saw a change in her and perceived that God had healed her.

Margie had a new lab report and showed us the comparison of the old with the new. It was medically documented that Margie's kidney functions were "NORMAL or BETTER." Hallelujah!

How to Pray for Those Who are Dying with Classic Unsaved Symptoms

Many people live in torment because they believe a loved one died without salvation and has gone to hell. The loved one may have been saved in the last seconds, in his spirit without anyone ever knowing about it. We cannot judge another person's heart at the moment of death, by the life he lived.

Go to Calvary and view the dying thief on the cross who was hanging beside Jesus. Everyone at the foot of the cross knew beyond a doubt that he was condemned; his mother was probably there too, and spent the rest of her life in anguish believing that her son would suffer a horrendous eternity. Only Jesus and the thief knew about their private conversation when Jesus pronounced, "Today shalt thou be with me in paradise" (Lu. 23:43 KJV).

When you pray for a terminally ill person whose lifestyle is condemning, your prayer can make a huge difference. You could ask God's Holy Spirit to come and have a private conversation with the spirit within the person. The Holy Spirit would tell him about righteousness in Jesus because that is one of his ministries. Also, he would give him assurance of salvation because that is another of his ministries. All of this could happen in his last redeeming second in this life. Then, in the next second, he would *be in Paradise!* "Absent from the body, present with the Lord" (2 Cor. 5: 6 KJV).

Remember, God is eager to hear your prayer: "*before they call, I will answer*; and while they are yet speaking, I will hear" (Isa.

65:24 NIV). Also, "The Lord is ... not wanting anyone to perish, but everyone to come to repentance" (2 Pet. 3:9 NIV). "If anyone sees his brother commit a sin that does not lead to death, *he should pray and God will give him life*" (1 Jn. 5:16 NIV).

The Unpardonable Sin

There is a sin that leads to death. I am not saying that he should pray about that" (1 Jn. 5:16 NIV). What is that sin? What if the one who is dying has committed the unpardonable sin?

The word blaspheme is connected with the unpardonable sin. It is commonly associated with vile words that are spoken, "Even God can't sink the Titanic!" Webster explained blasphemy as "contemptuous or irreverent speech about God or things regarded as sacred." But, that is not the whole story.

Do not presume anyone is doomed because of their profane mouth. They could have been bluffing for years, since some people try to maintain their image with harsh rhetoric. Probably, the thief of the cross had previously spouted off blasphemous words.

God had been repeatedly blasphemed by even his chosen people, the Israelites. "And all day long my name is constantly blasphemed" (Isa. 52:5 NIV). Paul the apostle said: "Even though I was once a blasphemer and a persecutor and a violent man, I was shown mercy because I acted in ignorance and unbelief" (1 Tim.1:13 NIV).

Nevertheless, that is not the unpardonable sin. God still loved the Israelites and provided a way whereby they might be redeemed. Ultimately, Jesus died so even the vilest of these could be saved.

Jesus did his part. Next comes the believing and receiving. When the sinner believes that Jesus died for his/her sins and wants Jesus to be his Lord, the Holy Spirit will come to live within his heart. Now, at this point is where the sinner raises his "Go" or "Stop" sign. He can accept or reject the Holy Spirit.

The next three verses will explain the unpardonable sin. There is another way to blaspheme:

"Everyone who speaks a word against the Son of Man [God extended in human form, Jesus] will be forgiven, but anyone who blasphemes against the Holy Spirit will not be forgiven" (Lu. 12:10 NIV).

The unpardonable sin is blasphemy against the Holy Spirit *by forsaking him*. Read on:

> This is what the Sovereign Lord says: In this also your fathers blasphemed me *by forsaking me:*
> Ezekiel 20:27

> But whoever blasphemes against [permanently forsakes] the Holy Spirit will never be forgiven; he is guilty of an eternal sin.
> Mark 3:29

Clearly, the unpardonable sin is not what is spouted from the lips; it is "who" is rejected in the heart. But, if the profanity includes final rejection, it has eternal consequences.

The dooming sin is probably rare and cannot happen by accident. It is committed by the person who deliberately hardened his/her heart against God by deciding, with finality, to keep his sins and reject God's Spirit of Holiness. Salvation cannot happen if the Holy Spirit does not enter a person's heart, by faith in Jesus' atoning blood; *He* is the transformer of the spirit. "Therefore if any man be in Christ, he is a new creature: old things are passed away; behold all things are become new" (2 Cor. 5:17 KJV). Without the transforming power, old things *have not* passed away and *nothing* has become new.

The explanation of the blasphemous rejection of God's Holy Spirit may be simplified this way: When God's Holy Spirit taps on the hearts' door, there is a sign, "DO NOT ENTER!"

If you are praying, or have prayed at any time in the past, for a person who is not saved, I believe God heard and the answer is on its way, even if answered in the last few seconds of life. Remember the scripture: *"Before they call, I will answer."*

Rephrased, since God knows everything past, present and future, presume that God heard your prayer even before you prayed and he sent his answer on the way knowing in advance that *you would be* praying. God is not limited by time.

Pray for our Nation

At the top of the list in our Prayer Forms, we will pray for the leaders of our land. I want to expand that segment with an introductory prayer because the future of our nation is in jeopardy and our leaders desperately need God's guidance!

> I urge, then, first of all, that requests, prayers, intercession, and thanksgiving be made for everyone for kings and all those in authority, that we may live peaceful and quiet lives in all godliness and holiness. This is good, and pleases God our Savior, who wants all men to be saved and to come to knowledge of the truth.
> 1 Timothy 2:1–4 (NIV)

> If my people, who are called by my name, will humble themselves and pray and seek my face and turn from their wicked ways, then will I hear from heaven and will forgive their sin and will heal their land.
> 2 Chronicles 7:14 (NIV)

A Tsunami Power Prayer for our Nation
May we pray together:

Father, may your Living Water rain upon our parched land. We need a deluge that will baptize us all in your Spirit. Therefore, we ask you to send a mighty Holy Spirit Tsunami. Let it start at the east coast from the tip of Maine down through the Florida Keys, and wash across our nation blowing away pride, ego, power and self indulgence from every home and every heart. Awaken the spiritually dead, humble the arrogant, and reveals your truth to all men.

Work mightily according to your transforming power filling each heart with your Spirit of Love. Transform the powerful and also the weak... the wealthy as well as the impoverished... the eldest to the infants... from the president to the man behind the plow.

Open the prisons in peoples' minds of low self esteem, addictions and whatever else that binds them. Free them to become all that you designed them to be. Empty the jails and fill the churches with people who are at peace with God and themselves. Inspire us to walk humbly in your strength so that our accomplishments will go beyond our greatest dreams for the prosperity of our families, our churches and our nation. May our compassionate generosity open as a flood gate into the world to the desperate multitudes.

Father, may your Holy Spirit Tsunami be the greatest revival known to man where your commandments are engraved in each heart: "Love God first and love your neighbor as yourself; don't kill, steal, lie or cheat." Give us wisdom to first rule ourselves before we try to rule others.

May *we the people* come alive in the light of Your Glory. May you be returned to your throne over our nation, prayers returned to our schools and your Commandments returned to our walls. May we truly be *one nation under God* which cannot be divided *with liberty and justice for all.*

Thank you, Lord, for hearing our prayer. We love you. Amen.

Prayer Forms will help to organize thoughts. Fill in the blanks and remember to mark prayer answers. Reviewing the many answers will inspire greater prayers.

VI: Ask Our Father "Thank You, Lord!"

My Personal Prayer Form

FOR WHOM	SUGGESTED PRAYER PRINCIPLES	SCRIPTURE
LEADERS: **National** - President Executive, Judicial and Legislative **State** - Governor, Senate, Congress **County** - Commissioner **City** - Mayor Commissioners **School** - School Board Administrators, Staff **Teachers** - All	Pray that our leaders will be saved and brought to the knowledge of Truth in order for our country to be a land of godly people who live in peace. Pray that our leaders will please God by their lives. Pray that God will give wisdom to each of our leaders as they make decisions regarding our welfare and safety. Pray that their spiritual, emotional, physical and material needs will be met. Pray they will understand God's will in spiritual matters and will be men and women of honor and integrity whose lives reflect the nature and character of Christ. Ask for them to have inner strength to stand courageously, patiently, and joyfully for what is right. Pray that the school officials and teachers will know the LORD personally and will be filled with His Spirit so they will be kind and patient, with wisdom and knowledge. May they have special concern for the progress of each student. Pray the teachers will be respected.	*First of all, then, I urge that entreaties and prayers, petitions and thanksgivings, be made on behalf of all men, for kings and all who are in authority, in order that we may lead a tranquil and quiet life in all godliness and dignity. This is good and acceptable in the sight of God our Savior, who desires all men to be saved and to come to the knowledge of the truth (1 Tim. 2:1-4).* *...if any of you lacks wisdom, let him ask of God, who gives to all men generously and without reproach, and it will be given to him (James 1:5).* *...ask that you may be filled with the knowledge of His will in all spiritual wisdom and understanding so that you may walk in a manner worthy of the LORD to please Him in all respects, bearing fruit in every good work and increasing in the knowledge of God; strengthened with all power, according to His glorious might, for the attaining of all steadfastness and patience; joyously giving thanks to the Father, who has qualified us to share in the inheritance of the saints in light (Col. 1:9-12).*

Christianity Alive! with Prayer Power!

My Personal Prayer Form

FOR WHOM	SUGGESTED PRAYER PRINCIPLES	SCRIPTURE
FAMILY: **Husband/Wife** **Dad/Mom** **Brothers/Sisters** **Children** **Other family members**	Pray that their spiritual, physical, emotional and material needs will be met. For those who are not saved, pray they will "...open their eyes that they may turn from darkness to light and from the dominion of Satan to God, in order that they may receive forgiveness of sins and an inheritance among those who have been sanctified by faith in Me (Acts 26:18)." Pray that they will live in the Spirit of Christ, walking in honor. Thank God for each family member and for their individuality - their personalities, talents and potential. (Focus on their positive qualities and do not report to God their failings) See each one as being a godly person, filled with the characteristics of Christ, Himself. That is, being patient, kind, loving, merciful, understanding, filled with wisdom and knowledge. Pray that each relative will always seek God. Pray that each one will reach the height of his/her potential and will be respected by his fellowman.	Beloved, I pray that in all respects you may prosper and be in good health, just as your soul prospers (3 John 2). Therefore be imitators of God, as beloved children and walk in love, just as Christ also loved you, and gave Himself up for us ... For you were formerly darkness, but now you are light in the Lord; walk as children of light (for the fruit of the light consists in all goodness and righteousness and truth), trying to learn what is pleasing to the Lord (Eph. 5:1,2,8-10 I came that they might have life, and might have it abundantly (John 10:10). Children are a gift of the LORD (Ps 127:3). As for me, I shall behold Thy face in righteousness; I will be satisfied with Thy likeness when I awake (Psalm 17:15). The LORD has looked down from heaven upon the sons of men, to see it there are any who understand, who seek after God (Psalm 14:2). As for God, His way is blameless; The word of the Lord is tried; He is a shield to all who take refuge in Him (Psalm 18:30).

VI: Ask Our Father "Thank You, Lord!"

My Personal Prayer Form

FOR WHOM	SUGGESTED PRAYER PRINCIPLES	*SCRIPTURE*
FRIENDS:	Thank God for your friends and ask Him to increase the realm of your Christian friends	*A friend loves at all times...(Prov. 17:17).*
	Pray for courage and boldness to tell those who do not know God as Father, the good news of salvation. If you are not absolutely certain that they have been* born again *do not presume they are.*	*The harvest is plentiful, but the workers are few. Therefore beseech the LORD of the harvest to send out workers into His harvest (Matt. 9:37,38).*
Children's Friends		*Greater love has no one than this, that he lay down his life for his friends (John 15:13).*
Neighbors	Pray for salvation and blessings for all neighbors.	*This I command you, that you love one another (John 15:17).*
	Pray that the Jews all over the world will recognize Jesus Christ as their Messiah. Ask God to reveal to your Jewish friends that you have a special love for them because they are God's chosen people. Pray that your family from generation to generation will always love and respect them.

God notices how the Jews are treated. It is an awesome responsibility to be kind to them because God "*will bless those who bless them*" and will "*curse those who curse them*". (Remember Jesus was the Jewish Messiah and we, by faith in Him, have become "*sons and daughters of Abraham*" in God's eternal spiritual family.) | *For I am not ashamed of the gospel, for it is the power of God for salvation to every one who believes,* <u>*to the Jew first*</u> *and also to the Greek (Rom. 1:16).*

Now the LORD said to Abram...'And I will bless those who bless you, and the one who curses you I will curse' (Gen. 12:1,3). |
| Jews - all | | |
| Enemies | Pray for those who are your least favorite - those who harass, injure or continually offend you. Pray for their salvation and transformation of their nature and character. Ask God to change your attitude toward them. | *...love your enemies, do good to those who hate you, bless those who curse you, pray for those who mistreat you (Luke 6:27,28).* |

Christianity Alive! with Prayer Power!

My Personal Prayer Form

FOR WHOM	SUGGESTED PRAYER PRINCIPLES	*SCRIPTURE*
EMPLOYMENT: Employers/Employees	Thank God for your job and your employer (or) employees. Ask God to bless each one with His Spirit and meet each physical, emotional and material need. Pray for wisdom to work with each one. If you are an employer, ask God to help you to find ways to increase their wages, or benefits. Pray for harmony as you work together toward a common goal. Pray that God will help you to be an exemplary employer/employee. Ask God to bless the leadership of the company and each person who has a part in its operations. Ask for patience, understanding, wisdom and knowledge to prevail as each one gives his best with honesty and integrity. Pray especially for those who are difficult to work with. Ask God to help you so you won't be the difficult one. Pray that the company will always have money to pay each employee a fair wage promptly.	*Masters, (employers) grant to your slaves (employees) justice and fairness, knowing that you too have a Master in heaven. Devote yourselves to prayer keeping alert in it with an attitude of thanksgiving (Col. 4:1,2).* *...I will be a swift witness against...those who oppress the wage earner in his wages... (Mal. 3:5).* *Servants, obey in all things your masters according to the flesh; not with eye-service, as menpleasers; but in singleness of heart, fearing God (Col. 3:22).* *Whatever you do, do your work heartily, as for the LORD rather than for men; knowing that from the LORD you will receive the reward of the inheritance. It is the LORD Christ whom you serve (Col. 3:23-24).* *Do not take money from anyone by force, or accuse anyone falsely, and be content with your wages (Luke 3:14).*
Those who are sick	Think about each sick person you know and ask God to heal him/her and bless him/her according to His love and compassion. Pray for all who are in hospitals. Thank God for hearing your prayer, and for the answers He is sending. Amen.	*Is anyone among you sick? Let him call for the elder of the church, and let them pray over him...and the prayer offered in faith will restore the one who is sick...(Jas. 5:14,15).* *The effective prayer of a righteous man can accomplish much (James 5:16)*

VI: Ask Our Father "Thank You, Lord!"

My Personal Prayer Form

Name	Personal Written Prayer	Prayer Answers

Don't Forget to Say, "Thank You"
Does God See Us as One of the Nine?

> As [Jesus] entered a village there, ten lepers stood at a distance, crying out, "Jesus, Master, have mercy on us!" He looked at them and said, "Go show *your*selves to the priests." And as they went, they were cleansed of their leprosy.
>
> One of them, when he saw that he was healed, came back to Jesus, shouting, "Praise God!" He fell to the ground at Jesus' feet, thanking him for what he had done. This man was a Samaritan.
>
> Jesus asked, "Didn't I heal ten men? Where are the other nine? Has no one returned to give glory to God except this foreigner?" [*Except this foreigner,* implies there were Israelites among those who did not say, "Thank You."]
>
> Luke 17:12–18 (NLT)

Are we among those Israelites? How often do we forget to tell God how much we appreciate what he has done for us?

An example of profound gratitude: Rosie and Brenda are in our Ladies Bible Study Class. Rosie wrote:

> For twelve years, our daughter seized every day from six to one hundred times, with every kind of episode. We took her to seven neurologists and hospitals all over Texas.
>
> Brenda never knew what it was like to play outdoors or attend any social activities. We seldom went to church, or anywhere else. She wore a monitor so she could be watched constantly. She went to school, but spent a lot of time in the nurses' office.
>
> We started attending the First Baptist Church in Rio Hondo Texas and felt a sense of peacefulness. Though she was heavily medicated, she was tolerating the exposure. She and I started attending the Ladies Bible Study Class and the ladies anointed her with oil and prayed fervently for her. Immediately, the seizures became less frequent. They continued to pray.

VI: Ask Our Father "Thank You, Lord!"

Now, it has been two years since she completely stopped seizing. She had two E.G.G.s and the doctor could not believe the results that came back normal. He had another doctor read them and sure enough, they were NORMAL.

He asked me if I had done anything different with her. I told him that Jesus Christ had performed a miracle. And, I told him about the Ladies Bible Study class and how the women still pray for her. He asked me to pray for him so he could help other patients.

Brenda is living a normal life. There is no way her dad and I can ever thank God enough for the greatest miracle! "THANK YOU, LORD!"

Sample Prayer

Ask Our Father "Thank You Lord!"

Thank you for loving us, your children, so much that you want to hear and answer our prayers.

I know that your ways and thoughts are so much higher than ours that it is not easy for us to think in that realm. Please help us to ask for and believe in you for all that you want to provide.

First, we ask for your Holy Spirit to come and work mightily, according to your glorious transforming power our lives, our family's lives, friends and all mankind.

Many people have dire needs; some are physical, mental, emotional, financial and broken relationships. Please help each person, because you alone have insight and power to provide.

May your Holy Spirit flow over our nation like a mighty Holy Spiritual Tsunami. Thank you for hearing our prayer and for the many lives that you are in the process of transforming and blessing.

Thank you for all of our prayer answers. In the name of Jesus and for his glory, we pray. Amen.

Living Christianity Assignment

Bible Study—Research in the back of your Bible the subject of prayer to learn more about asking and receiving.

> We have confidence before God and receive from him anything we ask, because we obey his commands and do what pleases him.
> I John 3:21–22 (NIV)

Prayer—Select a prayer partner for agreement prayer. Learn to pray together, even over the telephone. Expand your intercession time.

> Fast, with a righteous life: "Then you will call, and the LORD will answer; you will cry for help, and he will say" Here am I."
> Isaiah 58:9 (NIV)

Works—Express your love to others. When you see someone who needs a smile, give them one of yours. Observe their needs and add them to your Intercession List.

> Do not forget to do good and to share with others, for with such sacrifices God is pleased.
> Hebrew 13:16 (NIV)

VII:
Repent to Our Father
"I am So Sorry, Lord"

"Forgive us our debts"

> If we confess our sins, he is faithful and just and will forgive us our sins and purify us from all unrighteousness.
>
> 1 John 1:9 (NIV)

VII:
Repent to Our Father
"I am So Sorry, Lord."

"Forgive us our debts"

- Five Steps from Sin to Answered Prayer

    - Sins Recognized
    - Sins Repented
    - Forgiveness Received
    - Obedience Reinstated
    - Harmony Restored

- Walking in His Footsteps
- Sample Prayer: Repent to Our Father "I'm So Sorry, Lord!"
- Living Christianity Assignment

VII:
Repent to Our Father
"I am So Sorry, Lord."

"Forgive us our debts"

Five Steps from Sin to Answered Prayer

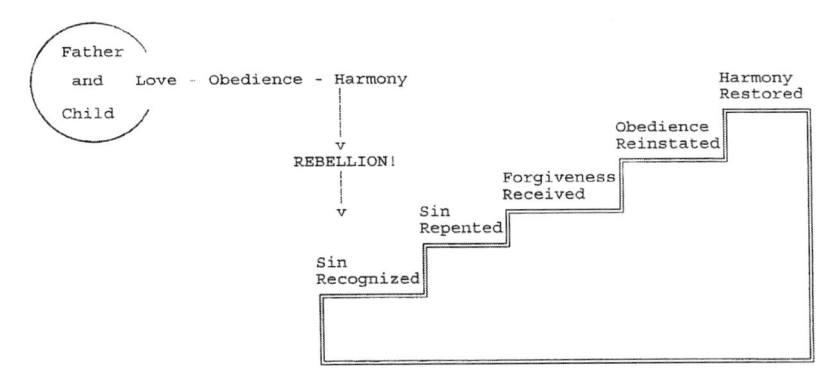

```
 ┌─────────┐
 │ Father  │
 │  and    │  Love - Obedience - Harmony                    Harmony
 │ Child   │         │                                      Restored
 └─────────┘         │                              ┌──────────────
                     v                              │  Obedience
                 REBELLION!                         │  Reinstated
                     │                  ┌───────────┘
                     │                  │ Forgiveness
                     v         ┌────────┘ Received
                               │  Sin
                               │  Repented
                    ┌──────────┘
                    │   Sin
                    │ Recognized
      ──────────────┘
```

Sin breaks harmony with *Our Father* and short-circuits our prayer life. With un-repented sin we cannot enter into the holy realm where there is *power* in prayer. First, we must get our relationship straightened out with *our Father*. This is a family affair. Similarly, in any family the child who is loving and obedient is in a better position to make large requests than one who is disobedient. We cannot hide anything from *our Father*.

For the word of God is living and active. Sharper than any double-edged sword, it penetrates even to dividing soul and spirit, joints and marrow; it judges the thoughts and attitudes of the heart. Nothing in all creation is hidden from God's sight. *Everything is uncovered and laid bare before the eyes of him to whom we must give account.*

Hebrews 4:12–13 (NIV)

Five Steps from Sin to Answered Prayer

The five steps are 1. Sin Recognized 2. Sin Repented, 3. Forgiveness Received, 4. Obedience Reinstated. 5. Harmony Restored.

Some people vehemently declare, "I don't sin." Scripture states, "...all have sinned and fall short of the glory of God" (Rom. 3:23 NIV). "If we claim we have not sinned, we make him out to be a liar and his word has no place in our lives" (1 Jn. 1:10 NIV).

Truth is, since Adam and Eve sin has spread like an insidious virus into epidemic proportions.

Sin Recognized

We may define sin as any thought or action that is contrary to God's nature, character, and expressed will. "All wrongdoing is sin" (1 Jn. 5:17 NIV). Analyzing how Scripture defines sin will help us to recognize our weaknesses.

Long before Satan tempted Eve, Lucifer resided in the heavenly realm the closest to God. He became highly impressed with his status. Sin was born with a subtle thought and gradually transformed angelic Lucifer into Satan. Through spiritual imagery we might see into that ancient heavenly drama: Lucifer was the most beautiful, glorious, powerful and prestigious angelic being in the heavenly host. Through the prophet Ezekiel, God said,

> You were the model of perfection, full of wisdom and perfect in beauty. You were in [Heavenly] Eden, the garden of God;

> every precious stone adorned you: ruby, topaz, and emerald, chrysolite, onyx, and jasper, sapphire, turquoise, and beryl. *Your* settings and mountings were made of gold; on the day you were created they were prepared.
>
> You were anointed as a guardian cherub, for so I ordained you. You were on the holy mount of God; you walked among the [brilliantly sparkling] fiery stones. You were blameless in *your* ways from the day you were created till wickedness was found in you.
>
> Ezekiel 28:12–15 (NIV)

The first sin entered Lucifer as a flicker of pride. God said, "Your heart became proud on account of your beauty, and you corrupted your wisdom because of your splendor" (Ezek. 28:17 NIV). The tiny seed of leaven grew until Lucifer was consumed with conceit.

Vanity caused dissension as he dared to assume an opposing opinion to God. Soon, unrestrained ambition welled within as he *said* in his heart, "…I will raise my throne above the stars of God…I will make myself like the Most High" (Isa. 14:13, 14 NIV).

Lucifer began to think of himself to be as good as, if not better than, God. Harmony was severed. As he moved among the heavenly hosts promoting his cause, unrest turned into insurrection. One-third of the angels joined him in his quest for supremacy. Deceived and blinded by pride and grandeur, he could not see the adverse effects.

All did not go as Lucifer had planned since sin cannot abide in the holy sphere of righteousness. When eviction was apparent, he became more vociferous in his new role as adversary. The malignity of sin rapidly spread.

Lucifer's nature changed dramatically. Now, *nothing* would stand in his way! He mastered the art of deception. Feelings of anger, rage, and murder filled his heart as he became totally unscrupulous in all things. Sin took its toll on the once beautiful Lucifer. He became Satan the epitome of evil!

You and I are neither as evil as Satan, nor as holy as Jesus. Sin, in varying degrees, is present in each of our lives. Sin also begins as a thought with us. Jesus said, "... from within, out of men's hearts, come evil thoughts, sexual immorality, theft, murder, adultery, greed, malice, deceit, lewdness, envy, slander, arrogance, and folly" (Mk. 7:21,22 NIV).

We also have *thought* sins, like Jesus said, "... anyone who looks at a woman lustfully has already committed adultery with her in his heart" (Matt. 5:28 NIV). Going into deeper water, it is not uncommon for people to mentally craft false gods as they establish their philosophies and priorities. Common today, like Lucifer, *Humanism* negates dependency upon God.

Again like Lucifer, attitude sins like pride and self-righteousness are sometimes hard to detect in ourselves. It is easy to pray, like the Pharisees, "God, I thank you that I am not like other men, robbers, evildoers, adulterers, or even like this tax collector" (Lu. 18:11, 12 NIV).

Godly men can be impressed with their own holiness. R. A. Torrey writes,

> Many and many a man in answer to prayer has been endued with power and thus has wrought great things in the name of the Lord, and when these great things were accomplished, instead of going alone with God and humbling himself before Him, and giving Him all the glory for what was achieved, he has congratulated himself... become puffed up, and God has been obliged to lay him aside. The great things done were not followed by humiliation of self, and prayer to God, and so pride has come in and the mighty man has been shorn of his power.[76]

Other subtle sins are *judging and criticizing*. They can easily slip in under the guise of *discernment*. As we draw closer to God and become more aware of our sins, we notice other people's sins too. Jesus said, *"Why do you look at the speck of sawdust in your brother's eye... ?"* (Matt.7:3 NIV).

VII: Repent to Our Father "I am So Sorry, Lord"

Sins of omission are perhaps the most subtle; apathy is their silent cohort. The greatest of these is prayerlessness, which is failure to communicate with *our Father*, and failure to intercede in prayer for others. Samuel said, "...far be it from me that I should sin against the LORD by failing to pray for you" (1 Sam. 12:23 NIV). John R. Rice confesses:

> My greatest sin, and *your*s, is prayerlessness. My failures are all prayer-failures. The lack of souls saved in my ministry is primarily because of lack of prayer, not because of lack of preaching. The withering away of joy in my heart, sometimes, is the fruit of prayerlessness. My indecision, my lack of wisdom, my lack of guidance comes directly out of my prayerlessness. All the times I have fallen into sin, have failed in my duties, have been bereft of power, or disconsolate for lack of comfort, I can charge to the sin of prayerlessness.[77]

Jesus considers sins of omission a serious offense:

> Depart from me, you who are cursed, into the eternal fire prepared for the devil and his angels. For I was hungry...you gave me nothing to eat, I was thirsty...you gave me nothing to drink, I was a stranger...you did not invite me in, I needed clothes...you did not clothe me, I was sick and in prison...you did not look after me. They also will answer, "Lord, when did we see you hungry...thirsty...a stranger...needing clothes...sick or in prison, and did not help you?" He will reply, "I tell you the truth, whatever you did not do for one of the least of these, you did not do for me."
> Matthew 25:41–45 (NIV)

The strongest definition of sin is *rebellion against God*. The prophet Samuel relayed God's message to Israel's King Saul, "...rebellion is like the sin of divination, and arrogance like the evil of idolatry...you have rejected the word of the LORD...he has rejected you as king." (1 Sam.15:23 NIV).

We all know that the symbol for rebellion is a clinched fist. I shudder as I remember seeing a Christian woman who blamed God for her circumstance by raising her fist and shouting, "God, I am angry with you!"

One of the most self-willed women I have ever known had a serious head injury when she was involved in a dune buggy accident on Padre Island, when she was not supposed to be there. I heard her say, as she lay in the Neurological Intensive Care unit of the hospital, "I learned a long time ago the best thing to do is keep *your* mouth shut, and do what you want to do anyway." Clearly, that meant she had developed a lifestyle of defying authority.

Some people attribute their headstrong rebellion as their inherited *stubborn streak*. They glibly say, "You know I'm red-headed," or "My grandfather was Irish." Utter frustration prevails between the stubborn person and God; right and wrong are in direct conflict.

There is no giving-in; God can't change and the stubborn won't! It reminds me of a donkey sitting in the road, tugging at his master's rope.

There are subtle sins and glaring sins, but no hidden sins. God knows all about them. Scripture warns, "…you may be sure that *your* sin will find you out" (Num. 32.23 NIV). An infamous example happened back in the days when modesty was the social norm. Two obscure young women posed together for nude photographs. Later, one became Miss America and the sin became national news.

Regrettably, sexual sins, even among our national leaders are no longer headline news. Some leaders also keep Ethics Committees busy on other infringements.

In recognizing our sins, honesty before God is essential. Andrew Murray writes, "Let us be assured that God will not judge us according to the perfection of what we do, but according to the honesty with which we yield ourselves to lay aside every known sin, and with which we accept conviction by the Holy Spirit of all our hidden sin."[78]

The Holy Spirit convicted the Israelites on the Day of Pentecost when Peter preached his powerful gospel sermon:

> Men of Israel, listen to this: Jesus of Nazareth was a man accredited by God to you by miracles, wonders, and signs, which God did among you through him, as you yourselves know. This man was handed over to you by God's set purpose and foreknowledge; *and you, with the help of wicked men put him to death by nailing him to the cross.* But God raised him from the dead, freeing him from the agony of death, because it was impossible for death to keep its hold on him.
>
> … When the people heard this, they were *cut to the heart* [*deeply convicted*] and said to Peter and the other apostles, "Brothers, what shall we do?" Peter replied, "Repent and be baptized, every one of you, in the name of Jesus Christ for the forgiveness of *your* sins. And you will receive the gift of the Holy Spirit.
>
> Acts 2:22–24; 37–38 (NIV)

Many people don't have to be convicted. They are painfully aware of their sins. One man told me, "God can't forgive what I have done." Truth is, God does not keep separate records for big and little sins: This includes murderers and fibbers. God is eager for everyone to come to Him. The price has already been paid.

Sins Repented

Scripture clearly warns that repentance is essential. God spoke through Ezekiel,

> Why will you die… For I take no pleasure in the death of anyone… Repent and live!
>
> Ezekiel 18:31, 32 (NIV)

> Jesus said, "Repent, for the kingdom of heaven is near."
>
> Matthew 4:17 (NIV)

> John came… preaching a baptism of Repentance for the forgiveness of sins.
>
> Mark 1:4 (NIV)

> Repent... turn to God, so that *your* sins may be wiped out.
> Acts 3:19 (NIV)

Confession of sin may not be repentance. Many people openly discuss their sins and don't even mind telling God about them. However, they do not regret them enough to stop doing them... A desire to change, resulting from godly sorrow over unrighteousness, accompanies true repentance. D. L. Moody writes about Spurgeon exposing Pharaoh's unrepentant heart.

Speaking of Pharaoh's words, *"Entreat the Lord that He may take away the frogs from me,"* Spurgeon says: "A fatal flaw is manifest in that prayer. It contains no confession of sin. He says not, 'I have rebelled against the Lord; entreat that I may find forgiveness.' Nothing of the kind; he loves sin as much as ever. A prayer without penitence is a prayer without acceptance."[79] Pharaoh only wanted to get rid of the frogs.

Many sinners sob over getting caught but would commit the act again if they thought they could get away with it. Gloria Leigh writes,

> I've watched folks run through a sinner's prayer, shed buckets of tears at the altar and sniffle, "I've been bad." All the Christians get excited, cry with them, hug their necks and exclaim about how the angels are rejoicing in Heaven... then they feel like fools by Friday... when word gets back that the new *saint* is back out there doing whatever he was doing on Saturday before he *repented*.[80]

This story is worth reading again: In *Loving God*, Chuck Colson tells about the gangster, Mickey Cohen. When Mickey was asked if he would like to become a Christian, Mickey said he thought he'd really like that.

VII: Repent to Our Father "I am So Sorry, Lord"

> Billy Graham prayed with him. Of course, it was a front page news item and everyone talked about it for weeks. Later, it was rumored that he was still involved up to his ears in crime, gambling casinos, and his nationwide bookie establishment. When confronted, he was genuinely surprised. "Well, there are Christian movie stars, Christian athletes, and Christian businessmen. Why can't there be Christian gangsters?" Mickey Cohen, of course, was not saved. And he was appalled at the idea of giving up his career. His summation? "If I have to give up all that, count me out."[81]

Men of vile character who are smug in their unrighteousness need to fall on their faces in deep remorse... in terror of judgment.

When we are serious about repenting, God is quick to forgive. D. L. Moody writes in essence:

> When Job was humbled and said, "My ears had heard of you but now my eyes have seen you. Therefore I despise myself and repent in dust and ashes." Then, the tide turned. It was when Isaiah cried out before the Lord, "I am undone," that the blessing came. It was when David said, "I have sinned!" that God dealt in mercy with him.[82]

Repentance is action and brings visible results. It heads a life in another direction. I heard a preacher say, "Repentance is like a person driving down the expressway and deciding he wants to go in the opposite direction. He has to do more than just decide. He must take action by looping under the expressway and heading the opposite way. God offers us no option to repentance: "Take *your* evil deeds out of my sight! Stop doing wrong" (Isa. 1:16 NIV).

Persistent refusal to repent *could* lead to committing the unpardonable sin, which is *final deliberate rejection of God's Spirit of Holiness*. If a person stubbornly clings to his sins with no intention of repentance, God will eventually give up on him, and His rejected Holy

Spirit will leave. The LORD said, "My Spirit will not contend with man forever..." (Gen. 6:3 NIV). Without the convicting power of God's Spirit, the habitual sinner will feel no guilt. Old time preachers used to call this "sinning away your day of grace."

Adding to this, the Apostle Paul wrote, "Since they did not think it worthwhile to retain the knowledge of God, he gave them over to a depraved mind, to do what ought not to be done" (Rom. 1:28 NIV). Without the convicting power of God's Spirit, the habitual sinner will feel no guilt.

Before stepping into quicksand with whatever addiction is captivating the thoughts, we must read this warning:

> If we deliberately keep on sinning after we have received the knowledge of the truth, no sacrifice for sins is left, but only a fearful expectation of judgment and of raging fire that will consume the enemies of God. Anyone who rejected the law of Moses died without mercy on the testimony of two or three witnesses. *How much more severely do you think a man deserves to be punished who has trampled the Son of God under foot, who has treated as an unholy thing the blood of the covenant that sanctified him, and who has insulted the Spirit of grace?*
>
> Hebrews 10:26–29 (NIV)

We cannot be so bogged down in sin that God won't forgive if we are serious about repentance. Michael Booth wrote a deeply emotional song that conveys in essence, "There are places in my heart that I don't even want to go." Be assured, *every* sin has been covered by Jesus' blood at Calvary. When we come clean, Jesus will say, "What sin?"

Forgiveness Received

Forgive means "to pardon; to cease to bear resentment against; to cancel" (Webster). We are set free innocent again. Daniel writes, "The Lord our God is merciful and forgiving" (Dan. 9:9 NIV).

After we have received forgiveness, if the feeling of guilt and condemnation remains, or returns, it could be Satan, the accuser, reminding us of our sins. We can banish those thoughts by announcing: "I have repented and I'm not doing those sins any more. Jesus Christ is my Lord; he has paid the price for my sins!" Be gone! Case settled.

Obedience Reinstated

Obedience is the opposite of rebellion. Once we are forgiven we must act differently. Jesus said, "Produce fruit in keeping with repentance" (Luke 3:8 NIV). "Learn to do right! Seek justice, encourage the oppressed. Defend the cause of the fatherless, plead the case of the widow... If you are willing and *obedient*, you will eat the best from the land" (Isa. 1:17, 19 NIV). "The eyes of the Lord are on the righteous... his ears are attentive to their prayer" (1 Pet. 3:11, 12 NIV).

Obedience to God is not so regimented that we can't decide issues for ourselves. He allows us great flexibility in exercising our own wills, within the protective framework of His love and laws of righteousness.

Harmony Restored

During the Glorietta Christian Writer's Conference in New Mexico's Sangre De Cristo Mountains, I strolled through the beautiful Glorietta Prayer Garden. Sun shining through the Aspens made them appears to be covered with brilliant shimmering lemon drops. An occasional golden leaf floated downward. A crow cawed while geese glided on a lake nearby. I thought, "Oh My! How peaceful and beautiful."

I thought of Adam and Eve being cast out of *their* Garden of Eden lest they also eat of the Tree of Life and live forever in their fallen state. Then, I thought about Jesus *being* The Tree of Life when He said, *"I am the way and the truth and the life"* (Jn. 14:6 NIV). He has also redeemed us from all of the sinful apples we have ever eaten. The Tree of Eternal Life, in Him, is ours now.

In the cool of the day, I blissfully walked and communed with *Our Father* in *my* Garden of Eden.

Walking in His Footsteps

We have all seen little children happily walking behind their dads in his footprints. The prints are big and the stride is long. The child is in step with his/her dad walking in the spirit of sweet harmony. There are times the dad playfully, carries his child on his shoulders. It is all about love.

Sample Prayer

Repenting to Our Father

Our Father,

We pray as David prayed, "Search me, O God, and know my heart; test me and know my anxious thoughts" (Ps. 139:23 NIV). Reveal our sins so that we can repent. Father, we are truly sorry for each sin.

Please forgive us when we are impatient, critical and judgmental. Help us to clearly discern right and wrong, yet not judge others. Also, we do not want to be *righteous in our eyes* only in *your*s.

Forgive us for the sin of prayerlessness. We do not spend as much time with you as we should. We also know that this disappoints you. And, we miss the tremendous blessings of coming into your presence.

Father, we love you with all my hearts. Thank you for hearing our prayers, forgiving our sins and making a way for us to live in love and harmony with you and with each other.

Living Christianity Assignment

Bible Study—Read Psalms chapter 1–20. King David had a heart for God.

> The word of God is living and active. Sharper than any double-edged sword, it penetrates even to dividing soul and spirit, joints and marrow; it judges the thoughts and attitudes of the heart. Nothing in all creation is hidden from God's sight. Everything is uncovered and laid bare before the eyes of him to whom we must give account.
>
> Hebrews 4:12–13 (NIV)

Prayer—Ask God to reveal *your* sins. Repent and accept God's forgiveness.

> If our hearts do not condemn us, we have confidence before God and receive from him anything we ask, because we … do what pleases him.
>
> I John 3:21–22 (NIV)

Works—Fault-finding Quarantine: Do not criticize. Rather, look for each person's good qualities. Remember, our lives are an open book, our attitudes tell it all.

> Create in me a pure heart, O God, and renew a steadfast spirit within me.
>
> Psalms 51:10 (NIV)

VIII:
Forgive Others? "But, Lord!"

"As we also have forgiven our debtors"

> But if you do not forgive men their sins, *your Father* will not forgive *your* sins.
>
> Matthew 6:15 (NIV)

VIII: Forgive Others? "But, Lord!"

"As we also have forgiven our debtors"

- As We Also Have Forgiven Others? "But, Lord"
- "Give and it Shall be Given Unto You" Forgiveness
- The *Stone Throwing* Boomerang Principle
- Beware of the Root of Bitterness!
- We Must Also Forgive Ourselves
- Forgiveness Heals
- Good News, the Charges Have Been Dropped!
- Forgive Others "But, Lord…!"
- Living Christianity Assignment

VIII:
Forgive Others? "But, Lord!"

"As we also have forgiven our debtors"

Un-forgiveness has risen to epidemic proportions. Our courts are jammed and insurance companies are staggering under the weight of so many *charges against our fellowman*. Plaintiffs are *going for the jugular vein* over minor infringements that should simply merit, "It was an accident, or a misunderstanding." We all know that they are not only padding the cost of the actual damages, but they are also adding astronomical charges for such things as mental anguish and inconvenience. *Nothing* is forgiven.

The saddest part of these stories is yet to come. These plaintiffs have set God's law into motion: "Do not judge, and you will not be judged. Do not condemn, and you will not be condemned. Forgive, and you will be forgiven" (Lu. 6:37 NIV).

"Do not be deceived: God cannot be mocked. A man reaps what he sows" (Gal. 6:7 NIV).

Some day these plaintiffs may desperately need forgiveness and may not receive it, unless God's mercy intervenes. They may be sitting on *the other side* of the courtroom as the defendant. As Christians, we must settle things quickly before the matter goes to court. To know how to do this, we much pray for wisdom and divine guidance.

Christians are supposed to act differently. The Apostle Paul admonishes those in the church of Corinth because they are taking each other to court

> If any of you has a dispute with another, dare he take it before the ungodly for judgment instead of before the saints? Do you not know that the saints will judge the world? And if you are to judge the world, are you not competent to judge trivial cases? Do you not know that we will judge angels? How much more the things of this life!
>
> Therefore, if you have disputes about such matters, appoint as judges even men of little account in the church! I say this to shame you. Is it possible that there is nobody among you wise enough to judge a dispute between believers? But instead, one brother goes to law against another—and this in front of unbelievers!
>
> 1 Corinthians 6:1–6 (NIV)

Forgiveness is not an easy spiritual principle. Yet, it is something *everyone* has to deal with. You and I have had hurtful, even devastating conflicts that we may have buried in our past and have tried to erase from our memory.

Our Father has much to say about forgiveness. It is not an option; it is *imperative,* so that our hearts may be pure before God. The following imaginary dialogue correlates scriptures:

As We Also Have Forgiven Others? "But, Lord..."
An Imaginary Dialogue with God

"Lord, do you mean I am to ask you to forgive me *in just the same manner* as I have forgiven those who have offended me?"

"Yes, my child, for it is written, *'Pray, then, in this way... forgive us our debts, as we also have forgiven* our debtors'" (Matt. 6:9, 12 NIV).

VIII: Forgive Others? "But, Lord!"

"But, Lord, does that mean that I must forgive others *before* I come to you for my forgiveness?"

"It is written, 'When you stand praying, if you hold anything against anyone, *forgive* him, *so that your Father* in heaven may forgive you *your* sins'" (Mk. 11:25 NIV).

"But, Lord, *he* is the one who hurt *me. He* ought to apologize."

"My child, think about that. Apology and forgiveness is not the same."

"Oh, I see, even a heathen may happily receive an apology from the one who offends him. Whereas, forgiveness must come from the injured person."

"It is also written, 'If you are offering *your* gift at the altar and there remember that *your* brother *has something against you,* leave *your* gift there in front of the altar. *First* go and be reconciled to *your* brother [apologize for *your* guilt]; *then* come and offer *your* gift'" (Matt. 5:23, 24 NIV).

"All right, Lord, I will apologize for my part. But, I don't know if I can forgive; he hurt me so badly. Do you know what he did?"

"Yes, I know all about it, but I was hurt far more than any man when I died at Calvary. Yet, in my pain I prayed, *'Father, forgive them, for they do not know what they are doing'*" (Lu. 23:34 NIV).

"But, Lord, I feel more revengeful than forgiving."

"My child, it is written, 'Do not repay anyone evil for evil. Be careful to do what is right in the eyes of everybody. If it is possible, as far as it depends on you, live at peace with everyone. Do not take revenge, my friends, but leave room for God's wrath, for it is written: It is mine to avenge; I will repay, says the Lord. On the contrary: If *your* enemy is hungry, feed him; if he is thirsty, give him something to drink... overcome evil with good'" (Rom. 12:17–21 NIV).

"I also want you to forgive quickly: 'in *your* anger do not sin: Do not let the sun go down while you are still angry, and do not give the devil a foothold'" (Eph. 4:26, 27 NIV).

"That means, with un-forgiveness and bitterness, *your* spiritual strength will deteriorate and the devil will take advantage of you. It is written, 'See to it that no one misses the grace of God and that no bitter root grows up to cause trouble and defile many'" (Heb. 12:15 NIV).

"It is further written, 'Get rid of all bitterness, rage, and anger, brawling and slander, along with every form of *malice*'" (Eph. 4:31 NIV). "You felt revengeful? 'Study malice.'"

"Lord, I see *malice* means: ill will; spite; desire to injure another; criminal intention. A malicious person's spirit is evil, malignant and could be fatal."

"Yes, far more serious, malice is also characteristic of those who are not part of my kingdom, for it is written, 'They have become filled with every kind of wickedness, evil, greed, and depravity. They are full of envy, murder, strife, deceit, and *malice*... slanderers, God-haters...'" (Rom. 1:29–31 NIV).

"But, Lord, this is not the first time he has hurt me. How often do I have to forgive?"

"My child, I will tell you the same thing I told Peter when he asked that question, 'not seven times, but seventy-seven times'" (Matt. 18:22 NIV).

"That means, forgiveness must be a part of *your ongoing lifestyle:* 'Be kind and compassionate to one another, *forgiving* each other, just as in Christ God forgave you'" (Eph. 4:32 NIV).

"Few people realize the consequences of refusing to forgive. Consider this abbreviated parable of mercy in Matthew 18:23–35:"

A king wanted to settle accounts with his servants. A man who owed him ten thousand talents was brought to him. The king ordered that he and his wife and his children and all that he had be sold to repay the debt. The servant begged and the king canceled the debt.

But when that servant went out, he found one of his fellow servants who owed him [only] a hundred denarii. He began to choke him. "Pay back what you owe!"

VIII: Forgive Others? "But, Lord!"

The other servants told the king, so he called the wicked servant "I canceled all that debt of *your*s because you begged me to. Shouldn't you have had mercy on *your* fellow servant?"

In anger the king turned him over to the jailers to be tortured, until he should pay back all he owed [which would be impossible]. Jesus said, "This is how my heavenly Father will treat each of you unless you forgive *your* brother from *your* heart."

Rephrased: "That means, *You* will be the one who stubbornly retains the 'sin of un-forgiveness,' *in spite of the fact that Our Father wants to forgive you.*"

"It is written, 'As God's chosen people ... clothe *your*selves with compassion, kindness, humility, gentleness, and patience ... forgive whatever grievances you may have against one another. Forgive as the Lord forgave you'" (Col. 3:12, 13 NIV).

"But, Lord, *how* can I forgive?"

"My Child, I understand this is difficult, but you must '*forgive your brother from your heart*'" (Matt. 18:35 NIV). Try these steps:

Decide to forgive

Determine to forgive

Tell me that you forgive him/her

Be specific about the offense

Ask me to help you with a spirit of forgiveness

Tell him/her that you forgive

Ask me to bless him/her

"All right Lord, I'll forgive, but I don't want to have anything to do with him/her ever again."

"Then you haven't forgiven. But I tell you who hear me: Love *your* enemies, do good to those who hate you, bless those who curse you, pray for those ... who mistreat you" (Lu. 6:27 NIV).

"Lord, I will try, but I can't forget."

"My child, it is written, 'I can do everything through him who gives me strength'" (Phil. 4:13 NIV).

"Meditate upon his/her good qualities, and not the hurtful circumstances. Think about: 'whatever is true...noble...right...pure...lovely...admirable...think about such things. Whatever you have learned or received or heard from me, or seen in me put it into practice. And the God of peace will be with you'" (Phil. 4:8, 9 NIV).

"After you have forgiven and prayed for the one who has injured you, then Our Father will heal your mind and emotions because it is written, 'He heals the brokenhearted, and binds up their wounds'" (Ps. 147:3 NIV).

"After the healing process, you may remember the circumstances, but they won't be so important to you anymore. There will be no more pain in remembering. *Your* former enemy could become a friend. These are *Our Father*'s ways."

"Thank you, Lord. I forgive."

"Give and it shall be given unto you" Forgiveness

"Give and it shall be given unto you" can also apply to forgiveness *and* un-forgiveness. Think about the scripture:

> Give, and it will be given to you. A good measure, pressed down, shaken together and running over, will be poured into your lap. For with the measure you use, it will be measured to you.
>
> Luke 6:38 (NIV)

Clearly, that means *whatsoever* we give we shall receive. For example, if we give love, we will receive love. If we give to the poor, God will be sure that we receive a "good measure, pressed down, shaken together and running over" dumped right into our laps. If you need time, give of your time in the Lord's work and somehow he will make the clock tick slower. God rewards his generous loving children.

Also, that means when you forgive, at some point when you need it you will be forgiven. If you give "un-forgiveness" then you will receive un-forgiveness. *Greed* works along the same lines.

We set events in motion with the way we live. Love and forgive. This will please *Our Father*.

The Stone Throwing Boomerang Principle

> The teachers of the law and the Pharisees brought in a woman caught in adultery. They made her stand before the group and said to Jesus, "Teacher, this woman was caught in the act of adultery. In the Law Moses commanded us to stone [to death] such women. Now what do you say?"
>
> …Jesus bent down and started to write on the ground with his finger. When they kept on questioning him, he straightened up and said to them,
>
> "If any one of you is without sin, let him be the first to throw a stone at her."
>
> Again he stooped down and wrote on the ground. [He could have been listing the names of those who had committed the same sin even within their thoughts.]
>
> At this, those who heard began to go away one at a time, the older ones first, until only Jesus was left, with the woman still standing there. Jesus straightened up and asked her, "Woman, where are they? Has no one condemned you?" "No one, sir," she said. "Then neither do I condemn you," Jesus declared. "Go now and leave your life of sin" (Jn. 8:3–11 NIV).

Noteworthy is the fact that *women* were stoned to death, but where were the men who participated? Why were the men throwing the stones?

Now, Jesus puts the shoe on the other foot with a *thought sin* illustration: "…anyone [man] who looks at a woman lustfully has already committed adultery with her in his heart" (Matt. 5:28 NIV).

Which Christian, man or woman, can honestly say, "I have never had a lustful thought"? It is not rare to hear that even a really good Christian fanaticized, and then succumbed to the temptation.

Certainly, infidelity may leave a marriage partner feeling mortally wounded and rejected. However, if the injured partner would honestly review his/her own *sensual thought history*, it could go a long way in balancing out the wrong, in their own mind.

Even so, both marriage partners being found guilty won't make anyone righteous, or justify wrong. In the eyes of Jesus, the only difference between the two sinners is—*one committed* and *the other speculated*. Jesus called them both, "adulterers."

Furthermore, a vindictive spouse who persistently makes degrading remarks can ultimately destroy the husband/wife's self worth until their life isn't worth living.

The exception: If your marriage partner is a habitual adulterer, with no remorse and no intention to change. Then, you have two choices: You have biblical grounds for a divorce. Or, you can continue living together, and pray for a changed lifestyle.

If the injured partner recognizes his/her own frailty, they may want to drop the stones. This could make the guilty one deeply appreciative and more loving.

If the perpetrator changes and *really* wants forgiveness then, forgive and drop it. We don't have any wiggle room here because God said, "*Forgive!*" That means if you have a wounded martyr complex, drop that too. And, *never* use the adulterous situation for bribery or as a weapon.

Sex can be a weapon; withholding sex can be a fatal to a marriage. The Bible tells us that "Each man should have his own wife and each woman her own husband. The husband should fulfill his marital duty to his wife, and likewise the wife to her husband. The wife's body does not belong to her alone but also to her husband. In the same way, the husband's body does not belong to him alone but also to his wife." (1 Cor. 7:2–4 NIV). This does not give a license to physically abuse, just to love.

The Bible instructs us to love and respect: "Each one of you also must love his wife as he loves himself, and the wife must respect her husband" (Eph. 5:32–33 NIV).

It is possible to have a better marriage than ever. Both partners should devote their thoughts to remembering their love at the marriage altar. Rekindle. Then, when along the way, hurtful memories pop up sidetrack them by thinking about *your new love*.

The best plan is to move forward: Forgive, love and honor him/her *as though it never happened*. Then, God will be pleased, and you may have the best marriage ever, from this day forward.

Beware of the Root of Bitterness!

There are many reasons to harbor bitterness. It is impossible for imperfect people to live in a society together without having occasional misunderstandings that lead to confrontations, in varying degrees. When we are injured or offended, we must guard against bitterness taking root in our hearts. Not only will it obstruct our victorious Christian walk, it also has a deteriorating effect on our lives.

In *Seasons of Life* Charles Swindoll writes about a marine who allowed the root of bitterness to grow. Thirteen years after World War II, the marine spoke with vile language of the tortures he had endured in a Japanese prison. "He was still fighting a battle that should have ended… In a very real sense, he was still in prison."[83]

I, personally, remember facing a crucial decision with bitterness. On the highway between Gladewater and Kilgore, Texas, two drunks, who were racing their cars to the next beer hall, came over a hill side by side and crashed into my parent's car. My mother, age 43, was killed and my dad was seriously injured.

The phone rang in our apartment in Germany. I was at the stove cooking supper. The news was devastating. Our friends came and left. Since I was only twenty and had never experienced so great a tragedy, I guess I thought the world was supposed to stop. Later in the evening, I realized, "Supper still had to be cooked." Life goes on.

I had two options. I could be consumed with the desire to vent my grief face to face with them, which was impossible because I was in Germany and they were in intensive care. Or, I could turn the matter over to God and continue life the best I could since bitterness could not bring my mother back. I also realized that with my intense grief I could not handle any more emotions. So, I chose to drop *that* issue. Soon, I felt nothing but pity toward them.

Recently, I was rummaging through archived materials and found the newspaper article about the accident. For the first time, I saw the names of the men. I called "information" for their phone numbers. One could not be found. At the home of the second man, a woman answered the phone. I told her who I was and that I just wanted to talk with her husband. She said that her husband died a few weeks ago and his life had been miserable from the injuries. I said, "Oh, I am so sorry." I have never held bitterness. I just called to talk with him. Her grief touched my heart and I closed with, "May God bless you." Now, this was not sanctimonious on my part; it was the peace that comes only from God.

Root of Bitterness

```
        LOVE          KINDNESS
    JOY         ♡        GOODNESS
  PEACE                   GENTLENESS
   PATIENCE              FAITHFULNESS
      SELF-CONTROL
```

The fruit of the Spirit is love, joy, peace, patience, kindness, goodness, faithfulness, gentleness, self-control...
Gal. 5:22

A LIFE IN HARMONY WITH GOD

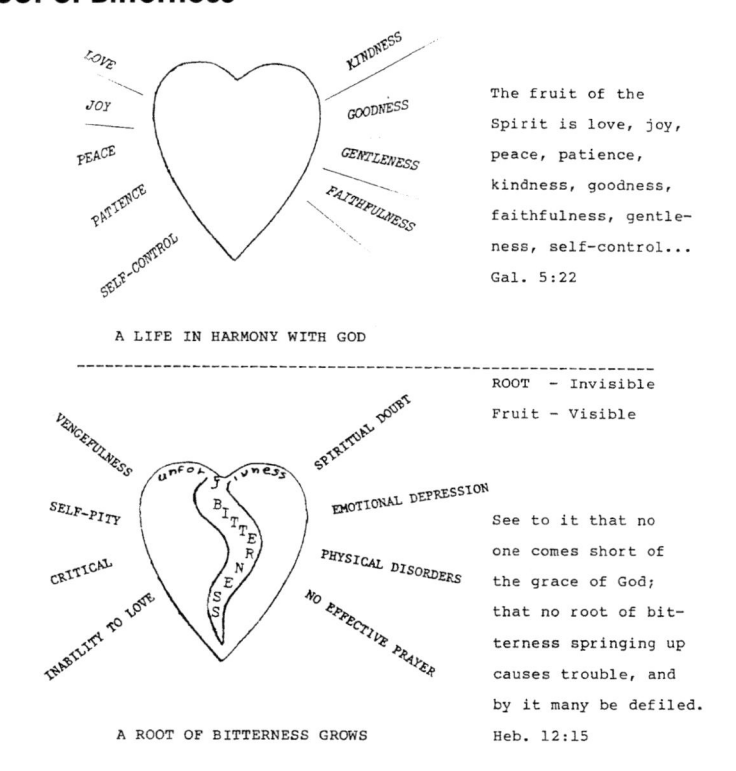

ROOT - Invisible
Fruit - Visible

```
  VENGEFULNESS      SPIRITUAL DOUBT
                unforgiveness
  SELF-PITY      BITTERNESS    EMOTIONAL DEPRESSION
  CRITICAL                    PHYSICAL DISORDERS
    INABILITY TO LOVE       NO EFFECTIVE PRAYER
```

A ROOT OF BITTERNESS GROWS

See to it that no one comes short of the grace of God; that no root of bitterness springing up causes trouble, and by it many be defiled.
Heb. 12:15

Years ago, I knew a woman who held bitterness against a man in our church. Although she knew that God said it was imperative to forgive, she nurtured her vindictive spirit. I did not inquire about the reason. She even tried to get her close friends to take up her cause. Later, cancer struck her gall bladder and life slowly dwindled. Our pastor visited with her shortly before she died. Knowing about her grudge, he asked if she wanted to confess any unforgiveness. She said, "No."

A distant woman who did not know this, called a friend of mine *who, coincidentally, was studying the physical effects of spiritual attitudes.* The woman said, "Do you remember the pretty gray-haired woman who attended our church? I dreamed about her last night. Her face expressed pain as she tried to tell me something. Finally, she said, 'It's so bitter. The taste in my mouth is so bitter.' What do you think this means?"

My friend, knowing the woman in the dream well, believes the Lord used this distant person to bring out an illustration on how *bitterness affects the spirit.*

Far worse, inflamed hatred can boil over and murder. I saw on CNN World News a minister being interviewed at the scene of the mass murders at Columbine High School, Littleton, Colorado. He said that while he was waited through the long hours while the swat teams were searching the school, he was analyzing two atrocities that were vying for world headline news.

The other carnage was happening in Yugoslavia. President Slobodan Milosevic was perpetrating a massive ethnic cleansing campaign against the citizens of Kosova. The Serb army burned villages, killed thousands, and drove homeless multitudes across borders. The minister concluded, after his analysis, that *hate* was the common factor that filled the hearts of those who committed both, the carnage in Columbine and in Yugoslavia.

We Must Also Forgive *Ourselves*

How often do we flinch with a remembrance of something we did, or said, that has come back to haunt us? It may be easier to forgive others than it is to forgive ourselves. How often do we beat ourselves over the back with a psychological whip? I have this problem even though I can't think of anyone whom I need to forgive, or ask for forgiveness.

Since Jesus has already covered every dumb thing you and I have ever said or done, we too, need to wipe the slate clean.

With God's system of forgiveness, we need not drag the bad encounters of our yesterdays through our tomorrow. We must be in harmony with *our Father* as we live in peace with each other. This puts us in the spiritual realm where there is power in prayer.

VIII: Forgive Others? "But, Lord!"

Forgiveness Heals

A woman who had received her hearing told me that she had to forgive others before God healed her physically. She said,

> I believe that Jesus paid for my healing when he died, according to Isaiah 53:4, 5. And, resentment kept me from receiving when others prayed for me. First, I was bitter toward my grandfather for molesting me when I was a child.
>
> Second, my dad was an alcoholic and had brutally punished me. Third, I resented my mother for leaving the room and turning up the radio when my dad beat me. I lived with fear and pain.
>
> I heard a lesson on forgiveness. The teacher said, "You must forgive, *even if the ones who offended you are dead.* This is the only way bitterness can be purged."
>
> Finally, with God's help, I forgave them and was freed from the pain of those memories. Soon after that, the Lord also restored my hearing.

Years after her liberation from a German concentration camp, Corrie ten Boon faced the guard who had mercilessly forced her and other women to stand naked in freezing weather, causing her sister's death. The guard's outstretched hand asked for her forgiveness. Facing that stark moment of decision, she testified:

> "Jesus, help me!" I prayed silently. "I can lift my hand. I can do that much. You supply the feeling." And so woodenly, mechanically, I thrust my hand into the one stretched out to me. And as I did, an incredible thing took place. The current started in my shoulder, raced down my arm, sprang into our joined hands. And then this healing warmth seemed to flood my whole being..."I forgive you, brother!" I cried. "With all my heart!"[84]

In her home in Holland, Corrie wrote about her observations of victims of Nazi brutality: "Those who were able to forgive their former enemies were also able to return to the outside world and rebuild their lives, no matter what the physical scars. Those who nursed their bitterness remained invalids."[85]

Recently, Dr. Ernie Gottmann, a close friend who was in General Patton's army when they liberated the German death camps said, "The stench permeated the air from miles away. When we entered the barracks, the prisoners looked like leather stretched over bones and the only sign of life was eyes that just stared." Those, and many other, atrocities were painfully embedded in his memory.

After realizing that forgiveness was not an option. He finally dealt with his bitterness. And, with great relief was set free.

Sometimes forgiveness must reach over broader and deeper roots of bitterness. While in Tango, the Ivory Coast, and Cameroon, part of what was known as the Slave Coast, "Pope John Paul II ... asked modern Africans to forgive the Christians who for four hundred years uprooted millions of Africans ... and took them into slavery in Europe and America."[86] Recently, with world news coverage, he also asked forgiveness for not defending the Jews against Hitler.

More recently, how can we forgive the terrorists for killing more than three thousand innocent people when they destroyed the World Trade Center Twin Towers in New York? That is only one of their major attacks on America. More lives were lost in New York than in Pearl Harbor. The radical Muslims are still plotting our *total* annihilation. Only God can tell us what to do.

In this era of rampant divorce and broken homes there are multitudes of justified reasons for bitterness between husbands, wives, children, grandparents. Through a divorce in the family, I developed the philosophy "Let the dust settle, and keep on loving." I knew that love would eventually win. I'm so glad that I did because eleven years later, our precious granddaughter, who was now a young lady, came down the escalator into the airport lobby, and we showered her with yellow roses and balloons. For the entire family, there was only love. That is God's way. Such joy!

VIII: Forgive Others? "But, Lord!"

Good News: Charges Have Been Dropped!

Through my years as a Bible teacher, I have been in court to give spiritual support to individuals who were in desperate trouble. Let's review how Christ drops our charges through a scenario of forgiveness. Let's envision a young man who faced negligent manslaughter charges: Fear marked his face as he stood before the judge. White knuckles showed from his clenched fists. For months he had wavered between hope and despair. Braced for the worst, he waited for the verdict. The judge rose and said, "The charges have been dropped!" Then he pounded the gavel with finality.

"The charges have been dropped!" resounded in the young man's mind. He struggled to grasp the significance. This was a new thought. "What does it mean? Am I free? Can I go?" Jubilantly, he realized, "Yes that *is* what it means. I am free. There are no charges against me!"

The legal process stayed in motion while the plaintiff enforced the charges. However, when the charges were dropped, the defendant was free. Though he could have been guilty no one remained to accuse him. Similarly, as Jesus said to the adulteress, "Woman, where are they [*your* accusers]? Has no one condemned you?... neither do I condemn you... Go now and leave *your* life of sin" (Jn. 8:10, 11 NIV).

You and I stood before God with "sealed indictments" against us. They contained accurate records of every sin, and each sin carried a death penalty: *"The wages of sin is death"* (Rom. 6:23 NIV). Without hope and means to make restitution for our sins, Jesus mercifully assumed our charges. And with them, He received the most gruesome death penalty possible—scourging and crucifixion.

Jesus prayed when He hung on the cross, *"Father, forgive them, for they do not know what they are doing"* (Lu. 23:34 NIV). You and I helped to drive the nails into His hands and feet with our sins. The soldiers at the foot of the cross stood in awe as the earth quaked and the sky turned dark. With awakened faith, they said, *"Surely, he was the Son of God!"* (Matt. 27:54 NIV). With *our* awakened faith, you and I also received forgiveness with our records marked, "Paid in Full!" In essence... atonement was made... the charges were dropped... and *we are free*!

Jesus also paid for the sins of those *who have injured us*. Therefore, we must not bind them to the charges. Similarly, an innocent man asked me to find out if another person, who thought he was guilty, would give him a chance to explain what really happened. It was imperative for him to know so the issue could be settled in his mind. He was psychologically bound to the circumstances until they could resolve the situation. Sad to say, she ignored the plea. Too often, we curl up with our wounds, justifiable or not, and do not realize the *guilty*, or the one presumed guilty one, is suffering too. Forgiveness will unlock the chain that binds the two together.

Our forgiveness could set up a chain reaction. A lifestyle of forgiving others may have a more profound effect than we realize. It could influence history. Lorans Cunningham, Founder and Director of Youth with a Mission, writes:

> The truth of the power of forgiveness was made clear to me last year when I was a guest of the prime minister of Tonga and received an audience with the king. The king is not a man who expresses a close relationship with God, but as I spoke with him, he showed me how a non-Christian had taught him to respect the power of forgiveness. He [the king] explained he had read a book by Chiang Kai-shek which told about an incident in which he [Chiang Kai-shek] talked with a Russian advisor...
>
> He asked the advisor, "Why is it you hate Christianity so much?" The advisor replied, "We cannot take over without a revolution, and a revolution is impossible with love; and love, of course, is forgiveness. With the Christian way of loving and forgiving, there can't be all this bloodshed and revolution and take over for a godless cause."[87]

We will have fewer conflicts with others when we try to understand them and have compassion when they err. Remember,

VIII: Forgive Others? "But, Lord!"

All temperaments are not the same, nor are all the circumstances which surround people the same in every case. Make allowance for temper, training, nationality, education [or lack of it], and circumstances. Under the right influences we have seen weak people become strong, sour people become sweet, and ill-tempered people become sane and reasonable.

Remember, too, that many men are better than they appear. Richard Baxter, after the closest contact with the severest Puritans of the Commonwealth, and the most licentious cavaliers of the Restoration, writes in his old age: "I see that good men are not so good as I once thought they were, and ... few men are as bad as their enemies imagine."[88]

"But one thing I do: forgetting what is behind and reaching forward to what is ahead, I pursue as my goal the prize promised by God's heavenly call in Christ Jesus." (Phil. 3:13, 14 NIV).

Sample Prayer

Forgive Others? "But, Lord!"

Our Father,

Thank you for forgiving me. Now, I want to forgive everyone who has ever hurt me. Go with me through my memories and reveal situations where I harbor bitterness. [meditate]

Father, this situation with _____ [name] comes to my mind.

I don't see how I can forgive him/her for _____ [name]. However, I am determined to drop these charges and loose us both from these circumstances. Please help me.

Thank you for forgiving me, and for forgiving him/her. Please bless this special person in every way.

Thank you for hearing my prayer and for your reassuring answers.

VIII: Forgive Others? "But, Lord!"

Living Christianity Assignment

Bible Study—Read Philemon and learn about how Paul asked the master of a run-awayslave to forgive the slave.

> Be kind and compassionate to one another, forgiving each other, just as in Christ God forgave you.
> Ephesians 4:32 (NIV)

Prayer—Ask God to reveal any bitterness againts others who have harmed you. Determine to forgive and ask God to help mend these relationships.

> Pray for those who persecute you.
> Matthew 5:44 (NIV)

Works—Make restitution for your part in broken relationships. Write letters, make payments, phone or visit. If they do not respond, leave the results to the Lord.

> But I tell you who hear me, love your enemies, do good to those who hate you.
> Luke 6:27 (NIV)

IX:
Tempted, Tested, Triumphant

"And lead us not into temptation"

> No temptation has seized you except what is common to man. And God is faithful; he will not let you be tempted beyond what you can bear. But when you are tempted, he will also provide a way out so that you can stand up under it.
>
> 1 Corinthians 10:13 (NIV)

IX:
Tempted, Tested, Triumphant

"And lead us not into temptation"

- We Live In a Mine Field of Temptation
- Good and Evil Often Look the Same
- Evil Lurks in the Paths of Temptation

  - Lust of the Flesh Physical
  - Lust of the Eye Material
  - Pride of Life Spiritual

- Beware, Lest We Become the Stumbling Block!
- We Have Power to Escape
- God Will Help Us through Our Temptations
- Steps to Power over Temptation
- Temptations can be Terrifying
- Sample Prayer: Tempted, Tested and Triumphant
- Living Christianity Assignment

IX:
Tempted, Tested, Triumphant
"And Lead us not into Temptation"

Why would Jesus instruct us to pray, "Lead us not into temptation" when it is contrary to God's nature to tempt anyone?" This question is asked in many Bible study groups because Scripture informs us that, "When tempted, no one should say, 'God is tempting me.' For God cannot be tempted by evil, nor does he tempt anyone" (Jas. 1:13 NIV).

We Live in a Mine Field of Temptation

In response to that question, obviously God knows that temptations surround us daily and Jesus has always said, "Follow Me." We might compare this with a demolition expert saying, "Follow me" through a mine field. Jesus knew that *"Lead us not into temptation"* would be prayed from the human viewpoint; from sheep that need to recognize their weakness and realize they are prone to wander. We might pray, "Lead us away from areas where temptation is strong because we do not trust ourselves to withstand them."

This prayer makes us more aware of temptations and our need for our Shepherd who will lead us through the narrow paths of righteousness. "The LORD himself *goes before you* and will be with you; he will never leave you nor forsake you. Do not be afraid..." (Deut.31:8 NIV).

Good and Evil Often Look the Same

We need a flashing red warning light, *"TEMPTATION AHEAD!"* because distinguishing between good and evil is not always easy. Since temptation is *anything* that diverts our attention from living in God's will, we may be tempted to do so many good things like numerous church activities that we disregard study of God's Word and communion with Him. Our zeal for charitable causes may result in neglect of our families. We may also be tempted to do right things with wrong motives. Some people have donated vast sums of money to charities with the sole motive to immortalize their name.

Situation Ethics is a popular philosophy that says right and wrong may fluctuate according to the situation. "My wife doesn't understand me," commonly *justifies* adultery. There are individuals who have murdered with no remorse. Satan capitalizes on this philosophy and relegates truth into *shades of gray.* "Woe to those who call evil good and good evil." (Isa.5:20 NIV).

Satan also appeals in areas that seem good, and his cohorts *"masquerade as servants of righteousness"* (2 Cor.11:15 NIV). He used this approach with Eve in the Garden and with Jesus in the wilderness. After all, what harm is there in eating an apple, or turning stones into bread, especially if one hasn't eaten for forty days?

The truth is temptation is not bad. Resisting is good; yielding is sin. Enticement can serve a useful purpose as we exercise our will. Resisting can strengthen us to say "No" when the next, perhaps more difficult, temptation confronts us. Most importantly, resisting honors God when He sees us holding firm to his laws of righteousness. Jesus firmly said, "No."

Eve said, "Yes." Like Eve, after we sin we also are tempted to shift the blame. Adam started the whole thing when he said, "Eve made me do it." Then, we know that Eve passed the blamed on to the serpent. In reality, *"Each one is tempted when, by his own evil desire, he is dragged away and enticed"* (Jas.1:14 NIV).

IX: Tempted, Tested, Triumphant

We could be on a slippery slope if we don't *know* God's word. When Jesus quoted God's word, Satan cast doubt, "Now, hath God said?" He can sound convincing, if we don't know what God *really* said. When we can't stand on the written solid ground, we will tilt to our own tainted judgment. "He [Satan] gains his point, if he can but bring men from dependency upon God, and fill them with an opinion of their self-sufficiency."[89]

Evil Lurks in the Paths of Temptation

Let's scout the mine field: Temptations make three basic promises that appeal to our physical, material and spiritual desires. "Everything in the world the cravings of sinful man, the (1) lust of his eyes and the (2) boasting of what he has (3) and does, comes not from the Father but from the world" (1 Jn.2:16 NIV).

1. You will do something that feels good—Lust of the flesh
2. You will have something that you see—Lust of the eye
3. It will make you feel important—Pride of life

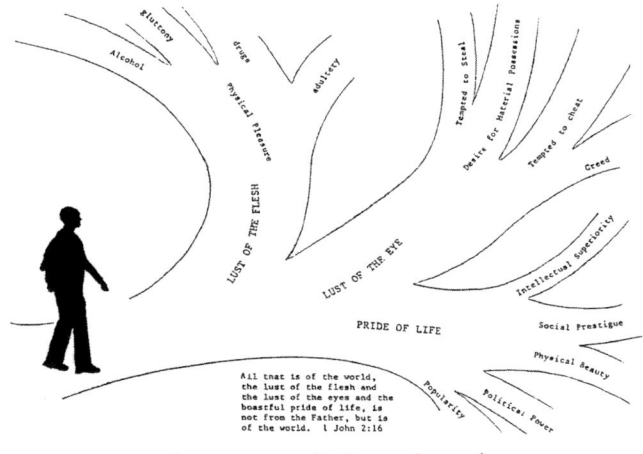

(see page 378 for larger image)

Satan used his basic three when he tempted Eve and Jesus. "When the woman saw that the tree was (1) good for food ... (2) pleasing to the eye, and ... (3) desirable for gaining wisdom, she took some and ate it" (Gen.3:6 NIV).

Satan's goal was to entice Jesus to heed him: to prove pridefully that He was God's son, and to act out of His own sufficiency rather than depend on God. Jesus refused to yield; Satan could not manipulate Him. We read,

> Then Jesus was led by the Spirit into the desert to be tempted by the devil. After fasting forty days and forty nights, he was hungry [his weakest moment]. The tempter came to him and said, "*If* you are the Son of God [prove it], tell these stones to become bread" [lust of flesh—physical].
>
> Jesus answered, "It is written: 'Man does not live on bread alone, but on every word that comes from the mouth of God.'"
>
> Then the devil took him to the holy city and had him stand on the highest point of the temple. "*If* you are the Son of God," he said, "throw yourself down. For it is written: 'He will command his angels concerning you, and they will lift you up in their hands, so that you will not strike *your* foot against a stone' [pride of life spiritual]"

Satan quoted scripture too. Jesus answered him, "It is also written: 'Do not put the Lord *your* God to the test.'"

> Again, the devil took him to a very high mountain and showed him all the kingdoms of the world and their splendor. "All this I will give you," [lust of the eye material] he said, "if you will bow down and worship me."
>
> Jesus said to him, "Away from me, Satan! For it is written: 'Worship the Lord your God, and serve him only.'"
>
> Matthew 4:1–10 (NIV)

Satan offered Jesus the easy way out; He could have the world without going to Calvary. Although in heeding, Satan would have become Jesus' master. Instead, Jesus focused on His mission, and redeemed everyone who *had* succumbed to Satan's temptations.

This was a phenomenal testing of wills. Satan was battling for ultimate power; Jesus was battling for the souls of all mankind. Whoever won would be the master.

Satan's tactics are the same today. He combats with us to be our master. Do we listen? Let's evaluate our most vulnerable areas.

Lust of the Flesh Physical

The popular philosophy, "If it feels good, do it!" appeals to the lust of the flesh. Scripture identifies these lusts, as they are listed in the characteristics of man's sinful nature:

> Sexual immorality, theft, impurity and debauchery; idolatry and witchcraft; hatred, discord, jealousy, fits of rage, selfish ambition, dissensions, factions and envy; drunkenness, orgies, and the like. I warn you, as I did before, that those who live like this will not inherit the kingdom of God.
> Galatians 5:19–21 (NIV)

Listed first, "sexual immorality" is probably the strongest of the fleshly lusts. Throughout the Bible so many people committed adultery that the terminology is repeatedly used in Scripture to symbolize alienation of affection from God to *other things* idols. "I gave faithless Israel [Northern Kingdom] her certificate of divorce and sent her away because of all her adulteries. Yet, I saw that her unfaithful sister Judah [Southern Kingdom] had no fear; she also went out and committed adultery" (Jer. 3:8 NIV).

The list goes on...

It is easy to let "Idolatry and witchcraft" zip right past us because we don't have a little golden calf sitting on our mantles, or a séance in our schedule books. The truth is, *whatever* we love the most, above God, is an idol. Our checkbooks reveal a lot about our priorities.

Following those, are probably the most impetuous temptations that relate to emotional conflicts with others: "hatred, discord, jealousy, fits of rage, selfish ambition, dissensions, factions and envy." Revenge retaliates.

The "uncontrolled tongue" is probably the most common and most frequent of the temptations. We may often be tempted to spout off, or have the last word in a discussion, which could become a heated debate that accelerates into World War III.

This was happening to young lady. Later, I said, "Honey, please remember that many times the best thing to let the storm settle so you can choose a more receptive time to express *your* thoughts. That does not necessarily mean you forfeit standing up for what you believe. Remember too, the other person will feel less threatened when you keep the volume down. Now, don't let this or any other such episode steal *your* joy and cause you to get stuck in the midst of a bygone situation. Ask God to give you wisdom to know how to handle things like this in the future."

When I was young, my daddy had a word of wisdom. He said, "The best way to stop an argument is to eliminate *your* half." I found that it worked, when I tried it.

"Wisdom is the ability to take God's word and apply it to every circumstance of life."

Lust of the Eyes Material

The second category of temptation is the *lust of the eyes*. We want something that we see.

> Tucked in tissues inside an envelope scanned with the rest of the president's [a CEO's] mail were two silver forks, a knife and a teaspoon, all engraved "The White House." A corporate guest pocketed the silverware at a power lunch in the

White House and foolishly bragged...His boss dressed him down and...mailed back the booty.[90]

The desire for riches has always been a problem. Paul writes, "People who want to get rich fall into...many foolish and harmful desires that plunge men into ruin and destruction. For *the love of money* is a root of all kinds of evil. Some people, eager for money, have wandered from the faith and pierced themselves with many grieves" (1 Tim. 6:9, 10 NIV).

Some people have worked compulsively for wealth, resulting in family neglect and divorces. Families have been divided when The Will was read. Men have notoriously fought over riches.

> You want something but don't get it. You kill and covet, but you cannot have what you want. You quarrel and fight. You do not have, because you do not ask God. When you ask, *you do not receive, because you ask with wrong motives*, that you may spend what you get on *your* pleasures.
>
> James 4:2, 3 (NIV)

It is easy to become so enthralled with making money that there is no time for God. Scripture warns, "Again I tell you, it is easier for a camel to go through the eye of a needle than for a rich man to enter the kingdom of God" (Matt. 19:24 NIV). *Obsession* with making money, with disregard for God, could also happen to the poor. Jesus said, "Watch out! Be on your guard against all kinds of greed; a man's life does not consist in the abundance of his possessions" (Lu. 12:15 NIV).

Pride of Life—Spiritual

God said, "I hate arrogance" (Prov. 8:13 NIV). Also, "Pride goes before destruction, a haughty spirit before a fall." (Prov.16:18 NIV).

While I was attending the Billy Graham Assn. Decision Magazine School of Christian Writing in Minneapolis, I met a former occult priest. After discussing Christianity vs. the Occult,

Fletcher Edwards gave me written permission to quote: "The occultist develops self, glorifies self with self-realization. The Christian sets self aside, glorifies God and assumes the Jesus nature."[91] Jesus humbled himself even unto death. Self-esteem characterizes Satan: "The devil is for nothing that is humbling."[92]

Self-esteem seeks power, authority, social prestige, financial prosperity, physical beauty, intellectual superiority, and has spiritual pride. Each of these temptations disregard humility, without which, there is no power in prayer.

Temptation for Power

During lunch, in jest I said to Bob, "I am writing my chapter on '*Lead us not into temptation.*' Tell me about *your* temptations, I don't want to write about mine." He instantly launched into a profound view:

> I believe the greatest temptation for *all* men is for power to dominate others. I cannot think of any sin that has brought more hell to this earth than the desire for power. Nations have gone to war over the desire for power. Kings, presidents, pharaohs, and czars built their empires by conquering. Alexander the Great wept because he thought there were no more worlds to conquer. Barbaric Hitler cremated over eight million people for more power. And, amazingly, I have never heard a sermon preached about the temptation for power.

Bob's response surprised me. I had never thought of either of us desiring power. Yet, I could see he was embarking on something big.

> Power represents prestige. At its ultimate level, it is man's search for immortality. Watch important leaders. They have one eye on what history books will say about them. Look at monuments men have built for themselves.
> Everybody, except those who have given up on life, plays the power game at some level. The struggle for independence,

then dominance, begins in the playpen as one toddler tries to maintain control of the toys and the other toddler. The teenager's car has to roar louder and zoom faster than any of his peers' autos. I have seen men accept higher level jobs with less pay to increase their status and power, while satisfying the all-important ego.

I caught the trend of Bob's thought. We agreed that the desire for power is the most obvious in a person who *must* control other people's lives, like a domineering mother, wife, or husband. They convey, "*I know best!*"

Many politicians proclaim this message as they get caught up in the melee for power. We all know that many conduct vicious and slanderous campaigns, lashing at their opponent's weaknesses and slanting their successes.

Chuck Colson, of Richard Nixon's Watergate men, said that the seduction of power is subtle, and that fine, well-meaning Christians fall under its weight daily. "Power corrupted me once and I know how easily I could be corrupted again. So I constantly relinquish it."[93] Barry Goldwater summarized the results of power in his well-known statement, "Power corrupts and total power corrupts totally."[94]

The lowest level of the power play is tragic. Some men who are frustrated from lack of power resort to wife-beating, rape, and child abuse to satisfy their male superiority. This all seems so obvious; yet, Colson said, "The seduction of power is subtle." It, like all temptations, gradually gains strength with each conquest, while concealing its monstrous consequences.

Desire for Authority

An insidious temptation that sounds tame is gossip. It is a rare person who never says *anything* negative about anyone. This backyard-fence sin makes the gossiper feel authoritative when *they know something the other person doesn't know* and they want him to know that they know.

An embellishment of the facts with vague innuendoes makes the story more dramatic and the tellers more *informed*. Accurate facts are not always relevant. The more lurid the story, the more innocent the tellers become, because it is something *they would never do*.

Combine the *desire for authority* with the *uncontrollable tongue*, and gossip can become a lethal weapon. "No man can tame the tongue. It is ... full of deadly poison" (Jas. 3:8 NIV).

There are many levels of authority that we strive to attain, and are reluctant to relinquish. Those who have never acquired status are caught in the struggle for it. Those who have given up in the struggle resorted to apathy.

What happens spiritually to those who surge forth to dominate? As these individuals climb over less ferocious climbers, power refuels their lust for power. Ultimately, their voices echo the one that resounded in the heavens eons ago as Lucifer declared, "I will raise my throne above the stars of God" (Isa. 14:13 NIV). For these, the sublime goal, humility, is always beyond their reach.

Our Father will transform and lead us to heights of which we never dreamed, not by climbing over others, but by carrying them with us.

Mother Teresa refused a banquet in her honor when she won the Nobel Peace Prize. Rather, she asked for the money that would have been spent, and fed a multitude of hungry people in Calcutta. For her life of humility lifting up her fellowman, she was given a state funeral in India reserved for only the highest dignitaries.

Elevation of Self in Social Prestige

The desire for social elevation starts at an early age. Little children like to show-off. The plea, "But Mom, *everybody* is doing it!" is heard in every teenager's home. Probably, many families sacrifice to belong to a prestigious country club. Social conscious young women are eager to join Junior Leagues. These organizations are good. I was a member of both. The question we must ask, regarding *any* organization, sport or business endeavor, "Do I live and breathe for them, to the exclusion of serving God?" It is likely many do and many don't.

Jesus, noticing how dinner guests were selecting places of honor, said,

> Do not take the place of honor, for a person more distinguished than you may have been invited. If so, the host ... will ... say to you, "Give this man your seat." Then, humiliated, you will have to take the least important place. [Rather], take the lowest place, so that when your host comes, he will say to you, "Friend, move up to a better place." Then you will be honored ... For everyone who exalts himself will be humbled, and he who humbles himself will be exalted.
>
> Luke 14:7–11 (NIV)

The status conscious mother of two of Jesus' disciples came to Him with a request: "Grant that one of these two sons of mine may sit at your right and the other at your left in your kingdom" (Matt. 20:21 NIV). Jesus denied her request and gave the formula for greatness:"... whoever wants to become great among you must be your servant, and whoever wants to be first must be your slave just as the Son of Man did not come to be served, but to serve, and to give his life as a ransom for many" (Matt.20:26,27 NIV).

Jesus taught the spirit of the servant nature when he washed his disciples feet. My grandmother followed his example. When I was a girl, I liked to go with her to her Primitive Baptist Church. The foot washing ceremony fascinated me. She lived the life of loving and serving her large family.

Elevation of self in Financial Prosperity

Some men boast of their financial ratings. Wall Street stays in a frenzy over buying and selling for profit. I heard of a tycoon who was ostracized from his smug social circle because he had to vacate his *six* million dollar mansion into a paltry *three* million dollar bungalow.

Elevation of Self in Physical Beauty

Spas and fashion shops thrive on people's vanity. Certainly, we want to look good, but God wants us to primarily be known for our good character and works, rather than for our glamour or muscles. (1 Tim.2:9 NIV). In Humility the Beauty of Holiness, Andrew Murray writes:

> It is when the truth of an indwelling Christ takes the place it claims in the experience of believers, that the Church will put on her beautiful garments, and humility be seen in her teachers and members as the beauty of holiness.[95]

Elevation of Self in Intellectual Superiority

The desire for intellectual superiority has spurred some individuals to the top in the academic world. We can assume that not every scholar is motivated purely by scientific curiosity or a desire to serve his fellowman. Although education is essential, and the attainment of high goals is very good, *preoccupation* with academics can become a god, and intellectual pride can become a besetting sin.

Titles arouse pride, such as General, Ambassador, Captain, or Doctor. I saw on television an example of a senator who reached a high goal, seemingly with status in mind. After Brigadier General Michael Walsh graciously said, "Yes, ma'am," and "No, ma'am," when answering questions, the senator replied "Could you say 'senator' instead of 'ma'am?'... I worked so hard to get that title. I'd appreciate it."

To put *attainment* in perspective, *Our Father* wants us to grow as Jesus grew in *"wisdom and stature, and in favor with God and men"* (Luke 2:52 NIV). He requires us to develop our talents, and puts no premium on slothfulness. He wants us to have pride in accomplishments, without being absorbed in vanity.

After God surveyed His creation, He saw that *"it was very good"* (Gen. 1:31 NIV). He also wants us to survey our accomplishments to see if we have done our best. Like earthly parents, God wants us, His children, to excel in every way. Eventually and without arrogance, He even plans for us to reign with Him" (2 Tim. 2:12; Rev. 20:6 NIV).

Elevation of Self in Spiritual Pride

Jesus recognized spiritual pride as a weaknesses when He said, "Fast in secret…give to the needy in secret…do not pray for the sake of being heard by others…" (Matt.6:18 NIV). He noticed the Scribes and Pharisees did all of these things wrong. "They make their phylacteries wide and the tassels on their garments long; they love the…most important seats in the synagogues; they love to be greeted…to have men call them 'Rabbi'" (Matt. 23:5–8 NIV). They even condemned Jesus for challenging their religious status.

That statement throws us into a self-righteous mode. *We* would *never* act like that! Recently, I heard through the grapevine that someone said that I was self-righteous. I immediately turned the other cheek and pronounced, "*She* is judgmental!" I simmered for a while in righteous indignation. Then, I thought, "Is God trying to get my attention since I am working on this chapter about temptation?" I prayed, "Show me, Lord." But first, I reminded Him about my exhausting efforts in the recent seminar *and* its glorious success. Then, I reeled out my list of other churchy accomplishments.

After all of that, the Lord reminded me of Job, the ancient biblical patriarch, and I squirmed. My *presumed* little evasive sin seemed inconsequential until I remembered what Job went through for doing the same thing.

Job was the most prominent and respected man in the Middle East at that time. His goodness was faultless. Although his spiritual pride left the door wide open for Satan to destroy everything he had, except his last breath. In the midst of agony, Job proudly declared, "I will not deny my integrity, never let go of it; my conscience will not reproach me as long as I live" (Job 27:6 NIV).

He also said, "I put on righteousness as my clothing...I was eyes to the blind and feet to the lame. I was father to the needy..." (Job 29:14–16 NIV). He even went so far as to challenge God to find fault. "Oh, that I had someone to hear me! I sign now my defense—let the Almighty answer me...I would give him an account of my every step; like a prince I would approach him."

Then, God set Job's record straight: "Brace *your*self like a man; I will question you, and you shall answer me...Can you bring forth the constellations in their season? Who endowed the heart with wisdom or gave understanding to the mind? Look at the behemoth, which I made along with you...Can you pull in the leviathan with a fishhook?...Who then is able to stand against Me?"...On and on until Job repented,

> Surely I spoke of things I did not understand, things too wonderful for me to know. My ears had heard of you but now my eyes have seen you. Therefore, I despise myself and repent in dust and ashes...
>
> Job 38, 40, 41 (NIV)

Now, with Job's humble heart, "the Lord made him more prosperous, and gave him twice as much as he had before...he died old and full of years" (Job 42: 10, 16 NIV).

Have we, like Job, ever been proud of being humble?

Beware, Lest We Become the Stumbling Block!

Others will find courage from our strengths and flounder from our weaknesses. Jesus said, "Things that cause people to sin are bound to come, but woe to that person through whom they come. It would be better for him to be thrown into the sea...than for him to cause one of these little ones to sin" (Lu.17:1, 2 NIV).

Peter was a stumbling block when Jesus needed encouragement. After Jesus told His disciples about His impending death, Peter rebuked Him, saying, "Never, Lord "This shall never happen to you"

(Matt.16:22 NIV)!" Jesus said to Peter, "Get behind me, Satan! You are a stumbling block to me; you do not have in mind the things of God, but the things of men" (Matt.16:23 NIV).

Of course, Peter said this out of love and did not realize he was presenting a temptation to weaken Jesus' resolve to follow through on His commitment to die for a divine purpose.

On the other hand, people tend to entice others to do whatever it is they are doing wrong, because it helps to justify their actions in their own minds. Scripture warns, "My son, if sinners entice you, do not give in to them" (Prov.1:10 NIV). We must not be their stumbling block!

I heard a person vehemently disclaim responsibility for *any* influence on other people. He declares, "I'll live my life and it's their responsibility to live theirs." This reminds me of the adage, "No man is an island unto himself."

People observe us. For example, if a non-Christian goes to a bar, gets drunk, and uses foul language, no one thinks anything about it. But if a person who is thought to be Christian does the same thing, he could confuse others who need to see a righteous example. As a result, the one who witnesses their actions could become disillusioned with Christianity. God *will* hold each of us accountable for our influence.

We Have Power to Escape

We can overcome temptation. Jesus is our high priest and our strength. We have His promises and His Presence:

> We do not have a high priest, who is unable to sympathize with our weaknesses, but we have one *who has been tempted in every way, just as we* are yet was without sin. Let us then approach the throne of grace with confidence, so that we may receive mercy and find grace to help us in our time of need.
>
> Hebrews 4:15, 16 (NIV)

Jesus combated life as an ordinary man and prevailed over all temptations. He accepted the vulnerable position of a newborn baby. Then, he grew up in a family with brothers and sisters.

To confirm Jesus earthly family, let's go deeper: "When the Sabbath came, he [Jesus] began to teach in the synagogue, and many who heard him were amazed:

> "Where did this man get these things, and what is this wisdom given to Him, and such miracles as these performed by His hands? Is not this the carpenter, the son of Mary, and brother of James and Joses and Judas and Simon? Are not His sisters here with us?" And they took offense at Him. Jesus said to them, "A prophet is not without honor except in his hometown and among his own relatives and in his own household."
>
> Mark 6:2–4 (NASB)

For Jesus to have been *tempted in every way, just as we*, it would have been necessary for him to have lived in a typical family setting where priorities, personalities, and problems have to be dealt with daily. Whereas, if Jesus had been reared in a home as an only *absolutely perfect child* with doting parents, how would he identify with those *years of temptations* that confront a typical family member.

We may assume his earthly father, Joseph, died sometime after Jesus was twelve because Scripture does not mention him again. Logically, being the eldest, Jesus assumed the responsibility of supporting the family by continuing in Joseph's trade as a carpenter. As he matured and struggled with responsibilities, he learned to identify with human passions, disappointments, frustrations, and grief. With four ordinary brothers and at least two sisters, he certainly had experience in conflict management. Probably, there were times when he wanted to toss all four brothers over Mt. Moriah.

We see further confirmation of Jesus' family. While Jesus was still talking to the crowd, his mother and brothers stood outside, wanting to speak to him. Someone told him, "Your mother and brothers are standing outside, wanting to speak to you..." He replied, "Who is my mother, and who are my brothers?"

With this question, Jesus took the physical family relationship as an illustration to introduce the imminent spiritual family in His Kingdom. Then, "pointing to his disciples, he said, 'Here are my mother and my brothers. For whoever does the will of my Father in heaven is my brother and sister and mother" (Matt. 12:46–50 NIV).

A Special Tribute to Mary, Jesus' mother: She was the purest of all women. Consummating her marriage with Joseph, after Jesus was born, in no way affected her exalted esteem. It shall always be as Elizabeth proclaimed in a loud voice: "Blessed are you among women, and blessed is the child you will bear!" (Luke 1:41,42 NIV).

Mary, above all women is to be perpetually honored and praised. It is unfathomable to be chosen by God to be the mother of Jesus, the Great "I AM!"—"I am the Light of the World, Bread of Life and Living Water." As it will be with all who trust in Jesus, Mary will reign with The King of Kings (2 Tim. 2:12; Rev. 20:6 NIV).

God Will Help Us through Our Temptations

> No temptation has seized you except what is common to man. And God is faithful; he will not let you be tempted beyond what you can bear. But when you are tempted, he will also provide a way out...
>
> 1 Corinthians 10:13 (NIV)

> Because he himself suffered when he was tempted, he is able to help those who are being tempted.
>
> Hebrews 2:18 (NIV)

An example of God's help in temptation happened in the Old Testament when God protected Abimelech, King of Gerar, from committing adultery. Abraham had told a half truth when he said that the beautiful Sarah was his sister, instead of his wife. God told

Abimelech in a dream that she was married. This scared him. Then, in another dream, God said to Abimelech, "*I know you did this with a clear conscience, and so I have kept you from sinning against me.* That is why I did not let you touch her" (Gen.20:3, 6 NIV).

As we walk in the paths of righteousness, Scripture instructs: "Make level paths for *your* feet and take only ways that are firm. Do not swerve to the right or the left; keep *your* foot from evil" (Prov. 4:26, 27 NIV). To stay on that firm path, there are steps we can take that will help us avoid evil.

Steps to Power over Temptation

- **Have a Firm Commitment**

To resist temptation our desire to please God must be stronger than the enticement. If we love God and draw near to Him, He will draw near to us" (Jas. 4:8 NIV). And, we will gain strength. Paul wrote, "Clothe *your*selves with the Lord Jesus Christ, and do not think about how to gratify the desires of the sinful nature" (Rom. 13:14 NIV).

- **Know God's Word**

Jesus responded to Satan's temptations: "*It is written…*" Satan knows how to slant Scripture to his advantage. We must study Scripture and know it so well that we instantly recognize a misquotation or wrong interpretation, and counter it with Truth. As Jesus quoted scripture in his temptations, God's Word is our weapon against Satan, too. It is the "*Sword of the Spirit*" (Eph. 6:17 NIV).

- **Pray**

Jesus told us to, "Watch and pray so that you will not fall into temptation. The spirit is willing, but the body is weak" (Matt. 26:41 NIV). Then, Paul wrote, "… the peace of God, which transcends all understanding, will guard *your* hearts and *your* minds in Christ Jesus" (Phil. 4:7 NIV).

- **Discipline Our Thoughts**

Since temptation enters as a thought, we must keep our thoughts under control. Paul writes, "...take captive every thought to make it obedient to Christ" (2 Cor. 10:5 NIV).

- **Select Companions and Activities**

Avoid obvious temptations. For example, young people should stay away from peers who would entice them to use drugs and alcohol and, watch porn. This is true for adults too. We all should choose friends who have values; we will find strength among those who have strength.

- **Walk on Water**

Take *your* eyes off the temptation and focus on Jesus. Peter said, "Lord, if it's you…tell me to come to you on the water." Jesus replies, "Come." Then, Peter got down out of the boat, walked on the water and came toward Jesus. But when he saw the wind, he was afraid and, beginning to sink, cried out, "Lord, save me!" Immediately Jesus reached out his hand and caught him. "You of little faith," he said, "why did you doubt?" (Matt. 14:28–31 NIV). When our storms rage, we too, must keep our eyes on Jesus and walk on water straight to Him.

- **Stay Busy about *Our Father's* Business**

We must be headed in a positive direction when temptations come. As we are *"about Our Father's business,"* walking in His Spirit, we will not be as tempted to *"gratify the desires of the sinful nature"* (Gal. 5:16 NIV).

Don't stall; keep moving forward. The light is green: "GO!"

- **When Temptation Comes, Simply Say, "No!"**

After the last temptation in the wilderness, Jesus commanded, "Away from me, Satan! For it is written: 'Worship the Lord *your* God, and serve him only" (Matt. 4:10 NIV). "Then the devil left him, and angels came and attended him" (Matt. 4:11 NIV). "Resist the devil and he will flee from you" (Jas. 4:7 NIV).

Now that we have reviewed the most common areas of temptation and the steps we must take to resist then, we must also be aware that temptations are not always subtle.

Temptations can be Terrifying

Early Christians were severely tempted to renounce their faith: "They were stoned; they were sawed in two; they were put to death by the sword. They went about in sheepskins and goatskins, destitute, persecuted and mistreated..." (Heb.11:37 NIV).

Dr. James Kennedy wrote in the Appendix of the book, *Tortured for Christ*. "The very mention of the name, 'Richard Wurmbrand,' conjures up in the mind the gripping record of 2,000 years of Christian martyrdom... This unbroken trail of blood is exemplified nowhere more graphically than in his classic book, *Tortured for Christ*..."[96]

Every Christian should read the book for a profound appreciation for all that Richard Wumbrand, and numerous other Christians, through the centuries, suffered. He was the founder of "The Voice of the Martyrs."

Tortured for Christ, confirms that Communism is an anti-Christ religion where Satan is in control against Christians. I wanted to know which nation was the most brutal against Christians so I called the "Voice of the Martyrs." The man who answered the phone said, "There is no doubt in my mind, North Korea."

Americans don't have to look outside our country to find enemies against Christianity. For example, we all know that Madaline O'Hare, an atheist, almost single handedly removed prayer from all public school functions in our nation. The ACLU is on the alert for any infringement of religion on public property; our military chaplains are restrained from praying, "In the Name of Jesus." Our freedom of speech to quote scriptures that address certain lifestyles is being challenged. The list goes on... As for our enemies *within;* we can hear their boots clicking.

The massive fundamental change in our government may seem relatively insignificant at this time, but the calendar is flipping. As the government accelerates in size and power, the rights of the citizens become fewer. According to Bible prophecy, ultimate government take-over will eventually evolve into a One World Global Government over which the Anti-Christ will rule during the Tribulation Period. And, followers of his arch enemy, Jesus Christ, *will be martyred.*

When temptation roars as a lion and we tremble in the blast of its breath, we must hold firm to our faith. Like Jesus, and the martyred Christians, we *must* keep God and his purpose for our lives so real that we would not forsake him, regardless of what we are facing. The martyrs' love for Christ was greater than their agonies.

Now, it has been made clear that the reason such atrocities continue to happen is our adversary [Satan] is still roaming around the world "seeking whom he may devour" (1 Pet.5:8 NIV).

Clearly, he is the one who inspires "man's inhumanities against man."

Reading to the end of the Bible: Satan will again be evicted. But, this time it will be to a much lower level to an eternal blazing tomb (Rev. 20:10 NIV). Whereas, martyrs for Christ will be elevated to Glory and will receive great rewards (1 Cor. 3:13–15; Rev. 20:4 NIV).

Before closing this section, Billy Graham will respond to a question that probably looms in each of our minds: "Why did God not send mighty angels to the godly men and women in desperate times?" Dr. Graham refers to the classic chapter of faith:

In the sufferings and death of these great saints not physically delivered, God had a mysterious plan.... Knowing this, they suffered and died by *faith*.... This latter part of Hebrews 11 indicates that those who received no visible help in answer to prayer will have a far greater heavenly reward because they endured by "faith" alone. But having died, they did enjoy the ministry of angels who then escorted their immortal souls to the throne of God. If the first part of Hebrews 11 is called "God's Hall of Fame," the second should be called, *"God's Winners of the Medal of Honor."*[97]

IX: Tempted, Tested, Triumphant

Sample Prayer

Tempted, Tested, Triumphant

Our Father,

Thank you for giving us freedom to make our own decisions regarding good and evil. We realize that we do not resist temptations as we should.

Help us to recognize temptations and have our minds so set on *you*, and our courage so strengthened *by your Holy Spirit*, that we will never give in or give up.

Thank You for hearing our prayers and for the power that we receive to overcome.

We know that storms of temptation are inevitable. And, our anchor is immovable.

Thank you, Lord, for being our anchor.

In the name of Jesus Christ our Lord, we pray. Amen

Living Christianity Assignment

Bible Study—Read Colossians and Galatians. Learn more about God's love for us. It will strengthen us when we face temptations.

> In all your ways acknowledge him, and he will make your paths straight.
> Proverbs 3:6 (NIV)

Prayer—Pray for wisdom and discernment to recognize your temptations. Ask God to fill you with His Spirit for strength to resist.

> Jesus said, "Get up and pray so that you will not fall into temptation."
> Luke 22:46 (NIV)

Works—When temptations confront you, simply say "No!" Stay away from people and places that entice you to do wrong.

> He restores my soul. He guides me in paths of righteousness for his name's sake.
> Psalms 23:3 (NIV)

X: Satan the Supreme Leader of Evil DEFEATED!

"Deliver us from the evil one."

> For our struggle is not against flesh and blood [humans], but against the rulers, against the authorities, against the powers of this dark world and against the spiritual forces of evil [satanic] in the [atmospheric] heavenly realms
>
> Ephesians 6:12 (NIV)

X:
Satan
The Supreme Leader of Evil
DEFEATED!

"Deliver us from the evil one."

- Exposing Our Enemy

  - Satan's Reality
  - Satan's Territory
  - Satan's Power
  - Satan's Rights
  - Satan's Strategy
  - Satan's Defeat and Destiny

- Overcoming Our Enemy

  - Our Goal
  - Our Spiritual Position
  - Our Authority in the Name of Jesus

- Our Strength
- Our Armor
- Our Weapons
- Victorious Overcomers

- The Battleground for the Mind Illustrated
- Do We Battle Satan, or Simply Trust *Our Father*?
- Sample Prayer: Satan The Supreme Leader of Evil Defeated!
- Living Christianity Assignment

X:
Satan
The Supreme Leader of Evil
DEFEATED!

"Deliver us from the evil one."

Many times Satan has us swirling in a whirlpool of negative circumstances because we do not recognize his hand in our affairs or realize victory over him is possible. Consequently, he works unchallenged, behind his invisible cloak. Jesus recognized Satan when He asked God to *"protect them from the evil one"* (Jn.17:15 NIV), and said to pray, *"deliver us from evil."* Billy Graham writes, "We are in a battle every day with the devil. There is a devil. There are demons."[98] In The Screwtape Letters, C. S. Lewis writes:

> The commonest question is whether I really, "believe in the Devil." Now, if by "the Devil" you mean a power opposite to God and, like God, self-existent from all eternity, the answer is certainly "No." There is no uncreated being except God...Satan, the leader...of devils, is the opposite, not of God, but of (the mighty angel) Michael.[99]

In regard to demonic adversaries and unsuspecting church members, Jack Taylor, past president of the Southern Baptist Convention, writes in his book, *Much More*:

> I am convinced that this group comprises the greater part of those whose names are listed [on church rolls]... there are those who suspicion that there is a war on but can't seem to decide whose side they are on. They would like to get by without committing themselves because they are trying to make the best of both worlds. Then there are those who have discovered that there is a war on but don't seem to be sure as to the outcome. They are discouraged... and defeated.
>
> Then... there are those who have discovered that there is a war on, know whose side they are on, and are certain of the outcome because Christ has already finished the victory. These are they who do not faint in the battle because they have learned... Victory is ours![100]

It is important for us to acknowledge our adversary and know his strategy, *"... in order that Satan might not outwit us... for we are not unaware of his schemes"* (2 Cor.2:11 NIV). We must recognize what is happening *before* we get caught up in a vicious cycle of sinister plots. Study our enemy, like every general does before going into battle. Scripture will unmask Satan and expose his ways.

Exposing Our Enemy

Satan's Reality

Satan has deceived many into believing he is nothing more than a mythical figure with horns and a pointed tail, wearing a comical red suit. Others joyously proclaim him to be a toothless lion. Neither is true.

> Satan is a vicious, invisible enemy, "who prowls about like a roaring lion, seeking someone to devour.
>
> 1 Peter 5:8 (NIV)

X: Satan the Supreme Leader of Evil DEFEATED!

> His goal is to steal, kill, and destroy us—all mankind!
> John 10:10 (NIV)

Satan's Territory

All people on earth, regardless of nationality, race or creed live in Satan's territory. After Lucifer's revolt, God banished him to earth. Scripture confirms his dominion.

> ...that ancient serpent...Satan...was hurled to the earth, and his (1/3 of the) angels with him.
> Revelation 12:7–9 (NIV)

> The whole world is under the control of the evil one.
> 1 John 5:19 (NIV)

> He is the "god of this age." [small "g"]
> 2 Corinthians 4:4 (NIV)

> [He is] ruler of the kingdom of the air, the spirit who is now at work in those who are disobedient.
> Ephesians 2:2 (NIV)

In the book of Job the Lord said to Satan, "Where have you come from?" Satan replied, "From roaming through the earth and going back and forth in it" (Job 1:7 NIV).

Since the Garden of Eden, Satan has not changed; he is still casting doubt on God's word to gain control over all who will listen. Since, then, all mankind has done his bidding and we don't have to look *closely*, the wars that have emerged are blatant.

When we say *all mankind*, we are not siding with any particular war since we are viewing evil from the perspective of eternal truths. The perpetrator's marching orders for religious wars are: "Kill the infidels!" This can broadly mean anyone who has a different philosophy. Throwing a dart at history:

> After the bloodbath of the Christian Crusades, when Saladin re-conquered Jerusalem for Islam in 1187, the Jews" (barred from the city by the Crusaders) were invited to return, and even the Western Christians, who had supported the crusading atrocities, were allowed back. In the 16th century, Ottoman Sultan Suleiman the Magnificent permitted the Jews to make the Western Wall their official holy place and had his court architect Sinan build an oratory for them there…"[101]

Wars are justified in the minds of the instigators. The Crusaders (1095–1291) thought they were serving God. Now, radical Muslims are willing to die for their righteous cause. Throughout history, whichever the nation or religion, enemies may trade sides when a new offence is sparked. The question is, "Who is planting thoughts of violence in their minds and motivating them to atrocities? It is not a God of love; it is Satan who is "seeking whom he can destroy." Christians, Muslims, Jews, Japanese, Germans, Russians, Africans… *all* get caught up in his traps.

For a simplified illustration, think of boys on school yard. There is generally a bully in their midst who revels in conflict. He can take two boys who already have a point of emotional stress and accelerate them into a major scuffle by saying to one, "You aren't going to let him get away with that!" Standing in the gathering circle, he gleefully prods them on. "HIT HIM AGAIN!"

Satan is a real pro. He can have the whole world at odds with each other in bloody conflicts. He begins by inspiring a relatively few *fanatics, for whatever reason,* to go on rampages.

"A man whose family was German aristocracy prior to World War II owned a number of large industries and estates. When asked how many German people were true Nazis, the answer he gave can guide our attitude toward fanaticism" In 'A German's point of view on Islam,'[102] he wrote:

X: Satan the Supreme Leader of Evil DEFEATED!

Very few people were true Nazis…I was one of those who just thought the Nazis were a bunch of fools. So, the majority just sat back and let it all happen. Then, before we knew it, they owned us, and we had lost control, and the end of the world had come. My family lost everything. I ended up in a concentration camp…

We are told…that Islam is the religion of peace, and that the vast majority of Muslims just want to live in peace.…

The fact is that *the fanatics rule* Islam at this moment in history. It is the fanatics who march. It is the fanatics who systematically slaughter Christian or tribal groups throughout Africa and are gradually taking over the entire continent in an Islamic wave. It is the fanatics who bomb, behead, murder, or honor-kill. It is the fanatics who take over mosque after mosque. It is the fanatics who zealously spread the stoning and hanging of rape victims and homosexuals.

Communist Russia was comprised of Russians who just wanted to live in peace, yet the Russian Communists were responsible for the murder of about 20 million people. The peaceful majority were irrelevant. China's huge population was peaceful as well, but Chinese Communists managed to kill a staggering 70 million people.

We all know that the Islamic fanatics destroyed the Twin Towers and killed more than 3,000 people. In retaliation, against building a mosque on the site, a pastor in a church in Florida planned to burn a Koran on an anniversary [September 11, 2010] of the bombing, Both had their *righteous* cause. We don't want to think about what *that* would have ignited. The issues are far from being settled. God does not want us to destroy, or retaliate. The cycle can be endless.

If both of the boys on the playground had turned on the bully, they could have gone away with their arms over each others' shoulders.

God does not want to *destroy infidels* by anyone's terms; he commands: "You shall not murder" (Exod. 20:13 NIV). He wants to *save the souls of all mankind* out of the world of Satan's domain. The same scripture in all languages applies to all people.

In the New American Standard Bible (NASB), we read:

> For God so loved the world, that He gave His only begotten Son, that whoever believes in Him shall not perish, but have eternal life.
>
> John 3:16 (NASB)

In the Arabic Life Application Bible (ALAB), we read the same words:

الْوَحِيدَ، ابْنَهُ بَذَلَ حَتَّى الْعَالَمَ اللهُ أَحَبَّ هكَذَا لِأَنَّهُ
لَهُ تَكُونُ بَلْ بِهِ، يُؤْمِنُ مَنْ كُلُّ يَهْلِكَ لاَ لِكَيْ
الْأَبَدِيَّةُ الْحَيَاةُ.

John 3:16 (ALAB)[103]

Jesus said that two greatest commandments are: "Love the Lord your God with all your heart and ... Love your neighbor as yourself" (Mk.12:30–32 NIV).

Of course, "love thy neighbor" means love your fellowman regardless of race, color or creed. God gave me a special Persian friend, Victoria Shokri. She wrote "God is love" in Farsi: "Khodavand eshgh ast."

To me, she symbolizes peace loving Persian/Iranians. She was reared in Tehran, Iran and left when she was nineteen. Living now in California, I visualize her front porch with hanging baskets of flowers and her kitchen filled with an inviting aroma. She has an open door to her home and to her heart. We have bonded. She signed a note to me: "Asheghetam [Farsi for 'I love you'], Vicky."

This is the way it is with *Our Father*. It doesn't matter which, of the many languages the people of the world speak, he hears and sees with his loving heart.

X: Satan the Supreme Leader of Evil DEFEATED!

Satan's Power

In the book of Job, we see how Satan instigated disasters in peoples' lives. He caused the Sabeans to slay Job's servants, fire to burn up his sheep and shepherds, the Chaldeans to steal his camels and kill their caretakers, a tornado to hit his son's home and kill Job's children, and sores to cover Job's body (Job 1:12–70 NIV).

Satan has left evidence of his malicious handiwork strewn through the ages. For one, centuries after Job "a woman was there who had been crippled by a spirit for eighteen years. She ... could not straighten up at all ... Jesus said, "Then should not this woman ... whom Satan has kept bound ... be set free ... " (Lu.13:11- 16 NIV).

Satan's Rights

Satan has rights only because man gave them by listening to him. Satan came before God and accused Job of being loyal to him only because of his blessings. God responded to Satan's challenge with the obvious, *"Everything he has is in your hands,"* but you cannot have his life" (Job 1:12 NIV). In that statement, God acknowledged Job's freewill, Satan's realm over planet earth, and God's ultimate authority.

After Satan destroyed Job's children, his possessions, and left him near death, *Job refused to denounce God*. After Job's victory, "The Lord blessed the latter part of Job's life more than the first" (Job 42:12 NIV). His family, prosperity, and influence were greater. Now, his closest friends, who were the most influential patriarchs of the land reverenced Job's righteous relationship with God.

Satan also pressed his rights with the Apostle Peter. Jesus, not interfering with Peter's freewill, warned him, "Satan has demanded permission to sift you like wheat; but I have prayed for you, that your faith may not fail ... " (Lu.22:31,32 NAS).

Satan also sifts *us* like wheat; and, Jesus is praying for us, too, that our faith will hold. Are we going down in defeat using only our human capability?

Satan's Strategy

Today, Satan is still promoting his cause and acquiring followers. We may wonder, "Why would anyone choose to follow someone who is obviously evil?" Satan uses deception, often disguising himself in a cause representing truth and goodness (2 Cor. 11:14 NIV). He goes undetected as he diverts truth.

He is the "master of deceit and fraud, an enemy of all righteousness" (Acts 13:10 NIV). And he is the "father of lies" (Jn. 8:44 NIV); "accuser" (Rev. 12:10 NIV); and "tempter" (1 Thess. 3:5 NIV).

His main goal is to control man's mind: Dr. Torrey writes, "The awful, almost incredible blindness of men who are intelligent on other subjects" (like science and law) to the simplest and plainest truth about Christ is due to this blinding work of Satan."[104]

Some churches are under Satan's influence. They have impressive edifices, display intellectual sounding names, and expound humanistic philosophies. From their pulpits, deceived men proclaim spiritually fatal religious views.

Satan is becoming more brazen as the time approaches for him to make his big play as the dreaded antichrist. The church of Satan was founded in San Francisco in 1966 by Anton LaVey. Since that time, satanic churches have spread. In regard to their worship services, we see clearly his adversarial position. From Anton LaVey's Satanic Bible, Bob Larson quotes in his book *Satanism, the Seduction of America's Youth*,

> Since blasphemy is an integral part of worshiping Satan, LaVey includes outrageous invectives hurled against God...in addition...there is blatant pornography and sexism through The Satanic Rituals.[105]

Test the Spirits "Wolves in Sheep's Clothing"

I read an expose,' "Wolves in Modern Sheep's Clothing" by Rev. Gene Horton, Th. D. He quoted an anti-Christ theologian who was teaching in a *Christian University:* "Whether Jesus ever lived is a historical question that is interesting, but it is not fundamental to religion."

> Beware of false prophets, which come to you in sheep's clothing, but inwardly they are ravening wolves.
>
> Matthew 7:15 (KJV)

> Do not believe every spirit, but test the spirits to see whether they are from God, because many false prophets have gone out into the world. This is how you can recognize the Spirit of God: Every spirit that acknowledges that Jesus Christ has come in the flesh is from God, but every spirit that does not acknowledge Jesus, is not from God. This is the *spirit of the antichrist*, which you have heard is coming and even now is already in the world.
>
> 1 John 4:1–3 (NIV)

It is easy to find people who have the spirit of the anti-Christ. Recently, I saw a man sneer at the mention of Christ.

I read that, "One of the more obvious ways to spot false teaching is to be on the lookout for any attempt to diminish or put down the Godship of Jesus Christ. These portrayals range all the way from the concept of Him as a mere prophet, a teacher, a *good* man, a man of God, even conceding He is the Son of God but not God!"

Jesus is an extension of God manifested in human form for a divine purpose. He can lay his life down and take it up again.

The name Jesus means God with us. Jesus said, "I and the Father are one!" (Jn. 10:30 NIV); "Anyone who has seen me has seen the Father" (Jn. 14:9 NIV); "He is the image of the invisible God, the firstborn over all creation" (Col.1:15 NIV); "For in Christ all the fullness of the Deity lives in bodily form" (Col. 2:9 NIV); Jesus is "the radiance of God's glory and the exact representation of his being, sustaining all things by his powerful word" (Heb. 1:3 NIV).

If, through lies, deceptions, or half-truths, Satan can keep his naive followers unaware of eternal salvation that is available through Jesus Christ, then he maintains control without any further effort" (2 Cor. 4:4; 1 Jn. 5:19; Eph. 2:2 NIV).

I was shocked to see an arrogant false prophet on world television. He berated the Bible from his impressive sanctuary. And, in essence, said that (1) "he did not believe in the virgin birth of Jesus" (2) " it was not necessary to believe in Jesus Christ for salvation" (3) "the blood sacrifice was a barbaric and archaic concept that was not acceptable in our more informed era." Another scene on television showed him teaching a large group of attentive teenagers.

> For such are false apostles, deceitful workers, transforming themselves into the apostles of Christ...for Satan himself is transformed into an angel of light. Therefore it is no great thing if his ministers also be transformed as the ministers of righteousness; whose end shall be according to their works.
>
> 2 Corinthians 11: 13–15 (KJV)

Satan attacks our prayer time

He knows that we are weaker without our direct source of Divine power. Therefore, he uses diversionary tactics to distract us. He can cause the dog to bark, inspire friends to phone or visit and suggest distracting ideas.

Clearly, such a time happened in the home of our respected Chairman of the Deacons, Johnny Canville, and his wife, Ruth Ann. We had gathered to pray about a serious personal matter. We were on our knees in the living room. And, as we started praying the phone rang. Ruth went to the kitchen and had a brief conversation. She returned and we started praying again. The phone rang again...The third time Ruth went to the kitchen; I began to suspect this was more than a coincidence. I suggested, "Take it off the hook," while I thought, "This is a deliberate demonic hindrance." She returned to our frustrated prayer session.

Now, with the phone off the hook, it rang again. We stared at each other in disbelief. This time, Johnny went to the kitchen and saw across the room that the phone was indeed—off the hook. Seemingly in defiance, it rang again. He said, "The hair stood up on my arms!"

We had the last word as we resumed our prayer session in the Name of Jesus! Later, we verified with several technicians that it was not mechanically possible. Normally, we hear the "busy signal" when the receiver was off the hook.

The Prophet Daniel gives us a clue to the source of the problem. When he prayed, there was a mighty battle of satanic interference in the spirit world that delayed his prayer answer. Daniel had a terrifying vision and a voice spoke: "Since the first day ... *your* words were heard, and I have come in response to them. But the prince of the Persian kingdom resisted me twenty-one days. Then Michael, one of the chief princes, came to help me, because I was detained there with the king of Persia" (Dan.10:7, 10, 12–13).

It is logical to assume that, the *"prince of the Persian kingdom"* is still in the atmospheric realm over ancient Persia which is now Iran. Furthermore, since Lucifer was cast out of heaven with one third of the angels, they are over every nation around the world. That means, we too, have atmospheric dark angels that interfere and cause havoc in our lives.

Satan attempts to divert our prayers

Satan can deceive the petitioner by *causing prayer answers* when prayed to anyone or anything other than God. I heard a young man say, "I had a desperate prayer need and prayed to St. Jude, and he answered. So, now I *always* pray to St. Jude." This completely alienates God, who wants us to come straight to Him. Jesus said, "*This, then, is how you should pray: 'Our Father ... '*"

Satan puts surveillance on our Bible study time

False doctrine is convincing as long as we do not read the truth. Satan will try to keep us from reading the Bible by using three common lies: 1. Don't read the Bible, you won't understand it anyway. 2. You already know what is in it. 3. Read it later.

Satan plants imposters among the Christians

"While everyone was sleeping, his enemy came and sowed weeds among the wheat..." (Matt.13:25 NIV). Jesus said, "Allow both to grow together until the harvest... lest while you are gathering up the tares, you may root up the wheat..." (Matt.13:30,29 NAS). These weeds go to church but have no commitment.

A busy time for them is after a church service while driving home with their families and at Sunday dinner. They criticize the preacher, and *"take away the word that was sown"* by casting doubt on spiritual truths" (Mk. 4:15 NIV). They cause confusion and steal spiritual joy from others, including children.

Satan attacks our youth

Satan launched a major attack on the youth of our nation during the 1960's through deafening rock music. Garbled words ridiculed every moral value, promoted drugs, and incited rebellion against God, country and family. Long hair, faded shirts, ragged jeans and sandals became standard attire. Campus riots, flag-burnings, mind-altering drugs, and uninhibited sex began. Psychedelic lights and provocative dancing enticed our youth.

The "Virgin 50's became the Promiscuous 60's."

According to a Tom Brokaw CNBC Documentary[106], the era of the Baby Boomers began when the soldiers came home after World War II. They became the largest percentage of the population *age group* in U.S. history. In time, about 78,000,000 grew up to break the mold of our traditional concepts of life.

X: Satan the Supreme Leader of Evil DEFEATED!

It gained its foothold when turbulent youth protested the Vietnam War (1959–1975). They didn't see a purpose in the war and they didn't want to go.

During this era, we remember "Woodstock." The word conjures up memories of a trashed-out 600 acre field where an estimated 450,000 young people had gathered for the Aquarian Exposition Music Festival (Aug 15–18, 1969).

They just came to hear the music. After all, *everyone* will be there! Almost half a million fun loving young people were so spaced-out on drugs and alcohol that they were oblivious to everything, even the rain and muddy field. The frenzied guitars and the drumbeats set the mood; they were liberated from restraints. When God's laws move out Satan's lawless moves in.

Testimonies on television from those who were there: "We were stoned the whole time, we left a trail of wreckage"…"Blanket to blanket, body to body"…"Uninhibited sex"…"Embodiment of excess and degradation"…"We were a bunch of morons"…"Focused on self gratification"…"We changed everything."

The Beatles' blaring music blurred the moods and mind-set of that generation. The upside down cross symbolized what they called "Peace." It turned out to be a pivotal point in American history.

This does not mean *every* baby born in that era was raised with those concepts. Nor, does it mean there were no regrets at Woodstock. It is reasonable to believe that some sobered from a wild weekend and returned home to resume their traditional family lifestyle.

Even so, through the following decades the contagious free-spirit was like a virus that flowed through the corridors of schools affecting students from all echelons of life. Parents, teachers and law officials grabbed their dictionaries to look up the word "Marijuana." Young people were getting high and distraught parents were very low. Bob and I were two of the parents.

This largely independent generation grew up to become many of our top leaders today in government, industry and education.

According to the documentary, "They are in control of the White House, Congress, and three forth of the C.EO.s in Fortune 500 Companies. However, this does not categorize the entire generation. There are many who held to traditional values, and are in high leadership positions.

Nevertheless, his explains a lot about our cultural departure from the basics of our Founding Fathers. Now, in the progression of time, with a disregard for tradition and its values, numerous liberals are making their own laws and are strong proponents of abortion and homosexuality.

Satan ceases every opportunity. Today, he promotes his ideas through all Medias: television, radio, movies and magazines. The internet sends his message of hate and perversion throughout the world in lightening speed. He inspires scriptwriters and producers to create horror films that are beyond ordinary human imagination. These arouse some individuals to commit gruesome atrocities. Some video games inspire youth to kill. A teen reporter wrote a column in the *Valley Morning Star* that headlined, "Soul Blade Is So Real Wear Armor:"

> To each of the characters of this game, he has done something horrible. The Master Edge ending is when you see him 'truly' die. I say 'truly' because on the easy ending, you pick up his weapon and become truly evil, just like him ... Hmmm ... could he have escaped into *your* body? Of course. And that is how Soul Blade got its name. Because *your* soul is depending on the blade of *your* opponents.... [107]

These games are excellent training in brutality. It is no wonder desensitized children have taken guns to school and killed, with no remorse. In various ways, Satan also influences adults to murder. Too often, we read about a man brutally killing his wife and children or a mother drowning her five children in the bathtub.

X: Satan the Supreme Leader of Evil DEFEATED!

Satanic ceremonial sacrifices are truly shocking, such as animal and human mutilation. History records the brutal slaying of Mark Kilroy, the University of Texas student, in Matamoros, Mexico."

Satan tempts, deceives and perverts

Dr. Everett Koop, past Surgeon General, U. S. Public Health Service, is very interested in the effects of violence and pornography on our nation:

> I am involved now in a program that deals with violence ... including child abuse, spousal abuse, and abuse of the elderly ... When pornography crosses with violence, it presents a tremendous health problem with implications for morality and the mental health of the country.[108]

With only a few clicks on the keyboard, pornography can enter almost every home. Curious teenage boys are easy prey. On the grand scale worldwide, probably millions of *closet viewers* have swallowed the hook resulting in perversions, imprisonments ... pedophilias and even deaths.

More is never enough. When the mind becomes saturated, a demonic spirit from Satan can move in; then, the pedophile looses all sense of perspective. This could be the reason they have been deemed incurable. An inmate admitted, "When I get out of here the first thing I will do is go find a child. After all, what do you think I have been thinking about all of the time that I have been in here?"

There is no physical fix; it is a spiritual bondage. The Holy Spirit and the Name of Jesus is the only power strong enough to evict that which is demonic and set the victim free.

> Do you not know that the wicked will not inherit the kingdom of God? Do not be deceived: Neither the sexually immoral nor idolaters nor adulterers nor male prostitutes nor homosexual offenders nor thieves nor the greedy nor drunkards nor slanderers nor swindlers will inherit the kingdom

of God. And that is what some of you were. *But you were washed, you were sanctified, you were justified in the name of the Lord Jesus Christ and by the Spirit of our God.*

Flee from sexual immorality. All other sins a man commits are outside his body, but he who sins sexually sins against his own body. Do you not know that *your* body is a temple of the Holy Spirit, who is in you, whom you have received from God? You are not *your* own; you were bought at a price. Therefore honor God with *your* body.

1 Corinthians 6:9–11, 18 (NIV)

All mankind has fallen prey to Satan's enticements and deceptions in one form or the other. I cannot repeat enough: Jesus died in our place and paid for *every sin*, no matter what they may be...when they occurred...why they happened...or how strong the bondage may be. He wants to set everyone free and empower us to move forward and upward with him.

Satan's Defeat and Destiny

The triumphant conclusion! Jesus broke Satan's hold when he paid for our sins: "And having disarmed the powers and authorities, he made a public spectacle of them, triumphing over them by the cross" (Col. 2:15 NIV). "So that by his [Jesus] death he might destroy him who holds the power of death that is, the devil" (Heb. 2:14 NIV).

> His defeat was complete when Jesus declared, "It is finished"; he died and paid for our sins.
>
> John 19:30 (NIV)

> I am the Living One; I was dead, and behold I am alive forever and ever! And I hold the keys of death and Hades.
>
> Revelation 1:18 (NIV)

E. W. Kenyon writes,

> When Christ rose from the dead He not only had the keys to death and hell but He had the very armor in which Satan trusted. He has defeated the devil; He has defeated all hell and He stands before three worlds...heaven, earth, and hell...as the undisputed victor over man's destroyer. He conquered Satan before his own cohorts...his own servants in the dark regions of the damned, and there He stood...the absolute Victor and Master.[109]

Satan's ultimate destiny: "Then he [Jesus] will say to those on his left, 'Depart from me...into *the eternal fire prepared for the devil* and his angels'" (Matt. 25:41 NIV).

Overcoming Our Enemy!

In a capsule, these two scriptures tell us who we are, who the evil one is, what he does, and our dominance.

> We know that *we are children of God*, and that *the whole world is under the control of the evil one*. We know also that the Son of God has come and has given us understanding, so that we may know him who is true. And *we are in him* who is true even in his Son Jesus Christ. He is the true God and eternal life.
>
> 1 John 5:19–20 (NIV)

> The thief comes only to steal and kill and destroy; *I have come that they may have life, and have it to the full.*
>
> John 10:10 (NIV)

We all wonder, "If Jesus defeated Satan, why is he still on earth antagonizing us?" Paul Billheimer answers this question in Destined for the Throne. In the Foreword, Billy Graham wrote: "Every Christian who feels impelled to find a deeper dimension of Christian witness should not only read this book, but study it prayerfully, and apply its principles to his life."

Paul Billheimer wrote, "Although Christ's triumph over Satan is full and complete, God permits him to carry on guerrilla warfare. God could put Satan completely away, but *He has chosen to use him to give the Church on-the-job training in overcoming.*"[110]

Why do we need this training? When we are "born into Our Father's family" we are a new spiritual baby looking at a whole new world. We are saved from hell into eternal life, but we don't yet know how to walk in victory and stand in authority against a monstrous adversary. We must learn how to flex our spiritual muscles and reign. Watchman Nee wrote, "The principal work of over comers is to bring the authority of the heavenly throne down to earth."[111] Jesus promises:

> To him who overcomes, I will give the right to sit with me on my throne, just as I overcame and sat down with my Father on his throne.
>
> Revelation 3:21 (NIV)

> The sovereignty, power, and greatness of the kingdoms under the whole heaven will be handed over to the saints, the people of the Most High.
>
> Daniel 7:27 (NIV)

To become Victorious Overcomers, we must know our goal; realize the Divine Source of our strength; wear our full armor; wield our weapons; know our spiritual position; use our authority; and win on the battleground.

Our Goal

Jesus said, "I am sending you to them to open their eyes and turn them from darkness to light, and from the power of Satan to God, so that they may receive forgiveness of sins and a place among those who are sanctified by faith in me." (Acts 26:17, 18 NIV).

Our Spiritual Position

Christ is the head and we are the body. We must walk with perfect confidence in him and his judgment. In our unique position, we are His voice on the earth, carrying on His work when we are *in one* with His Holy Spirit.

> He has *rescued us from the dominion of darkness* [ruled by Satan] and *brought us into the kingdom of the Son* [ruled by Jesus].
> Colossians 1:13 (NIV)

> And he made known to us the mystery of his will... which he purposed in Christ... to bring all things in heaven and on earth together under one head, even Christ.
> Ephesians 1:3–10 (NIV)

> [He] made us alive with Christ... and raised us up with Christ and seated us with him in the heavenly realms *in* Christ Jesus.
> Ephesians 2:5, 6 (NIV)

> God placed *all things under his feet* and appointed him to be head over everything for the church, which is his body, the fullness of him who fills everything in every way.
> Ephesians 1:22, 23 (NIV)

Our Authority in the Name of Jesus

Jesus delegated authority to us when He said, *"All authority in heaven and on earth has been given to me. Therefore go..."* (Matt. 28:19, 20 NIV). He also said that *in my name* you will... have authority over evil" (Mk. 16:17, 18 NIV).

In the name of Jesus, "we are therefore Christ's ambassadors, as though God were making his appeal through us" (2 Cor. 5:20).

Christianity Alive! with Prayer Power!

According to Webster, authority means we have the power or right to give commands, take action, and administer justice. For example, Satan disregards his defeat until we take control. Similarly, a criminal can shove a policeman as long as the policeman permits it. Sad to say, it is easy for Christians to accept Satan's harassment, and then complacently whine, "Well, whatever is the Lord's will."

Authority is not parroting words. One must *know* the power of His backing. It does not have to yell. This became clearer to me while sitting in a court room. Federal Judge Filemon Vela was annoyed with the loud jack hammers in the street. Finally, he said to the bailiff in a conversational tone, "Take care of that." The man hurried out the door; he had no other choice.

Fascinated with the simple command, I mentally followed his footsteps...down the hall...down the elevator...out the front door...the jack hammers stopped. When the federal judge spoke, his authority was backed by the United States government. It superseded Brownsville, Cameron County, and Texas authorities.

Our authority comes from God. The highest name in heaven and in earth is the name "Jesus."

God exalted him to the highest place and gave him the name that is above every name, that at the name of Jesus every knee should bow, in heaven and on earth and under the earth. (Phil. 2:9–10 NIV).

Do we, like Judge Vela's speak softly, and expect all powers beneath the feet of Jesus to obey. Do we have assurance of our spiritual authority and expect a response without question? And, like the Centurion who knew the power of authority, replied, "Lord...*just say the word*, and my servant will be healed. For I myself am a man under authority, with soldiers under me. I tell this one, 'Go,' and he goes...'Do this,' and he does it" (Matt. 8:8 NIV).

I better understood *delegated authority* one day while helping my husband, who was president of the company. He asked me to supervise the remodeling of several tenant offices. When I made a decision regarding design and some materials, one of the subcontractors accepted the finality of the decision with the comment, "Wherever you go, Bob goes."

I thought about that, and realized Bob *was* the authority backing everything that I did. The workmen recognized this, and accepted my word as they would his. On a personal level, Bob has given me an unlimited Power of Attorney to use his name. This valuable document states:

> I appoint Frances Knight my lawful attorney-in-fact with full power and authority for me and in my name to pledge, mortgage, or execute deeds of trust for, possess, manage, lease, let, sell, convey, transfer, exchange or otherwise dispose of any or all of my property. Furthermore, I do expressly declare that the powers shall broadly include and embrace full and unlimited power and authority to do and perform on my behalf and in my place and stead and with equal validity, all other lawful acts... which I could do if I were present....

Bob said, "An unlimited power of attorney is the greatest expression of confidence one person can give another." E. W. Kenyon began *The Wonderful Name of Jesus* with this testimony:

> One afternoon, while giving an address on *The Name of Jesus* a lawyer interrupted me, asking: "Do you mean to say that Jesus gave us the 'Power of Attorney' the legal right to use His name?" I said to him, "Brother, you are a lawyer and I am a layman." He said, "If language means anything, then Jesus gave the church the power of attorney."
>
> Then I asked, "What is the value of this power of attorney?" He said, "It depends upon how much there is back of it, how much authority, how much power this Name represents."[112]

God promised through the prophet Isaiah, *"I will reveal my name to my people and they shall know the power in that name"* (Isa. 52:6 TB). The Apostles, Peter and John knew the power of His name. Peter said to the man who was born lame, "Silver or gold I do not have, but what I have I give you. *In the name of Jesus Christ of Nazareth, walk!" (*Act 3:6, 8 NIV). God's power healed the man. Exuberantly, he went walking, leaping, and praising God!

We must understand that the name of Jesus is not a spiritual amulet, as the seven sons of Sceva thought. They had no authority; Jesus was not their lord. They tried to invoke Jesus' name over a man who was demon-possessed: "One day the evil spirit answered them 'Jesus I know, and I know about Paul, but who are you?' Then the man who had the evil spirit jumped on them and ... gave them such a beating that they ran out of the house naked and bleeding" *(*Acts 19:13–16 NIV).

Jesus prayed, "Holy Father, Protect them *by the power of your name, the name you gave me* [Jesus]" (Jn. 17:11b NIV)

I remember a time when Jesus' name thwarted extreme fear. About midnight, a woman phoned and said that a mutual friend was suicidal. She asked if I could go talk with her.

I found our friend fearful, and indeed, at the point of suicide. After we talked, I decided to stay with her. As I dozed on a pallet by her bed, I sensed an *ominous dark cloud of fear* descending. I thought, "This is fear in its purest form." Even before it reached me, I was physically paralyzed with fear. Yet, spiritually, I *knew* what was happening! I *knew* who I was in Jesus Christ; and, I *knew* the power of His Name. With great effort I said, "*Jesus!*" The dark cloud of fear left instantly. I slept peacefully the rest of the night "Resist the devil and he *will flee* from you" (Jas. 4:6–8 NKJV).

In *Authority of the Intercessor*, J. A. MacMillan explains what happens when we stand in the name of Jesus.

> It is not because of an imposing faith, but that of an all-sufficient Name. The worker has no power of himself ... he is commissioned to wield the power of God. As he speaks ... in the name of Christ, he puts his hand on the dynamic force that controls the universe; heavenly energy is released, and his behest [order] is obeyed.[113]

X: Satan the Supreme Leader of Evil DEFEATED!

Authoritative prayer is effective when our life and mission is in harmony with God's nature, character, and will. Watchman Nee writes, "Authoritative prayer must abide in perfect agreement with Him regarding the work on earth ... It must rise from a heart with a depth of inner determination that the will of God shall be brought forth to proclaim, 'Oh Lord, this must be done!' We command what God has already commanded."[114]

E.M. Bounds writes about prayer power that is in harmony with God's will:

> God makes prayer identical in force and power with Himself, and says to those on earth who pray: *"You are on the earth to carry on My cause.* I am in heaven, the Lord ... the Maker of all ... Now whatever you need for my cause, ask me, and I will do it. Shape the future by *your* prayers ... Ask largely ... Do not abate [hold back] *your* asking, and I will not ... abate in my giving."[115]

Authority is also used in binding and loosing. Jesus said, "I tell you the truth, *whatever* you bind on earth *will be bound* in heaven, and *whatever* you loose on earth *will be loosed* in heaven" (Matt. 18:18 NIV). We restrain satanic influences and release their prey. According to Watchman Nee, "Ordinary prayer will be asking God to bind and loose, but authoritative prayer is using authority to bind and loose ... "[116]

In *The Authority of the Intercessor*, J. A. MacMillan reminds us that God told Moses to stop praying and wield his rod of authority, when the Israelites were trapped between the Red Sea and the Egyptian army. Moses cried unto God at the Red Sea (Exod. 14:15 NIV) to work on behalf of His people, only to receive the strong reproof: "Wherefore criest thou unto me? *Speak* unto the children of Israel that they go forward; but lift thou up thy rod, and stretch out thine hand over the sea, and divide it."[117]

We, too, must learn to *part the waters* through *impassable* circumstances. We must not stand whimpering on the bank and allow Pharaoh's army to hold us in bondage. When we lift up our heads, stretch out our rods of authority and march forward, God will fight our battles for us and *cause the water* to overwhelm our enemy. J. A. MacMillan writes,

> Increasingly they [the intercessors] realize that heavenly responsibility rests upon them for the carrying forward of the warfare... As they speak the word of command, God... stands behind His minister with all necessary power to bring forth that which has been commanded. His delight is in such co-working.[118]

Our Strength

Our strength is in the Lord and in his mighty power.
Ephesians 6:10 (NIV)

I can do everything through him who gives me strength.
Philippians 4:13 (NIV)

The one who is in you is greater than the one who is in the world.
1 John 4:4 (NIV)

We are continually being strengthened with all power according to his glorious might.
Colossians 1:11 (NIV)

My grace is sufficient for you, for my power is made perfect in weakness.
2 Corinthians 12:9 (NIV)

During the times when we feel tired and insignificant, remember that the spiritual giant, Elijah, had his moments of weakness; he was *a man just like us* (Jas. 5:17 NIV). He had three mighty victories and then ran in fear of mere words.

X: Satan the Supreme Leader of Evil DEFEATED!

1. He defeated eight hundred and fifty pagan prophets at Mt. Carmel.
2. He prayed for, and received, a mighty downpour of rain.
3. He outran a chariot.

Then Elijah was emotionally and physically drained and ran in fear from Jezebel's threatening *words*" (1 Kings 18:16–19:3 NIV).

Satan will likely intimidate us too when we are exhausted. We must remember during those times to rest "in the Lord and in His mighty power."

Our Armor

The Apostle Paul wrote, "Put on the full armor of God" (Eph. 6:13 NIV). Generally, when we think of armor we visualize a medieval warrior clanking around in his clumsy mail carrying a heavy shield and a huge spear. King Saul tried to outfit David in battle gear like this to fight Goliath. Christians have an invincible and less encumbering spiritual armor:

> Put on the full armor of God, so that when the day of evil comes, you may be able to stand … with the *belt of truth*… the *breastplate of righteousness* in place … *your feet fitted with the readiness* that comes from the gospel of peace … the *shield of faith* [confidence in God], with which you can extinguish all the flaming arrows of the evil one. Take the *helmet of salvation* and the *sword of the Spirit*, which is the word of God.
> Ephesians 6:13–17 (NIV)

I heard a preachers say, "Put on the *full armor of God* every morning." That won't work. The full armor is *who we are in Him*. Just as David rejected King Saul's clanky worldly methods by choosing *faith in God* and *his familiar slingshot*, we must also face the enemy clothed in our tried and tested spiritual armor our salvation, faith in God and His written Word. Though, it may be good to rehearse its benefits daily to build our faith.

Our Weapons

"The weapons we fight with are not the weapons of the world. On the contrary, they have divine power to demolish strongholds" (2 Cor.10:4, 5 NIV). They are: God's Word, Jesus' Blood, our testimonies and praise.

God's Word is our most powerful weapon

"The word of God is living and active. Sharper than any double-edged sword..." (Heb.4:12 NIV). It is called "the sword of the Spirit" (Eph. 6:17 NIV). We must respond to Satan's voice just as Jesus did: "It is written...."

Jesus' Blood and Our Testimonies are non-refutable weapons

As we tell about the blood Jesus shed for our sins, and give our testimonies about our changed lives, Satan cannot contradict us. "They overcame him by the blood of the Lamb and by the word of their testimony" (Rev.12:11 NIV).

Praise is Powerful

"God *inhabits the praises* of His people" (Ps. 22:3 KJV). As we studied in Chapter III, briefly: four examples of extraordinary events that happened when God's children used their powerful praising weapon are as follows:

1. The enemies of Israel destroyed each other in battle (2 Chron. 20:21–24 NIV).

2. The walls of Jericho fell (Josh. 6:2–5, 20 NIV).

3. Prison chains dropped off Paul's and Silas's feet (Acts 16:23–26 NIV).

4. The "glory of the LORD filled the temple…" (2 Chron.5:12–14 NIV).

When we praise God in all things and through all things, good and bad, God responds. First, our changed attitude will make a major difference in our response to the situations. This can start a chain of events.

Second, *our Father* is working from different perspectives. When we keep our eyes on Him, trust Him, and praise Him regardless of what we can see, hear or feel, we will be depending on him to solve the problem as no one else can. There is unfathomable power when our hearts reach God's heart in vibrant praise and utter trust.

Satan puts his hands over his ears and backs off. He doesn't want to be anywhere around such praise and worship to God.

Victorious Overcomers

"You, dear children, are from God and have overcome them, because the one who is in you is greater than the one who is in the world" (1 Jn.4:4 NIV).

> To him who overcomes and does my will to the end, I will give authority over the nations—
> Revelation 2:26 (NIV)

> He who overcomes will, like them, be dressed in white. I will never blot out his name from the book of life, but will acknowledge his name before my Father and his angels.
> Revelation 3:5 (NIV)

> To him who overcomes I will make a pillar in the temple of my God. Never again will he leave it. I will write on him the name of my God and the name of the city of my God, the

new Jerusalem, which is coming down out of heaven from my God; and I will also write on him my new name.

Revelation 3:12 (NIV)

The Battleground for the Mind

As an intercessor, our battleground is in the spirit realm where our prayer influences the one for whom we are praying. This is a battleground because our adversary is there too. In the following chart, we see how God's Holy Spirit and Satan vie for an individual's attention.

Though, the final choice remains with the one for whom we are praying, authoritative prayer activates a mightier work of God's Spirit, and thwarts Satan's power.

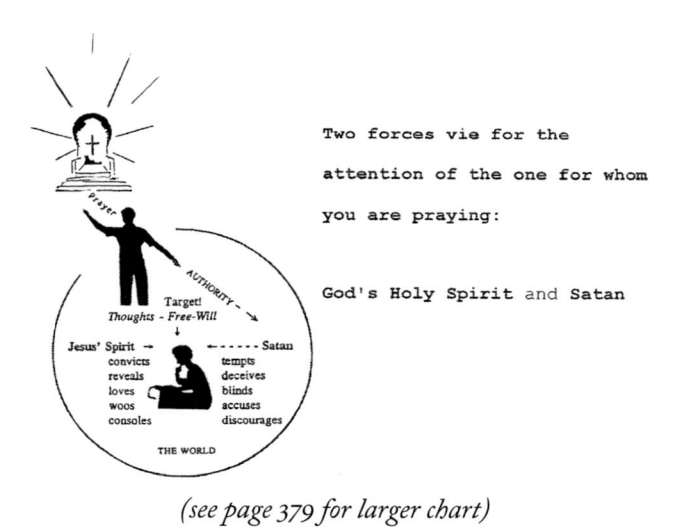

```
Two forces vie for the
attention of the one for whom
you are praying:

God's Holy Spirit and Satan
```

Target!
Thoughts - Free-Will

Jesus' Spirit →
convicts
reveals
loves
woos
consoles

← - - - - Satan
tempts
deceives
blinds
accuses
discourages

THE WORLD

(see page 379 for larger chart)

When Do We Battle Satan, or Simply Trust Our Father?

We have surveyed the battleground and felt the revelry of victory from the shadow of the Cross. Yet, we may still wonder, "How do I know when to fight Satan and when to simply trust *Our Father?*" Let's analyze the following steps:

- Size up the situation realistically.
- Talk to God about the details (Prayer).
- Ask His advice concerning the situation. His Spirit will reveal the answer in some way— that will verify in His written Word. (Prayer and Bible Study)
- Bind every hindering spirit away from the person or circumstance. (Warfare Authority)
- Declare the person or circumstance loosed in the Name of Jesus Christ. (Warfare Authority)
- Ask God to act in the circumstance, according to his divine wisdom and knowledge. (Prayer)
- Praise God for hearing our prayers and for the mighty work he is accomplishing. (Prayer of Thanksgiving and Praise)
- Stand firm and wait upon the Lord. (Faith)
- Trust him because the battle is the Lord's!

An Aggressive Prayer

"Father, for each one of Satan's harassments, I ask you to quadruple the effectiveness of my ministry. Thank you, Lord!"

As we are about Our Father's business, strengthened by His Spirit, commissioned with His authority, protected by His Presence, and wielding our weapons. How wonderful it is to see lives and circumstances released from the powers of darkness...

> Let the saints rejoice in this honor and sing for joy on their beds. May the praise of God be in their mouths and a double-edged sword in their hands [God's Word]... to bind their kings with fetters [demonic spirits], their nobles with shackles of iron, to carry out the sentence written against them. This is the glory of all his saints. Praise the Lord!
>
> Psalms 149:5–9 (NIV)

Sample Prayer

Satan The Supreme Leader of Evil Defeated!

Father, Please fill us with your Holy Spirit so that we will have discernment to recognize the sinister power of darkness that the Bible tells us are always present. We know that their goal is to steal all of our possessions and destroy everything that is of value to us including our self-confidence, our relationships, and our lives.

The Bible assures us that by the power of your indwelling Holy Spirit, we have authority over every satanic spirit. Teach us more about how to overcome intimidation and cause them to release their prey. Father, may those in spiritual, emotional and physical bondage by addictions be delivered and healed.

Father, for each time that Satanic powers harass us, we ask you to quadruple our blessings. You alone know the details of devious activities.

Thank you for hearing our prayer and for the mighty exploits that your word declares that we are to do.

We love you with all our hearts. It is in the name of Jesus Christ our Lord that we pray. Amen.

Living Christianity Assignment

Bible Study—Read Ephesians, our Christian Warfare Manual

> ...and his incomparably great power *for us who believe*. That power is like the working of his mighty strength, which he exerted in Christ when he raised him from the dead and seated him at his right hand in the heavenly realms, far above all rule and authority, power and dominion, and every title that can be given, not only in the present age but also in the one to come.
> Ephesians 1:19–21 (NIV)

Prayer—Ask *our* Father to teach you to stand in *your* heavenly position of authority.

> And God placed all things under his feet and appointed him to be head over everything for the church, which is his body, the fullness of him who fills everything in every way.
> Ephesians 1:22–23 (NIV)

Works—Fight the battle in the realm of prayer for your family and friends. They may not know about the powerful position of God's children on the battlefield with the enemy. Claim the victory for them and hold steady.

> The weapons we fight with are not the weapons of the world. On the contrary, they have divine power to demolish strongholds.
> 2 Corinthians 10:4–5 (NIV)

XI:
Victoriously Praise Our Eternal Father!

"For yours is the Kingdom and the Power and the Glory Forever."

> Now to the King eternal, immortal, invisible, the only God, be honor and glory forever and ever. Amen.
>
> 1 Timothy 1:17 (NIV)

XI:
Victoriously Praise Our Eternal Father!

"For yours is the Kingdom and the Power and the Glory Forever"

- Victoriously Praise Our Eternal Father!
- Thy Eternal Kingdom, Power, and Glory

  - Glimpsing "Thy Eternal Kingdom"
  - Glimpsing "Thy Almighty Power"
  - Glimpsing "Thy Shekinah Glory"

- Forever
- Sample Prayer: Victoriously Praise Our Eternal Father— "Lord, I See Your Glory!"
- Living Christianity Assignment

XI:
Victoriously Praise Our Eternal Father!

"For yours is the Kingdom and the Power and the Glory Forever."

As we approach the end of our prayer time, the earth and all its clamoring demands are obscured as we turn our thoughts to *our Father*'s Eternal Kingdom, His mighty power, and the brilliant light of His Awesome Glory. As we place our confidence in his consuming love and unlimited power victorious praise overflows!

For us to have this total confidence, we must hold a vision of God's kingdom, power and glory in our hearts. God drew back the heavenly curtain at different times in Scripture, so that we may "Tell of the glory of [His] kingdom and speak of [His] might, so that all men may know of [His] mighty acts and the glorious splendor of [His] kingdom" (Ps.145:10–12 NIV).

Rather than have a theological discussion of John's visions, I will spotlight Celestial Vignettes in the sequence as they are recorded:

"Thy Eternal Kingdom, Power, and Glory"
Glimpsing "Thy Eternal Kingdom!"

In Isaiah's vision, we see

> The Lord seated on a throne, high and exalted, and the train of his robe filled the temple. Above him were seraphs, each with six wings: With two wings they covered their faces, with two they covered their feet, and with two they were flying. And they were calling to one another: "Holy, holy, holy is the LORD Almighty; the whole earth is full of his glory."
>
> Isaiah 6:1–3 (NIV)

The prophet Daniel shares with us his vision:

> As I looked, thrones were set in place, and the Ancient of Days took his seat.
> His clothing was as white as snow; the hair of his head was white like wool.
> His throne was flaming with fire and its wheels were all ablaze
> A river of fire was flowing, coming out from before him.
> Thousands upon thousands attended him;
> Ten thousand times ten thousand stood before him
> The court was seated, and the books were opened.
> I looked, and there before me was one like a son of man [Jesus],
> coming with the clouds of heaven.
> He approached the Ancient of Days and was led into his presence
> He was given authority, glory, and sovereign power; all peoples, nations
> and men of every language worshiped him.
> His dominion is an everlasting dominion
> … and his kingdom … will never be destroyed.
>
> Daniel 7:9, 10, 13, 14 (NIV)

Stephen, a deacon in the first church in Jerusalem, saw into Heaven just before he was stoned to death. His face was as *radiant as an angels'* when he said "I see heaven open and the Son of Man standing at the right hand of God" (Acts 7:56 NIV).

In the last book of Holy Scripture we see John, the author of Revelation, as he was exiled on the Island of Patmos groping for words to depict a heavenly vision: "The one who sat there had the appearance of a jasper and carnelian. A rainbow, resembling an emerald, encircled the throne…" (Rev. 4:3 NIV).

Heaven is filled with glorious sights *and* sounds. Later, John heard the voluminous praising of a multitude of heavenly hosts, *"like the roar of rushing waters and like loud peals of thunder, shouting: 'Hallelujah! Our Lord God Almighty reigns'"* (Rev.19:6 NIV).

In the closing chapters John wrote:

> And I heard a loud voice from the throne saying, "Now the dwelling of God is with men, and he will live with them. They will be his people, and God himself will be with them and be their God."
>
> Revelation 21:3 (NIV)

> One of the seven angels said to me, "Come, I will show you the bride [the church of Christian believers], the wife of the Lamb. And he carried me away in the Spirit to a mountain great and high, and showed me the Holy City, Jerusalem, coming down out of heaven from God. *It shone with the glory of God, and its brilliance was like* that of a very precious jewel, like jasper, clear as crystal."
>
> Revelation 21:9–11 (NIV)

Glimpsing "Thy Almighty Power!"

At times in Scripture God's power is revealed through dynamic displays of the elements. We see with the prophet Habakkuk: "His glory covered the heavens and his praise filled the earth. His splendor was like the sunrise; *rays flashed from his hand, where his power was hidden*" (Hab. 3:3, 4 NIV).

Then, we envision the twenty-four elders around God's throne, prostrate as they worship God proclaiming: "We give thanks to you, Lord God Almighty, the One who is and who was, because you have *taken your great power* and have begun to reign" (Rev. 11:17 NIV).

John saw, "God's temple in heaven was opened, and within his temple was seen the ark of his covenant. And there came flashes of lightning, rumblings, peals of thunder, an earthquake, and a great hailstorm" (Rev. 11:19 NIV). "The temple was filled with smoke from the glory of God *and from his power*..." (Rev. 15:8 NIV). John wrote in Revelation 19:11–16:

> I saw heaven standing open and there before me was a white horse, whose rider is called Faithful and True. With justice he judges and makes war.
>
> His eyes are like blazing fire [judgment], and on his head are many crowns [ultimate reigning authority]. He has a name written on him that no one knows but he himself.
>
> He is dressed in a robe dipped in blood [that was shed for sins], and his name is the *Word of God*." ["In the beginning was The Word, and the Word was with God, and the Word was God...The word became flesh Jesus" (Jn. 1:1, 14 NIV).]
>
> The armies of heaven [those he had redeemed with his blood] were following him, riding on white horses and dressed in fine linen, white and clean.
>
> Out of his mouth comes a sharp sword [the Word of God] with which to strike down the nations [that turned against God]. "He will rule them with an iron scepter." He treads the winepress of the fury of the wrath of God Almighty [against un-repented, thus unredeemed sin].
>
> On his robe and on his thigh he has this name written: KING OF KINGS AND LORD OF LORDS.

XI: Victoriously Praise Our Eternal Father!

Glimpsing "Thy Shekinah Glory!"

She-ki-nah: the Hebrew word for the divine majestic presence or manifestation of God's Glory.[119]

My definition of God's glory: "The purity of God's holiness illuminated by the energizing power of His love shining with such heavenly brilliance no mortal's eyes can behold."

On the Mount of Transfiguration, Moses and Elijah appeared beside Jesus as His *"face shone like the sun, and his clothes became as white as the light"* (Matt. 17:2 NIV).

"His glory covered the heavens and his praise filled the earth. *His splendor was like the sunrise;* rays flashed from his hand, where his power was hidden" (Hab. 3:3, 4 NIV).

Ezekiel saw, "Like the appearance of a rainbow in the clouds... so was the radiance around him. This was the appearance of the likeness of the *glory of the* LORD. When I saw it, I fell facedown, and I heard the voice of one speaking" (Ezek. 1:28 NIV).

Later, as Habakkuk prophesied, "... the earth will be filled with the knowledge of the *glory of the* LORD, as the waters cover the sea" (Hab. 2:14 NIV).

When Jesus returns to earth, "The heavenly bodies will be shaken. At that time they will see the Son of Man coming in a cloud with power and *great glory"* (Luke 21:26, 27 NIV).

"For God, who said, 'Let light shine out of darkness,' made his light shine in our hearts to give us the light of the knowledge of the *glory of God* in the face of Christ" (2 Cor. 4:6 NIV).

The Son is the radiance of God's glory and the exact representation of his being, sustaining all things by his powerful word. After he had provided purification for sins, he sat down at the right hand of the Majesty in heaven (Heb. 1:3 NIV).

The power of Jesus' glory dramatically affected Paul on the road to Damascus. It blinded him physically and enlightened him spiritually: "Suddenly a light from heaven flashed around him. He fell to the ground and heard a voice say to him, 'Saul, Saul, why do you persecute me?'

'Who are you, Lord?' Saul asked. 'I am Jesus, whom you are persecuting,' he replied" (Acts. 9:3–5 NIV). Later, Paul reported, *"I could not see for the glory of that light..."* (Acts 22:11 KJV).

God's Holy Spirit gave me a vision. As I was praying I saw our Bible Study Classroom as a small church, with double doors wide open and a brilliant light pouring out through the doors. Inside, God's truth, purity and power was being proclaimed and as the women went forth, God's glory shone in their hearts and lives."

The devout eighteenth-century Christian Edward Payson saw the light of God's glory on his death bed when he said,

> The celestial city is full in my view. Its glories beam upon me. Nothing separates me from it but the river of death, which now appears as but an insignificant rill that may be crossed at a single step whenever God shall give permission.
>
> The Sun of Righteousness has gradually been drawing nearer, appearing larger and brighter as He approached, and now He fills the whole hemisphere, pouring forth a flood of glory, in which I seem to float in the beams of the sun; exulting, yet almost trembling, which I gaze on this excessive brightness, and wondering, with unutterable wonder, why God should deign thus to shine upon a sinful worm.
>
> My soul is filled with joy unspeakable. I seem to swim in a flood of glory, which God pours...upon me.[120]

We will need our transfigured bodies to behold the awesome power of God's glory. The miraculous truth is, one day we will be *like* Him in glory. Jesus said, *"The righteous will shine like the sun in the kingdom of their Father"* (Matt. 13:43 NIV).

In the Eternal City, His brilliant aura of holiness will light the city adding dazzling sparkle to the flawless precious gems that make its foundation and illuminating the pure translucent golden streets.

XI: Victoriously Praise Our Eternal Father!

His love will eternally flow through us as the river of Living Water, satisfying our souls with peace and instilling inexpressible joy.

We, God's sons and daughters, will spend eternity basking in the glory that Moses could not look upon, while listening to the mighty praising chorus of angels resounding in space. The music is amplifying the universe in beauty to the ear and to the heart, in the Kingdom lit with glory, forevermore.

The Eternal Kingdom with all its majesty, power, and glory is today's vision and tomorrow's reality. In this kingdom, the Father, the Son, and the Holy Spirit who are One, will no longer need separate identities. I believe that the face of God, *whom no one has seen or can see, who alone is immortal and who lives in unapproachable light"* (1 Tim. 6:16 NIV)," will finally be seen and adored. It will be the face of Jesus, the *"image of the invisible God"* (Col. 1:15 NIV).

Forever

During my worship, I have seen myself as a little child in the multitude of people near God's throne. For months, I was contented just to touch His throne. Then I thought, "There are so many people here that no one will notice if I just crawl upon the throne and nestle in the corner." I remained in that cozy spiritual position for months. I grew bolder as I realized my heavenly Father wouldn't mind if I crawled into His lap. Soon, I laid my head on His shoulder, and He wrapped His arms around me. There I will stay for eternity. John Newton wrote:

> When we've been there ten thousand years,
> Bright shining as the sun,
> We've no less days to sing God's praise
> Than when we first begun.[121]

Sample Prayer

Victoriously Praise Our Eternal Father
"Lord, I See Your Glory!"

Our Father,

May your spirit shine in us and through us. May that glow brighten as you transform us *"with ever-increasing glory"* (2 Cor. 3:18 NIV) and give us a clearer vision of *your kingdom, power and glory* until at last *"we shall see our Lord "face to face"* (1 Cor. 13:12 NIV).

Please hasten the day when we will live in your glorious Eternal Kingdom forever.

With all our hearts, minds, and souls we love you. We eagerly anticipate praising with the angels around *your* Throne, *"Hallelujah! Salvation and glory and power belong to our God"* (Rev. 19:1 NIV).

Holy, Holy, Holy, is the Lord God, the Almighty,
who was and who is and who is to come" (Rev. 4:8 NAS).
The Great "I AM"!

XI: Victoriously Praise Our Eternal Father!

Living Christianity Assignment

Bible Study—Read Revelation and learn about God's Kingdom, Power, and Glory, forever.

> Blessed is the one who reads the words of this prophecy, and blessed are those who hear it and take to heart.
> Revelation 1:3 (NIV)

Prayer—Pray humbly to your Father, The Great "I Am," and trust Him.

> Therefore I tell you, whatever you ask for in prayer, believe that you have received it, and it will be yours.
> Mark 11:24 (NIV)

Works—Let everything we do honor Our Father and bring glory to His holy name!

> Do it all for the glory of God.
> 1 Corinthians 10:31 (NIV)

XII:
"Amen" is not the End...

"Amen."

> The word of the Lord stands forever.
>
> 1 Peter 1:25 (NIV)

XII:
"Amen" is not the End...

"Amen."

- "AMEN" IS NOT THE END...
- Our Concluding Prayer
- Living Christianity Assignment

XII:
"Amen" is not the End...

"Amen."

"Amen" is more than a signal ending prayer, a period at the end of a sentence. Amen is the title of Christ who is all-in-all. He is "The Amen, the faithful and true Witness, the ruler of God's creation." (Rev. 3:14 NIV).

Jesus said, "I am the Alphabetical and the Omega, the First and the Last, the Beginning and the End." (Rev. 22:13 NIV).

"Amen" also signifies a unified spirit in the Body of Christ as petitions are lifted up that are in agreement with His will. King David wrote: "Blessed be the LORD, the God of Israel, from everlasting even to everlasting. And let all the people say, *'Amen.'* Praise the LORD" (Ps. 106:48 NIV)! Dr. Mary Relfe wrote,

In the largest Christian church in the world, Dr. Cho's Yoido Full Gospel Church in South Korea had about 53,000 worshippers in this service on the first floor, and about 500,000 on the upper thirteen floors. As Dr. Mary Relfe was speaking

> The congregation was graciously responsive so much so that I had to get in rhythm with them. They responded like a huge cheering section! After virtually every sentence, they would say a loud "Amen"! Following more affecting proclamations,

> the entire congregation would rise, lift hands heavenward, and repeat in unison, *"Amen! Amen!"*...
>
> Yodio Full Gospel is the only church which I have ever visited where the worshipers responded as described by Ezra: "And all the people answered, 'Amen, Amen' with lifting up of their hands" (Neh. 8:6 KJV).[122]

This confidence rests upon God's promises. Then, we trust God's power to cause his will to be brought forth. As we stand in our spiritual position with Christ Jesus, agreeing with him about the affairs of the earth that must be brought about, we may conclude our petition and assuredly proclaim, "Thus shall it be! Amen."

For the Son of God, Jesus Christ, who was preached among you ... was not "Yes" and "No" [It was not a wavering testimony] but in him it has always been "Yes." For no matter how many promises God has made, they are "Yes" in Christ. And so, through him the "Amen" is spoken by us to the glory of God (2 Cor. 1:19–20 NIV).

As the Bible draws near the end of the last chapter, Jesus proclaims:

> Behold, I am coming soon! My reward is with me, and I will give to everyone according to what he has done.
>
> Revelation 22:12 (NIV)

In the closing sentence of Holy Scripture (Rev. 22:21 NIV), John penned a tremendous unmerited blessing for us *signed by Christ, The Amen*:

> *"The grace of the Lord Jesus be with God's people,*
> *AMEN."*

XII: "Amen" is not the End...

Our Concluding Prayer

Now, through our study, may we have a greater love for our Heavenly Father; may we realize more clearly his abiding Presence and find strength to sustain us through whatever our earthly future holds. May our faith in him be so strong that we have absolute confidence in his love; and, may we receive the mighty prayer answers that we frequently need—until we are with Him in Glory!

In conclusion, let us pray:

> "Our Father in heaven,
> Hallowed be your name,
> Your kingdom come,
> Your will be done on earth as it is in heaven.
> Give us today our daily bread.
> Forgive us our debts,
> as we also have forgiven our debtors.
> And lead us not into temptation,
> But deliver us from the evil one.
> For yours is the kingdom
> and the power and the glory forever.
> Amen."

Living Christianity Assignment

Bible Study—Read the Bible through each year [about three chapters per day]. Faith will grow for a more victorious life and greater prayer power.

> Do not let this Book of the Law depart from *your* mouth; meditate on it day and night, so that you may be careful to do everything written in it. Then you will be prosperous and successful.
> Joshua 1:8 (NIV)

Prayer—Teach *your* family, children and grandchildren how to enjoy talking with God, by *your* example.

> Devote *your*selves to prayer, being watchful and thankful.
> Colossians 4:2 (NIV)

Works—Try to react to each situation in life as Jesus would. Our motto: "To be like Jesus."

> Let *your* light shine before men, that they may see *your* good deeds and praise *your Father* in heaven.
> Matthew 5:16 (NIV)

XII: "Amen" is not the End...

Author's Page for Readers

To all readers of this book: Please let me know how this book impacts your life.

I want to hear from you.

Web site: http://francesknight.tateauthor.com

My e/mail: f_knight@sbcglobal.net (note the underscore line between "f_knight")

Reader's Statement

What "Christianity Alive! with Prayer Power!" Has meant to me

_____

_____

_____

_____   _____

(Signature)   (Date)

My Prayer for You

Father, I come to you in the name of our Lord Jesus Christ asking you to bless beyond measure this special person who has just finished reading this book. Please help them to retain the principles of Christianity and Prayer for a more confident life in relationship with you. I know your love is incomprehensible and you will eagerly await his/her prayers. I know that you will answer each prayer according to your greater knowledge and wisdom. Let your peace settle each heart. Bless each family member and help with their greatest needs. Thank you for hearing this prayer and for the answers they will receive. We love you, Lord. Amen.

Author's Statement of Faith

The Bible is the infallible Word of God. It was written under the inspiration, and anointing of God. The overall theme of the Bible is God's plan for the redemption of mankind.

God is infinite and eternal. He exists as three persons Father, Son, and Holy Spirit.

Man sinned. Since the penalty of sin is spiritual death, everyone needs a redeemer.

Heaven and Hell are scripturally defined.

Jesus came to earth on a mission to die for mankind: The virgin, Mary, conceived by the Holy Spirit. Therefore, Jesus is true God and true man; He was the *only* one who could pay for sins with sinless blood.

He was buried, resurrected and ascended into heaven. All who personally receive Him, through faith, are declared righteous.

When a person confesses that he is a sinner and accepts Jesus as his/her Lord, he/she is spiritually reborn to be more like Jesus with a loving, caring nature.

The Holy Spirit is a witness for Jesus. He convicts the world of sin, righteousness, and judgment; he regenerates, seals, anoints, and sets apart the believer to a righteous life.

The indwelling Holy Spirit brings spiritual gifts which are special abilities for ministry in an extraordinary manner.

Christ ordained the observance of water baptism and the Lord's Supper, until He returns.

Jesus Christ will physically return to the earth one day as King of Kings and Lord of Lords.

And, believers will reign with him in His Eternal Kingdom.

Image Gallery

see page 36 for picture within text

Christianity Alive! with Prayer Power!

see page 37 for picture within text

see page 132 for picture within text

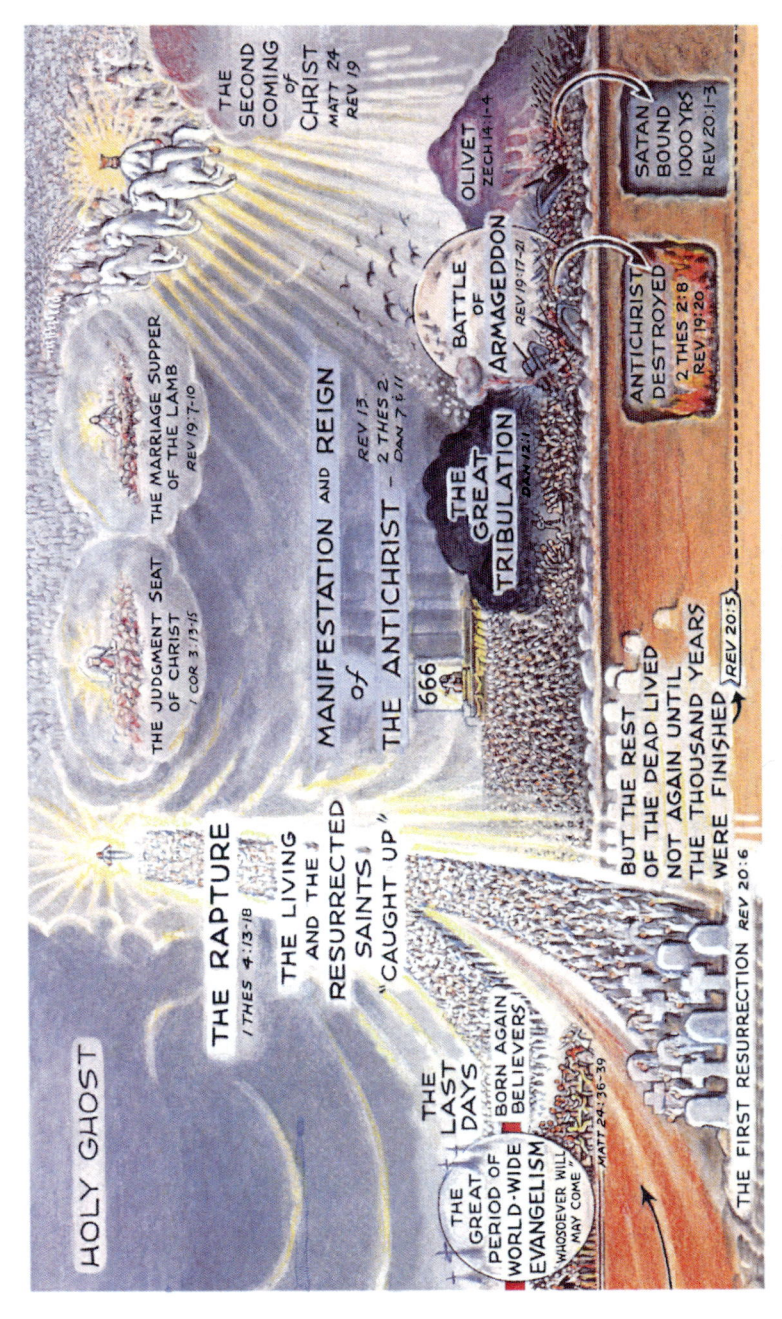

Image Gallery

see page 116 for picture within text

Christianity Alive! with Prayer Power!

see page 146 for picture within text

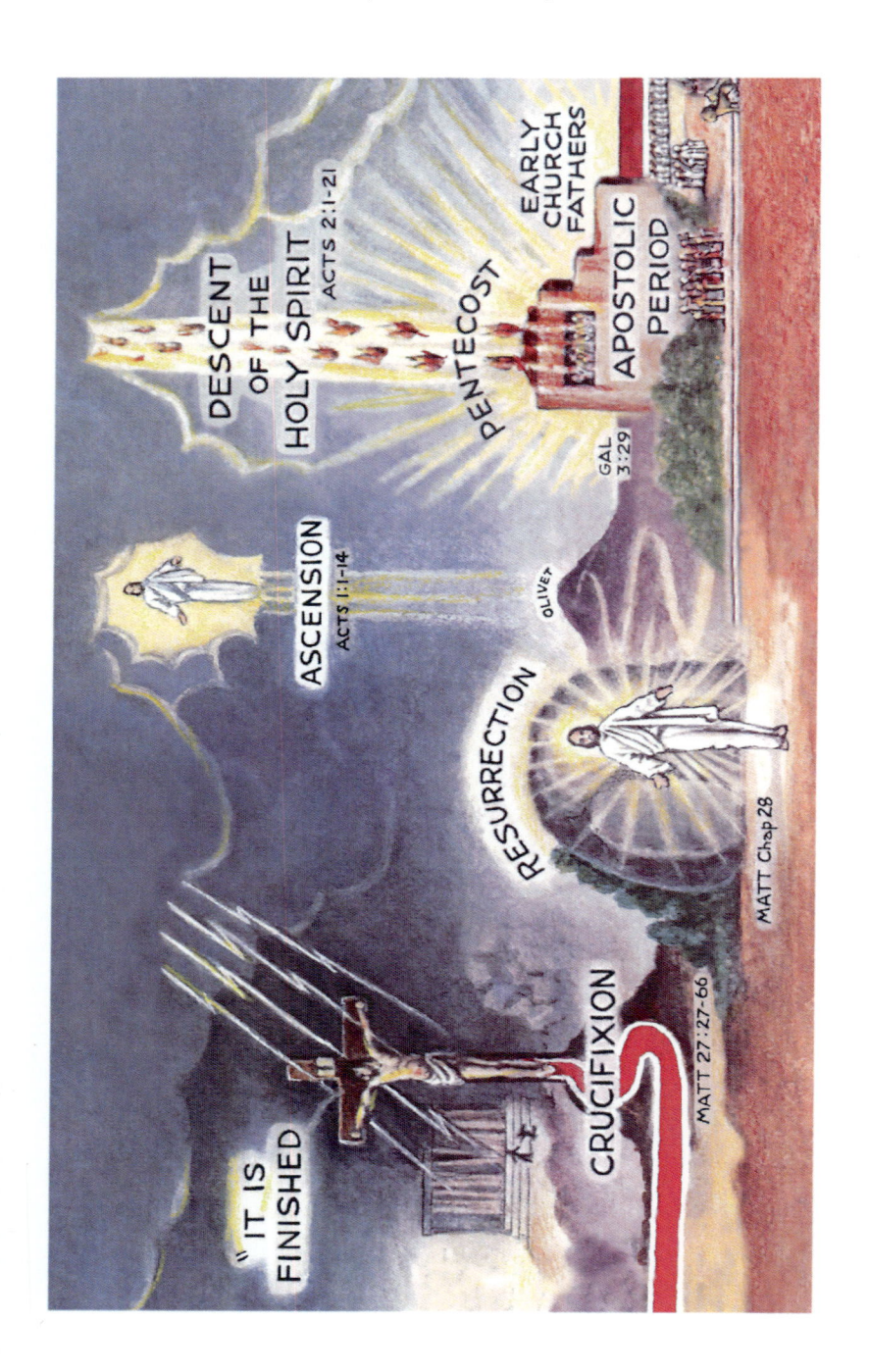

Image Gallery

"When the Gifts will Cease"—The Rapture

see page 171 for picture within text

375

Christianity Alive! with Prayer Power!

see page 45 for picture within text

Image Gallery

Intercessory Chart

GOD THE FATHER
A JUST JUDGE
JUSTICE MUST PREVAIL UNLESS MERCY INTERVENES

Attributes: HAS ALL KNOWLEDGE, HAS ALL WISDOM, PATIENT, COMPASSIONATE, GIVES COUNSEL, LOVING, KIND, UNDERSTANDING, MIGHTY, FORGIVING, MERCIFUL

The Father's attention is directed to the one who appeals.

...so will I do for my servants' sake, that I may not destroy them all (Isa. 65:8 KJV).

"Father, I come to You in the name of my Lord Jesus Christ to appeal to You in behalf of _____ (NAME)"

MOSES interceded for a nation
...But Moses said to the Lord...the Lord said, 'I have pardoned them according to your word' (Num. 14:13,20).

JOB interceded for his friends
...and My servant Job will pray for you. For I will accept him so that I may not do with you according to your folly... (Job 42:8).

SAMUEL interceded for the nation Israel
Samuel cried to the Lord for Israel and the Lord answered him (1 Sam. 7:9).

STEPHEN interceded for those who were stoning him.
'Lord, do not hold this sin against them' (Acts 7:60).

JESUS interceded for those who were crucifying Him.
'Father forgive them; for they do not know what they are doing' (Luke 23:34).

Those for whom we are to pray: ALL, LEADERS, Church, Family, Friends, ENEMIES, The Lost, The Sick

WE must intercede for all men
I exhort therefore, that, first of all, supplications, prayers, intercessions...be made for all men (1Tim.21 KJV).

see page 221 for picture within text

377

Christianity Alive! with Prayer Power!

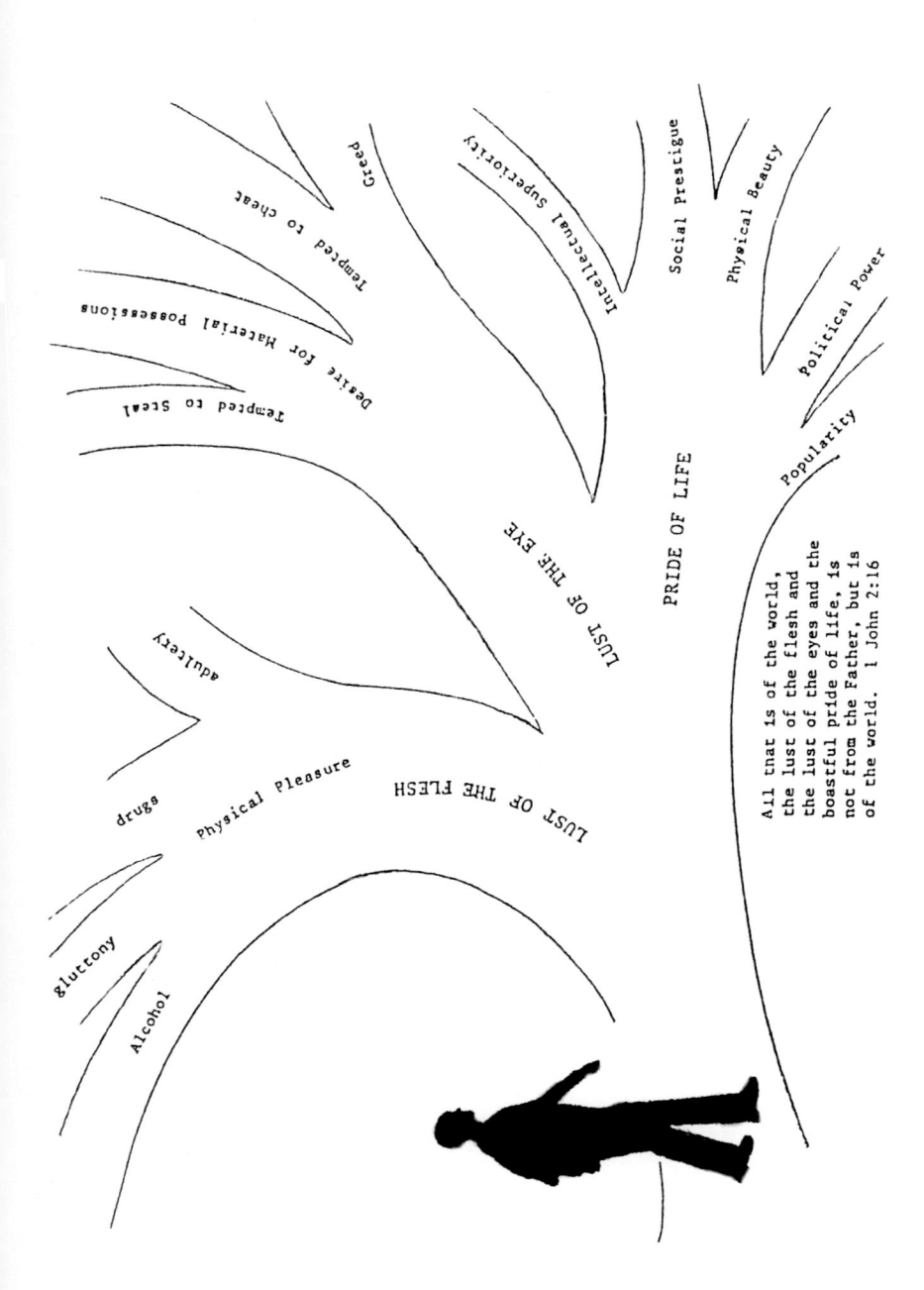

PRIDE OF LIFE
- Social Prestige
- Physical Beauty
- Political Power
- Popularity
- Intellectual Superiority

LUST OF THE EYE
- Greed
- Tempted to cheat
- Desire for Material Possessions
- Tempted to Steal

LUST OF THE FLESH
- Adultery
- Physical Pleasure
- Drugs
- Gluttony
- Alcohol

All that is of the world, the lust of the flesh and the lust of the eyes and the boastful pride of life, is not from the Father, but is of the world. 1 John 2:16

see page 289 for picture within text

378

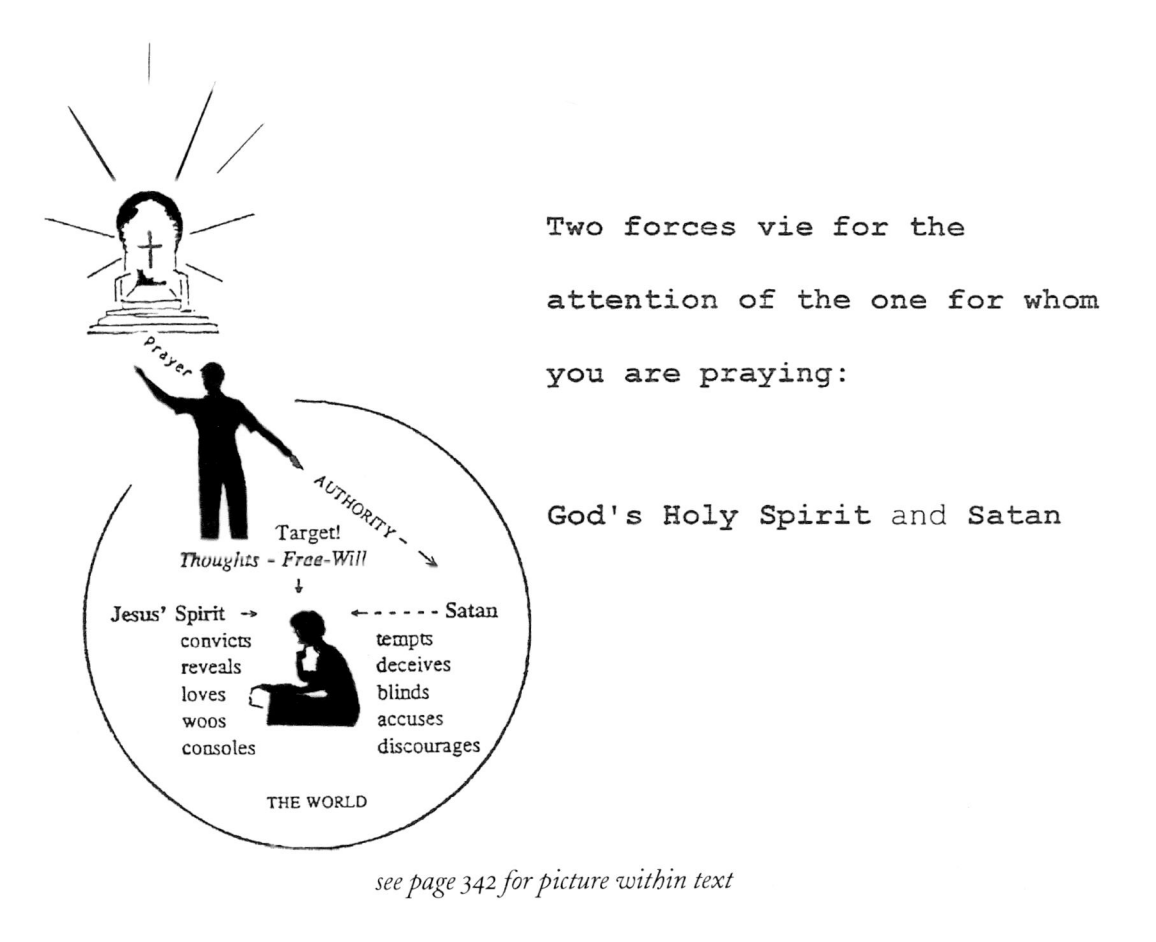

Image Gallery

Two forces vie for the attention of the one for whom you are praying:

God's Holy Spirit and Satan

see page 342 for picture within text

379

Endnotes

Introduction

1 Alfred Thompson Eade, *The New "Panorama" BIBLE Study Courses No. 1 "The Plan of the Ages,"* (New Jersey: Revell, 1966). Used by permission from Oak Knoll Publishing, Murphy, OR 97533. www.oakknollpublishing.com.

2 Henrietta Mears, What the Bible is All About (Calif.: Regal Books A Division of Gospel Light, 1998), p. 26.

Chapter I

3 A. W. Tozer, Pursuit of God (Penn.: Christian Publication, n. d.), p. 49.

4 Ibid., p. 50.

5 Thomas D. Segel, THE POLL SAYS WE STILL BELIEVE, Valley Morning Star, Harlingen, TX, Mar. 24, 1999, p. D2.

6 Rev. Bruce Green, M.A., Green has been a bridge-builder between Muslims and evangelical churches since 1983, Islam & Christianity–Compare Basic teachings and Beliefs (Rose

Publishing, 4733 Torrance Blvd. #259, Torrance, CA, 90503), Christianity, Cults & Religions Chart.

7   Ibid, passim.

8   Virginia Greek, The Blood Covenant, A Bible Study about God's Marvelous Plan of Salvation, Rio Hondo, TX. Passim. I give my gratitude to Virginia Greek for her research paper that helped me to more fully realize the importance of the Blood Covenant and to formulate my thoughts.

9   Alfred Thompson Eade, *The New "Panorama" BIBLE Study Courses No. 1 "The Plan of the Ages"*, The Garden of Eden–Study 2a,"(New Jersey: Revell, 1966, Oak Knoll Publishing, Murphy, OR 97533.

10   Ibid, Alfred Thompson Eade, Adam and Eve Exiled - Study 2b.

11   Gene Horton, Th.D., HEAVEN CAME DOWN, The JOY of Revival, (Dallas, Texas: Maple Springs Publishing Co., Inc.), pp. 6–8, Passim.

12   The Classic Writings of Billy Graham (N.Y.: Inspirational Press, A Division of BBS Publishing Corp. Permission from W Group, a division of Thomas Nelson, Inc. 14100 Nashville, TN, 37214–1000), back cover.

Chapter II

13   A. W. Tozer, *Pursuit of God* (Penn.: Christian Publications, n.d.), p. 50.

14   Hannah Whitall Smith, *The God of All Comfort* (New Jersey: The Christian Library, 1984), p. 10.

15 Chart: "100 Prophecies Fulfilled By Jesus," (Rose Publishing, Inc., 4733 Torrance Blvd., #259, Torrance, CA 90503) or www.rose-publishing.com

16 Wall Chart: Genealogy of Jesus Christ, (Rose Publishing, Inc., 4733 Torrance Blvd., #259, Torrance, CA 90503) or www.rose-publishing.com

17 Ibid. Chart: "100 Prophecies Fulfilled By Jesus," (Rose Publishing, Inc., 4733 Torrance Blvd., #259, Torrance, CA 90503) or www.rose-publishing.com

18 Catherine Marshall, *Beyond Ourselves* (N.Y.: Avon, 1968), pp.231, 232.

19 Dr. Oscar Thompson, Family Bible Study (Nashville, TN: LifeWay Church Resources of The Southern Baptist Convention, Vol. No. 4, Summer 2004), p. 66.

20 The Classic Writings of Billy Graham (N.Y.: Inspirational Press, A Division of BBS Publishing Corp. Permission from W Group, a division of Thomas Nelson, Inc. 14100 Nashville, TN, 37214–1000.) p. 79.

21 Ibid, pg 78.

22 David Wilkerson, "Nothing But Christ!" (Lindale, Texas, World Challenge, Inc., 1985), p. 2.

23 Carl Boberg, 1859–1940 Trans. by Stuart K. Hine, 1899 "How Great Thou Art," *Songs of Inspiration* (Burbank, Calif.: Manna Music, Inc., 1955), p. 2.

Chapter III

24 John Rudin & Company, Inc., *Book of Life* Systems Bible Study, "Historical Digest" (Chicago, Ill., Zondervan, 1980), p. 186.

25 Arthur W. Pink, Gleanings in Exodus (Chicago Moody Press, 1972), p.29

26 Dr. Doug Alexander, Associate pastor First Baptist Church, Little Rock, AK, Last church pastored - First Baptist Lenoir City, TN., permission by Karen Alexander-Doyel, 328 Silo Dr., Lenoir City, TN 37772.

27 Charles Wesley, R. E. Hudson, "Blessed Be the Name" Broadman Hymnal (Nashville, Broadman, 1940), p.279.

28 Mary Stewart Relfe, Ph.D., *Moments with His Majesty* (Pine Valley, CA: CSN Books, 2009, www.csnbooks.com), pg. 100, 101, 103.

29 Edward Perronet, Oliver Holden, "All Hail the Power," Broadman Hymnal (Nashville, Broadman, 1940), p. 1.

Chapter IV

30 Don Piper, 90 *Minutes in Heaven,* (New Jersey: Revell, 2004). Passim.

31 Alfred Thompson Eade, *The New "Panorama" BIBLE Study Courses No. 1 "The Plan of the Ages",* The Cross to Pentecost–Study 10b,11a, (New Jersey: Revell, 1966, Oak Knoll Publishing, Murphy, OR 97533, www.oakknollpublishing.com), (Photo #6).

32 Drs. Jack and Rexella Van Impe, catalogue, "Animals in Heaven? DVD," pg. 10.

33 Arthur Gordon, *PLUS The Magazine of Positive Thinking* (Carmel, NY: Guidepost Publication, 1995), p. 32.

34 Ibid, 90 *Minutes in Heaven,* pg. 21–33, passim.

35 Joy Dawson, *Intimate Friendship with God* (New Jersey: Chosen Books, Fleming H. Revell, 1986).p. 23.

Endnotes

36   Zion's Fire Magazine, Zion's Hope P.O. Box 121048, Clermont, FL 34712–1048, p.15.

37   Ibid., p.14.

38   Alfred Thompson Eade, The Millennial Reign - Study 11. Used by permission from Oak Knoll Publishing, Murphy, OR 97533. (Photo #6) www.oakknollpublishing.com.

39   E. M. Bounds, *Power Through Prayer* (Grand Rapids, Mich.: Zondervan Publishing House, 1962), p.71.

Chapter V

40   Catherine Marshall, *Something More* (New York: Avon Books, 1974), p. 245.

41   R.A. Torrey, What the Bible Teaches, (Fleming H. Revell, copyright 1898–1933), p. 2.

42   Alfred Thompson Eade, *The New "Panorama" BIBLE Study Courses No.* 1 *"The Plan of the Ages"*, (New Jersey: Revell, 1966, Oak Knoll Publishing, Murphy, OR 97533, www.oakknollpublishing.com). The Cross to Pentecost - Study 9b, 10a. (Photo #7)

43   Dr. Steven Carlson, Life Lessons Leaders Guide for Adults, One Lifeway Plaza, Nashville, TN 37234. Lifeway Christian Resources of the Southern Baptist Convention, Winter 2009–10, pg. 121.

44   R. A. Torrey, *How to Obtain Fullness of Power* (Pennsylvania, Whitaker, 1984), p. 142.

45   R. A. Torrey, *What the Bible Teaches* (New Jersey: Fleming H. Revell, 1933), p. 241.

46   Watchman Nee, *The Prayer Ministry of The Church* (New York: Christian Fellowship Publishers, Inc., 1973, p. 43.

47 Charles R. Swindoll, *Growing Strong in the SEASONS OF LIFE* " (Oregon: Multnomah Press, 1983), pp. 313, 314.

48 Robert Jamieson, D.D., A.R. Faced, a.m., David Brown, D.D., *COMMENTARY on the WHOLE BIBLE* (Michigan: Zondervan, rev. ed. 1961), p. 987. (Though the last verses of Mark were omitted from some earlier manuscripts, the principles are consistent with other verses. Jamieson, Faced and Brown state, "The overwhelming mass of MSS., versions and Fathers are in favour of the verses ... ")

49 Clay Price, Baptist General Convention of Texas, Research & Development office 214.828.5138 www.bgct.org, 333 North Washington, Dallas, TX 75246–1798.

50 Alfred Thompson Eade, *When The Gifts will Cease: The Rapture*–Study 10.

51 Alfred Thompson Eade, *When the Gifts will Cease:The Rapture*–Study 10." (Photo #8)

52 Watchman Nee, *Sit, Walk, Stand* (Illinois: Tyndale, Am. Ed. 1977), p. 69.

Chapter VI

53 Andrew Murray, *Helps in Intercession*, (Penn.: Christian Literature Crusade, 1970), p. 19.

54 John R. Rice, *Prayer–Asking and Receiving* (Tenn.: Sword of the Lord Pub., 1974), pg. 46, 47.

55 Catherine Marshall, *Adventures in Prayer* (New York: Ballantine Books, 1976), pp. 36, 37.

56 Mary S. Relfe, *Moments with His Majesty*, p. ix.

Endnotes

57 Arthur Wallis, *Pray in the Spirit* (Penn.: Christian Literature Crusade), pp. 125,126.

58 Annette Tewell, friend and school teacher, Leander, Texas

59 Leonard LeSourd, "Praying with Power for Others" (Lincoln, Va.: Breakthrough, nd), p. 2.

60 Catherine Marshall, *Beyond Ourselves* (New York: Avon Books, 1968), p. 238.

61 Gloria Leigh, "Diary of a Prayer Warrior," The Lighthouse Newsletter Vol. 7, Article 42.

62 David Wilkerson, "Six Reasons Prayers Are Not Answered," newsletter (Lindale, Tex.: David Wilkerson Min., nd.), pp. 1–4.

63 Arthur Wallis, *God's Chosen Fast* (Penn.: Christian Literature Crusade, 1970), p. 19.

64 Mary Stewart Relfe, Ph.D., *Moments with His Majesty* (Pine Valley, CA: CSN Books, 2009, www.csnbooks.com), p.119–121 passim.

65 Watchman Nee, *The Prayer Ministry of the Church* (New York: Christian Fellowship Publishers, 1973), p. 89.

66 *Ibid.*, p. 99.

67 J. A. MacMillan, *The Authority of the Intercessor* (Harrisburg, Pa.: Christian Pub., nd.), p. 10.

68 Watchman Nee, *Sit, Walk, Stand* (Wheaton, Ill.: Tyndale, 1977), p. 63.

69 Frances J. Roberts, *On the Highroad of Surrender* (Ojai, Calif.: King's Press, 1973), p. 46.

70 Bill Gothard, *The Power of Crying Out* (Sisters, Oregon: Multnomah Publishers, 2002), endorsements, preface.

71   Andrew Murray, *With Christ in the School of Prayer* (New Jersey: Fleming H. Revel, 1974), p. 58.

72   E. M. Bounds, *Power Through Prayer* (Mich.: Zondervan, 1962), p. 83.

73   E. M. Bounds, *The Purpose in Prayer*" (City, St., Pub., date), pp. 77, 89.

74   Book Fellowship International tract, "Victorious Praying", The Prayer of Committal by John Lindsay, (P.O. Box 164 N. Syracuse, N.Y. 13212), Tract N. 486, p. 2.19.

75   Norman Vincent Peale, Guideposts, (Carmel, N.Y., October 2000) Vol. LV, Issue 8, p. 60.

Chapter VII

76   R. A. Torrey, *How to Pray* (New Jersey: Fleming H. Revell, 1900), p. 72.

77   John R. Rice, *Prayer - Asking and Receiving* (Tenn.: Sword of the Lord Publishers, 942), p. 314.

78   Andrew Murray, *The Power of the Blood of Jesus* (New Jersey: Revell, n.d.), pp. 64, 65.

79   D. L. Moody, *Prevailing Prayer* (Chicago: Moody Press, n.d.), pp. 26,27.

80   Gloria Leigh, "What is Saved?" The Lighthouse Newsletter (Rio Hondo, TX, 78583, First Baptist Church, August 12, 1984), p. 2.

81   Charles W. Colson, *LOVING GOD* (Minneapolis: Grason, 1983), p. 89–92, passim.

82. Moody, *Prevailing Prayer*, p.27.

Chapter VIII

83 Charles R. Swindoll, *Seasons of Life* (Oregon: Multnomah Press, 1983), p. 166.

84 Corrie ten Boom, "I'm Still Learning to Forgive," Tract no. 7 (Westchester, Ill. 60153: 9825 W. Roosevelt, Good News Publishers, ND.), p. 4, Reprinted by permission from Guideposts Mag.," (N.Y.10512: Carmel, 1972).

85 *Ibid*, p. 3, 4.

86 "Pope Asks Forgiveness for Slavery," *Valley Morning Star*, (Harlingen, Texas 78550, Wed., Aug. 14, 1985), p. D1.

87 Lorans Cunningham, *Forgiveness Brings Healing* (Dallas: Christ for the Nations, Nov. 1978), p. 2.

88 System Bible Study, *The Book of Life* (Chicago: Zondervan, 1980), p. 735.

Chapter IX

89 Matthew Henry, COMMENTARY ON THE HOLY BIBLE (Nashville, TN, 1979), p.14, passim.

90 Valley Morning Star, NATIONAL BRIEFS, Associated Press (Harlingen, TX, 78550, Monday, Aug. 11, 1997, p. A7.

91 Fletcher Edwards, personal note, Aug. 1985. (I met Fletcher Edwards, a former occult priest, at a Decision Magazine School of Christian Writing. After discussing Christianity vs. the Occult, he put his comment in writing with permission to publish.)

92 Ibid. Matthew Henry, COMMENTARY ON THE HOLY BIBLE (Nashville, TN., 1979), p.14, passim.

93 Kathy D. David, "Charles W. Colson: Confronting Casual Christianity", *The Christian Writer Magazine* (Lakeland, Fl.: July, 1984), p. 11.

94 *Ibid.*, p. 11.

95 Andrew Murray, *HUMILITY The Beauty of Holiness* (New Jersey: Revel, n. .d.). p. 33.

96 Richard Wurmbrand, *TORTURED for CHRIST* (Bartlesville, OK 74005-2273, 1967, 1998), Appendix, Dr. James Kennedy.

97 Ibid, pg 79, 80.

Chapter X

98 Billy Graham, "Facing the Giants" *Decision Mag.* Vol. 27, No. 4 (Minn.: Billy Graham Evan. Assn., April 1986), p. 3.

99 C. S. Lewis, *The Screwtape Letters* (New York, N.Y.: MacMillan, 1973), p. vii.

100 Jack Taylor, *Much More* (Nashville, Tenn.: Broadman Press, 1972), p. 116.

101 Karen Armstrong, Islam: A Short History, TIME.com– Jerusalem, Islam's Stake, pg 2.

102 Paul E. Marek, "A German's point of view on Islam," written Jan.2, 2008, forwarded widely by Dr. Emanuel Tanay, MD, Wikipedia.

103 www.BibleGateway.com, Passage Look up, enter John 3:16; Select version, enter *Arabic Life Application Bible (ALAB)*.

104 R. A. Torrey, *What the Bible Teaches* (Revell, 17th edition, 1933), p. 529.

Endnotes

105 Bob Larson *SATANISM – The Seduction of America's Youth* (Nashville: Thomas Nelson Publishers, 1982), p. 110–114 passim.

106 Tom Brokaw Reports "Boomers!," CNBC documentary, April 3, 2010.

107 Arthur Gonzalez, "Soul Blade Is So Real Wear Armor," Valley Morning Star (Harlingen, TX., Oct. 9, 1997), Section C, pg. 1.

108 C. Everett Koop, M.D., Sc.D., "God's Plan for a Surgeon", *Decision Magazine"* (Minn.: Billy Graham Evangelistic Assn., Dec. 1985), p.30.

109 Jack Taylor, *Much More*, p. 115.

110 Paul E. Billheimer *Destined for the Throne* (Pa.: Christian Literature Crusade, 1975), p. 17.

111 Watchman Nee, *Prayer Ministry of the Church (*New York: Christian Fellowship Publishers, Inc., 1973), p. 99.

112 Kenneth E. Hagin, *The Name of Jesus* (Tulsa, Okla. Faith Library Publications, 1981), p

113 MacMillan, *The Authority of the Intercessor* (Harrisburg, Pa.: Christian Publications, Inc., MCMXLII), p. 7.

114 Nee, p. 98.

115 E. M. Bounds *Weapon of Prayer (*Chicago: Moody Press, 1980), pp. 24, 25

116 Nee, p. 103.

117 MacMillan, p. 8.

118 MacMillan, p. 10. Jesus delegated authority to His disciples, for all generations, when He said, just before ascending into heaven, "All authority in heaven and on earth has been given to

me. Therefore go and make disciples of all nations..."(Matt. 28:18–20 NIV).

Chapter XI

119 www.shekinahtoday.org

120 James Gilchrist Lawson *Deeper Experiences of Famous Christians* (Indiana: Warner Press, 1970) p. 266.

121 John Newton 1725–1807, "Amazing Grace," Early American Melody, Baptist Hymnal, (Nashville, Tenn.: Convention Press, 1956) p. 188.

Chapter XII

122 Mary Relfe, Moments with His Majesty, p. 103–104.

mostly

v
e
r
t
i
c
a
l

thoughts

MONOGRAPH
PUBLISHING

Copyright ©2012 Ralph Wright, OSB

All rights reserved. No part of this book may be reproduced or transmitted in any form or by any means, electronic or mechanical, including photocopying, recording, or by any information storage and retrieval system without permission in writing from the publisher.

Library of Congress Cataloguing-in-Publication data

Wright, Ralph OSB
Mostly Vertical Thoughts

Book and Cover Design by Ellie Jones
MathisJones Communications, LLC

Published by Monograph Publishing, LLC
1 Putt Lane
Eureka, Missouri 63025
636-938-1100

ISBN# 978-0-9850542-8-1

for Alex — we read to know we're not alone. C.S. Lewis

mostly vertical thoughts

Ralph Wright, OSB

PROLOGUE

"It is the honourable characteristic of Poetry that its materials are to be found in every subject which can interest the human mind" - so read the opening lines of the 'Advertisement' or Prologue to the Lyrical Ballads of Coleridge and Wordsworth published in 1798. After describing the poems that the book contains as 'experimental' Wordsworth, writing anonymously, goes on to say: "It is desirable that readers should not suffer the solitary word 'Poetry,' a word of very disputed meaning, to stand in the way of their gratification; but that while they are perusing this book, they should ask themselves if it contains a natural delineation of human passions, human characters, and human incidents; and if the answer be favorable to the author's wishes, that they should consent to be pleased in spite of that most dreadful enemy of our pleasures, our own pre-established codes of decision."

These poems, too, are offered for the pleasure of the reader whoever he or she may be. They are the product of the past fifteen or twenty years of my life as a monk. It is considered more hazardous these days to put one's 'vision' into poetry: people immediately feel uneasy and talk of propaganda. But perhaps it is when we cease to try to share our deepest thoughts, feelings and beliefs – about God and love and sin and silence and violence and hatred and union and distance and time and eternity – that our poetry ceases to please or to inspire. I would like my poetry to be read and loved not only by poets but also by the non-poet clientele of our world. Men and women of every walk of life and every interest. From those who program computers or punch cash registers to those vice-presidents who make multi-million dollar deals and survey the world through the dark one-way windows of tall buildings. For we all have to cope on an almost daily basis with belief, unbelief, love, loyalty, betrayal, union, violence, pain, ecstasy, joy, depression, sickness, anger and death.

The poems that follow are attempts to capture moments from these common experiences and to hold them up boldly and without shame for others to share. The Christian sees the dark side – sin, tragedy, separation, death. But he also sees the awesome beauty of all that God creates and the extraordinary dignity of Man re-created in Christ and called to share eternally in the intimate life of God. He already experiences in part the peace of his risen Lord and he believes that it is possible here and now to know, in some measure, the deep joy of union with God. He wants his faith to be reflected in his life and in his words for his deepest call is to give to others from his store – of life, of hope, of vision – whatever has been entrusted to him. If these poems are instances of this, I hope they may succeed in communicating a little of this vision especially to those who, perhaps seeing almost nothing hopeful, may be on the verge of opting for despair.

CONTENTS

Prologue	iv
Wordberg	2
Every Word Spoken	3
Cheery Thughts on a Rainy Morning	4
When God Made You	5
God Has an Exclusive Love	6
From All Eternity	7
If God had Been Indifferent	8
Although Dust	9
If God Loves Me	10
Our Sins	11
The Astronomical Nature of Your Love	12
The Gospel	13
Unquenchable Love	14
I Do Not Deserve the Joy	15
I Refuse to be Depressed	16
Humility	17
Infinite Patience	18
If We Can't See God	20
When the Lsst River	21
One Flesh	22
God's Love	23
Occurrence	24
Joy	25
As I Have Loved You	26
God Sees You	27
Covenant	28
A Spouse's Prayer	29
The Act	30
Conceive	31
Icon	32
Birthday Utterance	33
Mother of God	34

Every Christian Mother	35
The Mist Lifts	36
As Your Heavenly Father	37
Magnum Mysterium	39
The Wooing	40
Biography	43
Other Books by the Author	44

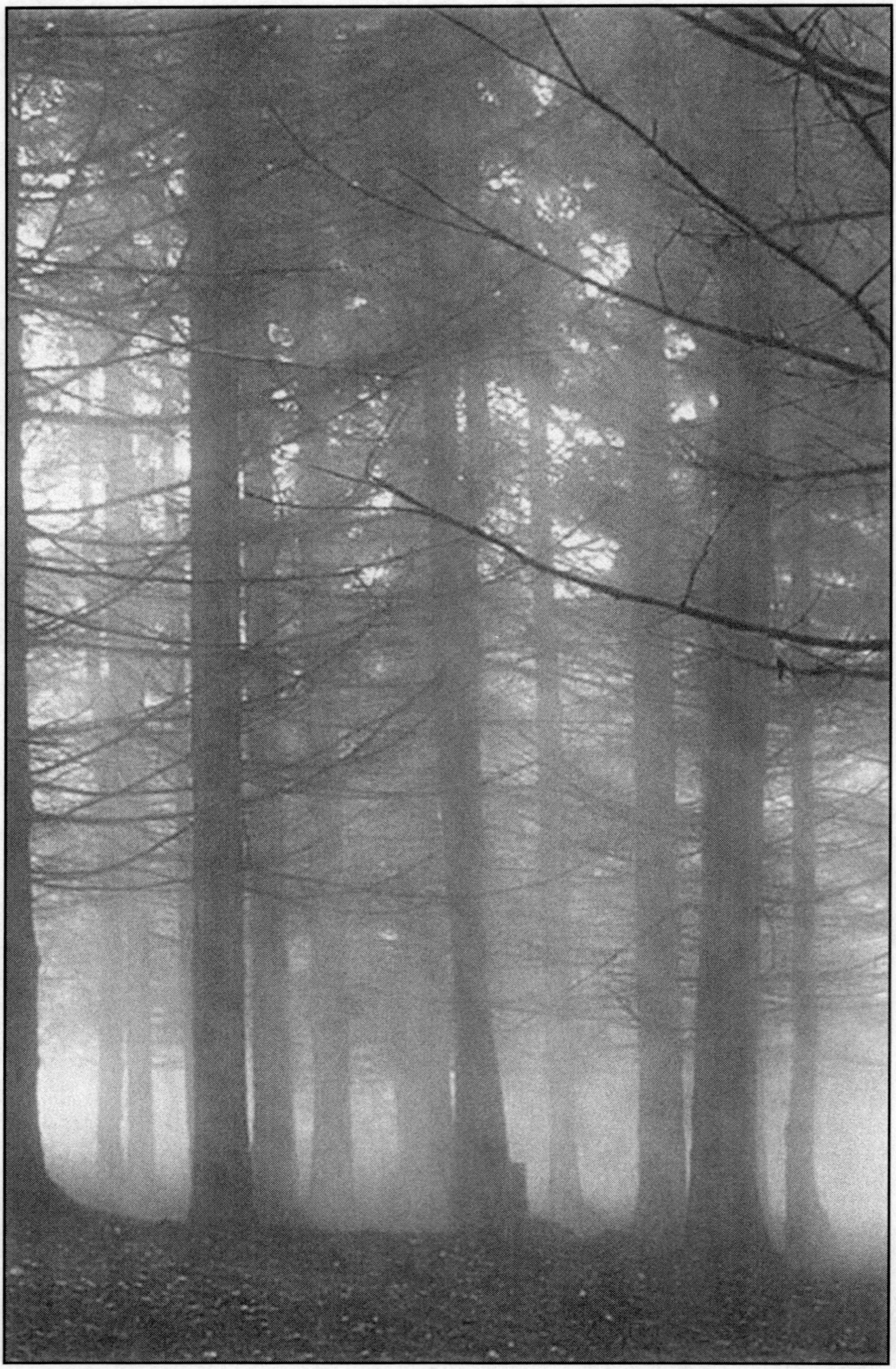

mostly

v
e
r
t
i
c
a
l

thoughts

WORDBERG

a
ninth
above
the
surface
the
rest
silence

EVERY WORD SPOKEN

every
word
spoken
is
as
past
as
pyramids
and
gone
forever

CHEERY THOUGHTS ON A RAINY MORNING

If You didn't need to
but only made me
because You loved me
what an unbelievably
marvelous being
I must be
designed
by the One Lover
only to be
perfectly beloved

WHEN GOD MADE YOU

When
God
made
you
there
was
silence
in
heaven
for
five
minutes.
Then
God
said:
"How come I never thought of that before?"

GOD HAS AN EXCLUSIVE

God
has
an
exclusive
love
for
each
person
he
creates.

FROM ALL ETERNITY

from all eternity
You made me
as if to be
your only spouse
in time
may I choose You
to be mine

IF GOD HAD BEEN INDIFFERENT

If
God
had
been
indifferent
to
you
he'd
have
made
someone
else.

ALTHOUGH DUST
(John 17 : 23)

Although dust
I am loved
by the one
eternal
Son of the Father
just as intensely
as this same Father
loves his one
eternal Son
O mystery
O majesty
O wonder
that what we
in our wildest dreams
could not conceive
has been
by God's own Word
quietly revealed

IF GOD LOVES ME

If
God
loves
me
as
much
as
he
loves
his
Son
I'd
better
watch
out
look
what
they
did
to
him

OUR SINS

our sins
do not
make God
love us less
but more
because
our need is greater

THE ASTRONOMICAL

The
astronomical
nature
of
Your
love
for
me
is
revealed
by
my
repentance
unbar
the
doors
and
let
the
dawn
light
blaze
in

THE GOSPEL IS

The
Gospel
is
that
we
are
each
unique
uniquely
made
uniquely
loved
uniquely
died for.

UNQUENCHABLE LOVE

If I could only see you, Lord,
as you are
a wild Lover
intent on loving
absolutely
each beloved—
unless prevented
by the wild horses of an untamed
savage will—
I would know the desire
in your heart
and would beg
on my knees
each day
the grace
to tame
my savagery
and so
unbar the door
and let my Beloved
enter
the quiet stable of a bridled heart.

I DO NOT DESERVE

I
do
not
deserve
the
joy
of
knowing
how
much
You
love
me.

I REFUSE

I
refuse
to
be
depressed
Lord
for
You
love
me

HUMILITY

Humility
is
hard
even
for
God
as
the
iron
passes
the
median
nerve
into
the
wood.

INFINITE PATIENCE

God lets
his Son
be stretched
against
the earth
and nailed
to the wood
of the world
behold
the mystery
of infinite
patience
that
God
should create
a being
able
to see
and love
or blindly
hate
then patiently
wait
and not
stop
the entire
show
when an innocent
child
weeps in the
night
or his Son
is stretched

against
the world
and brutally
nailed

IF WE CAN'T SEE

If
we
can't
see
God
in
the
hummingbird
why
should
we
see
him
in
the
Big Bang

WHEN THE LAST RIVER

When the last river has let its waters
meet the sea,
when the last cloud has let its rain
touch the waves,
when the last breeze has brought coolness
to the face of man
and the last sun has bowed its head
behind the mountains,
I will reach down and raise you up,
says the Lord,
to be with me, your brother,
for ever.

one flesh

GOD'S LOVE

God's Love means
giving
all
not once but
always

you can't give
more than
all
for if you've
given
all
you've got nothing more
to give

you can't give all
less than
always
for
if
you've given
all
just for
today
by dawn
tomorrow
you've given
nothing

but
God's love
means giving
all

OCCURRENCE

You might have been born in Hong Kong
when Ghengis Khan
was pounding the planet.
Or even today, eons away,
in London or Tokyo.
But somehow someone's kindly computer
decided
that you should be
roughly here
roughly now
and with four thousand million
currently elsewhere
I almost explode
with thanksgiving
as I blunder
like some beautiful rhino
casually out of the bush
into the path of your being.

JOY

Joy is momentary
freedom from
the distance that keeps
us apart
and the time that ends
our union
one day
the moment will be
eternal

AS I HAVE LOVED YOU

to lay down your life
for each other
each day
in every need

to serve each other
each day
on your knees
—even when they bleed

GOD SEES YOU

God sees you
as worth dying for
that much
He loves you

if God sees you
as that valuable
you must *be*
that valuable

if I see you
as God sees you
I will see you
as worth dying for

daily too

COVENANT

there is no substitute
for unconditional
surrender
no substitute
for giving
all

we cannot hold
anything back
and then pretend
that we have given
all

and giving all
is not an option
but a requirement
for each
conditional surrender
is the precondition
for temporary union

A SPOUSE'S PRAYER

I am made free
in the image of God
that my love may be total
for you and my God

may our love be faithful
through the grace of our God
may it also be fruitful
in people of God

THE ACT

Done without guile
the act gives
a whole life
in one brief while

done in faith
in the act is given
a total self
without condition

done that he
may have and may live
only what she
continues to give

done in the folly
of the leap and the cross
the sweet abandon
of total loss

done that the grain
that falls and dies
may create a harvest
of eternal lives

CONCEIVE

to bring
and to have brought
into being
through God

one called
to live forever
intimately
with God

what a stunning
mind-scalding
thing to do
and to have done

could anything
conceivably
be greater —
none

ICON

in the conjugal act
husband and wife
give themselves
totally
to each other
in love
and the result
in time
may be
a new person
– their child

in the Trinity
Father and Son
give themselves
totally
to each other
in love
and the result
eternally
is
a person
–the Holy Spirit

BIRTHDAY UTTERANCE

I have great joy
in knowing that you
have been
born
into the world
because
having been breathed
by God
into existence
you will never
be able
— like a bubble —
to pop
suddenly
back into nothingness

welcome
to this one great
champagne
dancing
party of being

and be
always
alive and utterly
grateful to Him
who
simply freely spontaneously
needlessly and
eternally
utters

MOTHER OF GOD

Fatherhood
the brief impulsive
ecstasy
of begetting

God gave his sons
with the baubles
and the tinsel
of the priesthood

a poor recompense
for the long
godlike creativity
of maternity

for which
from all eternity
God chose his daughters

EVERY CHRISTIAN MOTHER

every Christian mother
watches God
in her first-born
come
into the world
and with amazed
shocked
wonder
knows that the mystery
of Love
eluding
the handling of the mind
resembles more
twin squirrels
chasing each other
on either side
of a tree
than crashes of thunder
waking us at midnight
to Wagnerian lightning

THE MIST LIFTS

the mist lifts
for a moment
over the why of creation
as I see
God
making each person
with the identical
wonder and joy
of making
Jesus

'AS YOUR HEAVENLY FATHER'

because You see
in me
the one Jesus
You proclaim
the one excellence
— His word —
wherein no spot
or wrinkle
of evil or mediocrity
may be
for even a moment
found tolerable

because You love
in me
your only Son
therefore must I
love my enemies,
forgive those
who nail me naked,
give to all who ask and be
pure of every whim
of lust as lovely woman
crosses my path

because You love
in me
— distorted though I am
from birth —
all the one Jesus
that I am
You long so
long so

long so patiently, gently
for me to surrender
me to You
that in me You can say
—as in Jesus—
what I can
I will
I am

MAGNUM MYSTERIUM

the mystery
is how
we splice
our lives together
with that of Christ

THE WOOING

my whole life
is a love affair

my Lover haunts me
but he hides

he is patient
with my indifference
but never indifferent to it

he is gentle
with my infatuations
with the ravishing beauty
of his creation
but always jealous of them

he abides
my cautious steps
out over the ice of freedom
and my falling through
and refuses
to manipulate

he awaits that moment
when I choose

against my roaring
desires

that sacrificial dive
from the high board
into the unseen water
of the midnight pool

The momentary peace that is a poem.
Dylan Thomas

BIOGRAPHY OF RALPH WRIGHT, O.S.B.

Ralph Wright was born in Nottinghamshire, England, about 200 yards from Sherwood Forest on October 13, 1938. He was christened David Grant Melville Wright. His father, Monty Wright, was a mining engineer responsible for the coal mines of the Butterley Company. Five generations of the family had been involved in this Derbyshire company since it's foundation in 1790. David went to High School at Ampleforth College whence he won a minor scholarship in Classics to Pembroke College, Oxford. Deciding to spend two years doing his National Service before going to Oxford, he joined the Sherwood Foresters, was commissioned and spent a year in Malaya as a platoon commander, partly in the jungle, partly at the base camps. In 1969, on emerging from the army, he joined the Benedictine Community at Ampleforth Abbey in Yorkshire taking the name Ralph (pronounced Rafe) after the Derbyshire martyr, Ralph Sherwin.

Having completed his BA in Greats (Classics, Ancient History & Philosophy) at Oxford and his STL in Theology at Fribourg (Switzerland) he was ordained priest at Ampleforth Abbey on July 5, 1970. A month later, he left England, at the Abbot's invitation, to join the St. Louis Priory – the community's foundation in the United States. When the monastery became independent in July, 1973, he opted to become a permanent member of the newly independent house. Shortly thereafter, he became an American citizen. Fr. Ralph initially taught Latin, Greek, English and Religion in the St. Louis Priory School. In 1978, he was made Novice Master. He has been the Varsity Tennis coach on and off for over 25 years and Vocation Director for the community for about 20. Currently, besides running the Varsity tennis program and coordinating community efforts to attract vocations, he teaches Theology to the 11th grade, Creative Writing to seniors, and is Advisor in the School.

OTHER BOOKS BY FR. RALPH WRIGHT

Wild...
They Also Serve: Tennis, a Global Religion
Leaves of Water
On Leaves and Flowers and Trees
Seamless
Life is Simpler Toward Evening
All the Stars are Snowflakes
Perhaps God
Christ Our Love for All Seasons
Our Daily Bread
The Eloquence of Truth

Over 50 Hymns